MW00718742

To Philip:

I hope you enjoy reading my book. I value your friendship very much.

Richard Moetzke
12/15/99

Hush! A Demon Sleeps Beside Me

Hush! A Demon Sleeps Beside Me

A True Story of Violent Secrets, Betrayal and Courage

by

Richard E. Goetzke
and
Ted Schwarz

New Horizon Press
Far Hills, New Jersey

Copyright © 2000 by Richard E. Goetzke and Ted Schwarz

All rights reserved. No portion of this book may be reproduced or transmit-
ted in any form whatsoever, including electronic, mechanical, or any information storage or retrieval system, except as may be expressly permitted in
the 1976 Copyright Act or in writing from the publisher. Requests for per-
mission should be addressed to:
New Horizon Press
P.O. Box 669
Far Hills, NJ 07931

Richard E. Goetzke and Ted Schwarz
        Hush! A Demon Sleeps Beside Me

Interior Design: Susan M. Sanderson

Library of Congress Catalog Card Number: 99-70154

ISBN: 0-88282-190-3
New Horizon Press

Manufactured in the U.S.A.

2004   2003   2002   2001   2000   /   5   4   3   2   1

This book is inspired by and based on the actual experiences of Richard E. Goetzke. The personalities, events, actions, and conversations portrayed within the story have been reconstructed from extensive interviews and research, utilizing court documents, letters, personal papers, press accounts, and the memories of participants. In an effort to safeguard the privacy of certain individuals, their names have been changed, and in some cases, otherwise identifying characteristics have been altered. Events involving the characters happened as described: only minor details have been altered.

— ACKNOWLEDGMENTS —

The authors gratefully acknowledge the assistance of Mr. Robert Buckles, Jr. of Sarasota, Florida for his help in researching court records and news media files.

— CONTENTS —

Foreword

Red sky at night, a sailor's delight!
Red sky in the morning, a sailor's warning!

Old Sailor's Prophecy

In the pre-dawn darkness of Annacostia Beach, I watched the sun rise over Florida's Atlantic coast. I was alone with the sound of the surf and memories of an earlier sunrise. Lauren and I had been there with the magic of a new relationship, filled with hope and promise for a bright future. We had watched the gleaming fireball of sunrise peek over the horizon and paint the early morning sky with bright colors. The beauty of that morning the year before seemed prophetic. Everything seemed so right then, but in retrospect; an old sailing prophecy might have been more fitting, "Red sky at night, a sailor's delight! Red sky in the morning, a sailor's warning!"

In 1992, shortly after I met my wife Lauren, I began to keep a journal of our life together. The intended story line was quite different from what it is now. As time passed, our story became my daily journal of a passage through hell.

1

In late 1996, my journal went into a storage box along with countless hours of audio tape, newspaper clippings, court records, and other assorted memorabilia. There it stayed, sometimes rattling around like old bones of a family skeleton every time I opened the closet door. "Why open old wounds?" I asked whenever I would open the closet door and look at the box on the shelf. I would close the door and go on with whatever chapter of my life I happened to be living at the time. I knew it was there, waiting to be finished, waiting for closure. I was waiting for closure, too.

One day in 1998 I pulled the lid off the box and I looked inside. I knew that I had to finish the story. Left unfinished, I would never feel complete; or perhaps I would wonder for the rest of my life if it were really over. There were too many friends lost, too many years with my children long gone, and my career was in disarray.

I have always believed that each of us is placed on this earth to accomplish at least one special thing. I know that God put me here to do something special, perhaps not heroic, or earthshaking; but something significant that in some way helps another human being. Whether one chooses to believe or not, we often become each other's guardian angels. When I met Ted Schwarz I decided that the time was now; perhaps by our writing my story, I might become someone's guardian angel!

My decision to tell my story for all the world to see was not without serious soul searching, nor was it taken lightly. I kept thinking, *For all the world to see, then judge me!* Judgements about others sometimes come easy but living the experience which occasions them can be hard, as I well know. If my story brings truth and understanding to others, then all that has ever happened to me will become more meaningful.

Introduction

I grew up in the Midwest of the '50s; life was the American flag, mom's apple pie, John Wayne movies, and the American way. I was taught right from wrong in a stable family environment. I am sure my parents had their problems, but I never heard my father or mother so much as raise their voices to each other. Growing up in the clay bluffs and hills of western Iowa was a fun time that I shared with my friends.

When I was eight years old, I wanted to join the Marines. I never changed my mind about that. After I finished my second year of high school, my family moved east to New Jersey. Life there was a culture shock, a stark contrast to that of western Iowa, but life as a high school student anywhere was simpler than it is today. Peer pressure to use drugs did not exist, and students that did use drugs were often ostracized. For our class, a good time was the occasional beer in New York City where the legal drinking age was eighteen.

After I completed my junior year of high school, I convinced my father to sign my enlistment papers for the Marine Corps Reserve. The day after my seventeenth birthday, I became a member of the US Marine Corps Reserve

Air Wing, Squadron VMF 313 based at Floyd Bennett Field in Brooklyn. I graduated from high school and transferred to the regular Marine Corps. I was sent to Parris Island, South Carolina to endure the customary three months of hell called boot camp. One of the proudest days of my life was when I passed in review with the other Marines of Platoon 278 on graduation day. I was a full-fledged Marine!

I wanted to be a meteorologist, but I was assigned as a rifleman to an infantry battalion. I spent enough time living in the dirt and on APAs (amphibious transport ships) to be convinced that I had watched too many John Wayne movies as a youth. I had the good fortune to be company runner the day a personnel transfer order arrived for a posting in Norfolk, Virginia. That evening I packed my seabag, happily turned in my 782 gear (field gear), and boarded the bus for Norfolk, Virginia. While a member of the Marine Detachment there, I was introduced to law enforcement. As I neared the end of my tour of duty in the Marines, I seriously considered law enforcement as a future career.

I became a police officer with the Springfield, New Jersey Police Department a few years later. In the beginning of my career as a law enforcement officer, like many new officers, I thought of myself as a white knight on a charger, sworn to stomp out crime. That attitude changed as the reality of life as a street cop set in.

Some of the more meaningful assignments during my years as a law enforcement officer included working security details for Dr. Martin Luther King when he visited New Jersey. There were nights spent in the dark watching the front of Dr. King's motel room. I wondered why Dr. King was allowed to stay in a motel room where the door led directly to the outside.

Nearly a year-to-the-day after the last time I saw Dr.

King, he died outside his room at the Lorraine Motel in Memphis, Tennessee.

Through competitive examinations, I was fortunate to be promoted through the ranks; shortly I became a lieutenant. Soon afterward, I was appointed Executive Officer. I set about changing the police department in ways that were considered innovative. Five years later, I made a decision to enter the private security field. I became the Director of Security for the Franklin State Bank in Somerset, New Jersey. My career became a series of investigations, running the gambit from numerous bank robberies to organized crime involvement in loan frauds. Bank robbery was rampant in New Jersey. At the time, one of the FBI's most wanted, Frank Simmons, was leading gangs in high-profile bank robberies.

Bank robbery was organized then, and some of the losses were sizable. Mock-ups of banks were laid out in vacant factories in Newark where the gangs would practice robbing the targeted bank. When they struck, their total time in the victim bank averaged forty seconds. We nicknamed the gangs, calling them the "Lickity Splits." We introduced programs that succeeded in reducing robbery losses from more than $250,000.00 a year to $600.00. New technology was emerging to combat bank robbery crimes. We were successful in reducing robbery losses and increasing apprehension rates by use of what were referred to as dye-packs. The dye-packs had all the appearances of a stack of strapped currency. Once the unit was taken from the bank, it would activate in a short amount of time, spraying red dye, red colored smoke, and tear gas onto the currency and usually the bank robber. Through the dye-pack technique and by installing Plexiglas bandit barriers to protect the teller line, the "Lickity Splits" turned to other banks for their victims.

Three years later, recruited by the Barnett Bank of

South Florida, I moved to Fort Lauderdale. I thought that I had experienced everything related to bank fraud in New Jersey, but I found that working crimes against banks in South Florida was a challenge. Everyday there was something new. Ed Houston, my new Chief Executive Officer had given me one clear directive, "Keep the Federal Government out of the bank!" That meant trying to keep everyone honest in an environment and an economy crowded with drug dealers and money launderers.

Banking operations in the State of Florida in those years were in a constant state of flux, moving from small unit banks, to county-wide operations; then, to state-wide organizations. Interstate banking was the future. When I went to work in South Florida, I was assigned responsibility for the security of twenty-eight branches. Within eighteen months, that number grew to more than 180. My position, title, and salary also grew with the bank and I became Vice President and Director of Security for the East Coast.

South Florida is the bank fraud capital of the world. I met more con-artists there than I care to count. Bank losses in a single case sometimes amounted to $500,000.00, and even as high as several million dollars. I investigated more than one commercial loan fraud where the commercial property addresses were located in the middle of Biscayne Bay!

I always paid close attention to bank robbery related crimes. Unlike the forger or the embezzler, the bank robber always presented the risk of harm to a bank employee or a customer. There was plenty of opportunity in South Florida, and later in Virginia, to focus on bank robbers. I investigated more than one hundred bank robberies during the years I was a bank security executive. I wanted to be able to do more. For me, where the law was concerned, everything seemed clear cut and simple. There was God's law; there was common and statute law. There was right or wrong with no middle ground. I spent my years in bank security investigating major crimes and training bank employees on safety and security issues. It was immaterial whether a person had stolen twenty dollars or a million; it was wrong and they were responsible for their actions. If that made me a straight arrow, then that is what I was.

PART I

Believing in Fairy Tales

CHAPTER 1

Dry Champagne

As they waited for the ceremony to begin, Richard trembled with all the excitement of a teenager in the first throes of serious love. Lauren had the radiant beauty of a woman who, nearing forty, had an understanding of the true desires of her heart, yet she too seemed as nervous as a schoolgirl on the way to her first prom. All either of them was sure about was each other. That was why they held hands like adolescents going steady as they stood in front of the local magistrate who had been hired to perform the ceremony.

The wedding was a simple one compared with the ceremonies they had experienced for their first marriages. Then the events had to be bridal-magazine perfect, and they had been certain that the vows they took and the bliss they anticipated would last "forever." Neither had realized the surprises life could hold. For Lauren, it was realizing at a tender age that a high school romance did not a marriage make and later discovering that the man whose aggressive self-confidence made her feel loved and protected was actually so insecure that the slightest challenge could cause him to explode with violence. For Richard, it was realizing too late that putting in endless overtime on his law enforcement job in order to provide for his wife and small children would estrange him from those he held most dear.

Some of Richard's friends had expressed concern over the quick courtship, especially in light of his failed first marriage, and had urged him not to rush into things. However, he was certain about this woman and their love. That they had been given a second chance while young enough to have a long life together came as a delightful surprise for them both. They realized that what mattered most was being with loved ones and celebrating quietly in the clubhouse of the apartment complex where they would be making a future filled with the commitment and happiness that eluded them both in the past.

It was a cold day in Virginia, and the apartment manager had carefully built a fire to warm the recreation room and add an extra touch of romance to the occasion. Velvet folding chairs had been set up for the friends and neighbors witnessing the ceremony, and the large room had the comfortable feel of someone's cherished home. Off to the side was a small kitchen area where trays of caviar, shrimp cocktail, and cold cuts, along with chilled champagne had been set out for the reception. It would be a simple, quiet service; a time for shared joy before the couple drove to Virginia Beach for their honeymoon.

The first time around, Richard and Lauren saw their weddings as the start of fairy tales come true, a time when they and their friends were determined to eat, drink, and dance all night. They each thought their love was the most natural, the truest, the longest lasting the world had ever known, or so they believed during the days and weeks when they settled into their first homes. That was why they had not worked at their earlier relationships. That was why they ignored the subtle changes, the little frustrations that would build and build until what should have been a firm foundation became a wall of separation.

Now Richard and Lauren understood that the future

was not magic, that it would bring joy only with constant effort. Richard was ready for commitment, for richer or poorer, in sickness and in health. And Lauren understood that the greatest strength a man can have is shown through loving kindness. Neither had regrets for the failures they had known. Each preferred to thank the Lord that they had been given a new chance for happiness at a time when they finally had their lives together.

"Do you, Richard Goetzke, take Lauren...."

Neither Richard nor Lauren knew someone uninvited was watching them at the ceremony. But the woman did not take her eyes off them.

The bitch is doing it again, she thought. Hidden in the shadows, Hannah angrily stared at Richard, trying to figure out what Lauren saw in the bastard. He certainly wasn't Hannah's type. For one thing, he was an ex-cop and Hannah hated cops, especially Richard and others, who she believed had locked away the only man she ever loved. They had taken away her best friend. They had hassled her when she attempted to kill Lauren's previous husband.

Okay, so she hadn't really killed him. Tried hard, that's for damn sure. Put those bullets square in his body, certain she had struck something vital. No such luck, though. Anyone who tells you it's easy to shoot a son of a bitch doesn't know what he's talking about. Miss the heart, miss the brain, miss clipping an artery, and what have you got? A sniveling wretch of a cripple who's scared silly of you but still alive. Scared silly proved good enough to make Lauren miserable when he decided to get out of their marriage, but letting him live was not something Hannah desired.

Not that she'd make that mistake again.

Hannah studied Richard closely, knowing he would never notice her. He couldn't take his eyes off that sweet-talking bitch, Lauren.

Hannah should have worn her usual clothes that day

to show off her firm bust line, trim waist and the shapely legs she had maintained. That was why she favored tight blouses and short skirts. If you've got it, flaunt it, was the way she lived her life, especially as she got older.

The problem was her face. Where Lauren's skin was smooth and taut, like one of those women they show in cosmetics advertisements, Hannah's face was already showing the ravages of both time and the inner rage she never quite contained. Her jaw sagged, and the folds of skin made her look like she had a knife scar on her cheek. It was a hard face, the type you sometimes see in areas of extreme poverty, where each day is a fight for survival and women age well before their time. At twelve they look twenty-five. At twenty-five they're already past their prime. And at forty they look eligible for Social Security. That was the kind of face Hannah was developing, another reason to keep the bitch from ever knowing happiness with any man.

Not that Hannah was finished with life. Her body was enough to overcome her facial flaws when she wanted to turn on a man, even Richard. By chance, she had found herself in the St. Augustine, Florida area a few weeks earlier when Richard and Lauren traveled together to a hotel on Annacostia Beach. She had seen him, let him get a glimpse of her body, then watched as he hurried Lauren back to their hotel room, presumably to have sex. Hannah had to smile at the memory, certain that when Richard entered his beloved, his mind was actually on her, not Lauren.

"I take you in love as my partner for life, with the promise that I will always love you and make your happiness my joy!" said Richard. He spoke movingly, without illusions, knowing that he had learned from the mistakes of the past. He was entering this relationship as a mature adult, a man who had been given a second chance for joy.

After Lauren and Richard had taken their vows, the

magistrate spoke for two or three minutes about the difficulty people have staying together these days. He told the couple, "You will be successful if you take the time to nurture your life and to work together for your marriage." As Lauren and Richard looked deep into each other's eyes, they both knew he was right.

In minutes the ceremony was over. The couple kissed. Their friends applauded. And then they celebrated, enjoying food, drink, and one another. "To my darling wife, who has made all my dreams come true," Richard said, offering Lauren his champagne glass to imprint with her lips. Finally, they all went up to Lauren and Richard's luxurious apartment so they could open their presents.

Even though his background was law enforcement and he was trained to look out for suspicious people, that day he paid no attention to anyone or anything except Lauren. And, after all, he didn't know Hannah and could not imagine that she existed as a threat not only to his happiness but also to his life.

By one-thirty in the afternoon, three hours after the ceremony began, the new Mr. and Mrs. Richard Goetzke found themselves alone together. He took her in his arms and gave her a long, lingering kiss. Later, they changed out of their formal clothes, walked hand in hand down to their car in which their suitcases had been stored, and drove an hour to Virginia Beach for their honeymoon.

Left alone, Hannah was incensed. *A knife*, thought Hannah. This time she would use a knife. *Up close and personal.*

The gun had been a mistake. Not only did the bastard live, there was a time when she thought Lauren might try to get back together with him. Lauren had grown estranged from that husband when Hannah tried to kill him, but his near-death experience seemed to make him so pathetic, she knew the bitch felt bad for him and even considered going back to him to help him through his recovery. Instead, he had divorced her—not a complete victory for Hannah but a partial one she would have to accept.

In their new Lincoln Town Car, Lauren sat next to Richard. He was so different. There was gentleness to him, a loyalty in adversity that made him the perfect soul mate.

Wounding Richard, Hannah thought, would only bring Lauren closer to him. But losing Richard would cause the bitch to grieve as she had never done before. Hannah knew, as she left the party before she could be spotted, that Richard had to die.

Richard knew nothing of Hannah when Lauren and he got married. He certainly had not spotted her at the wedding, his mind and eyes too focused on Lauren to notice anyone else.

Neither Lauren nor Richard had ever felt so alive, so physically and emotionally sensitive to another person. Richard almost felt ashamed for never having experienced such pleasure in his first marriage. Though that relationship had had its passion as well. They did have two children, after all. But the passion was like a trumpet whose bell is muffled by a mute. It is only exciting when you had not yet experienced the full range of the instrument without restraint.

Such was the relationship Lauren and he discovered. Richard had never been so happy in his life, and he knew that with the effort he planned to put into the marriage this second time around, the strength of their love would only grow with each passing day.

CHAPTER 2

Imprints of the Past

While Richard and Lauren spent these early hours of their marriage wrapped in the rosy afterglow of their commitment, Hannah's festering hatred for Lauren and Richard seemed to feed off their growing love for each other. She was obsessed with the idea of being their invisible stalker, observing as much of their honeymoon as she could without their being aware that she had followed them after the wedding reception. Each of Richard's gentle caresses, each tender kiss served to intensify her rage.

Hannah continued to watch them when they returned home and when they took frequent weekend getaways. Richard and Lauren's love aroused more than anger in Hannah, but also brought back many painful memories of her failure to have a similar bonding with her previous husband.

That man, Norm Graybill, was the type much admired in parts of Virginia. He was as rugged as the land, as self-sufficient as the animals that made their homes amidst the rolling hills covered with trees, wild flowers, and little-used roads. He was good with his fists, skilled with a gun, and as comfortable living in a crude mountain cabin as he was surviving in the high-rise wilderness of the city. He was a successful builder who did much of the work on his construction sites himself. If there were flaws in him, they came from his rigidity and failure to understand those whose lifestyles did not mesh with his own.

Hannah and Lauren were both in Roanoke at the time Norm was thinking of taking a wife and settling down. They both had met the man and both found him appealing, though in quite different ways.

Lauren saw Norm as a potential protector. She looked upon so rugged and successful an individual as someone who would protect her forever.

Hannah had a quite different view. She saw Norm as a challenge. How far could she push him before he exploded? She liked driving men into rages. She liked engaging in a violence of her own. Norm was a man with whom she could have fun, even if others might have thought her idea of pleasure was rather perverted.

If there was a chance for Lauren to ever be close to Norm, it was during a time when they were together, walking in the woods. Norm saw the woods as a place to find dinner on the hoof—deer, wild turkey, and the like. Lauren was like Richard Goetzke, probably one of the reasons they ended up together. She saw the woods, the seashore, and other pastoral settings as places for quiet meditation. She enjoyed the beauty, the chance to escape from the cares of the world if only for a few hours. As a result, when Lauren and Norm came upon an abandoned wild turkey nest, Lauren saw a perfect but abandoned egg as a pet waiting to be born, while Norm saw the egg as a turkey sandwich waiting to happen. In fact, he had relatives who operated a farm on which they raised livestock to sell as meat. A wild turkey was food, nothing more. Besides, the abandoned egg was probably rejected for good cause. It was not worth bothering about.

Lauren, a woman with an intense love for animals, ardently disagreed. She gently, carefully picked up the egg despite Norm's teasing. She took it home, managing to keep the shell from cracking. She placed the egg in a Styrofoam cooler, using an electric light to simulate the heat of the mother's body, hoping it would hatch.

"When it does, there will be new life from the abandoned nest," she explained. When the egg hatched, Lauren was ecstatic.

From the first moment she saw the bird, Lauren fell in love. She immediately named it "Turkey Little" and nourished the hatchling by hand. Day after day she cared for the bird until it was a full grown tom. Knowing that Norm's family owned a farm, she asked Norm to see if he could arrange for her to take Turkey Little there for breeding.

The arrangement Norm made was quite different from what Lauren intended. She made daily visits to the farm, bringing Turkey Little treats and delighting in his antics. She watched him get big, fat, and delightfully sassy. She anticipated his being mated so there would be new babies to enjoy.

What Lauren didn't understand was that on a farm, only cats and dogs are pets, and often that is because they are working animals. When Turkey Little got big, Lauren thought there was more of him to love. Norm's relatives saw dinner. Even worse, when the bird was slaughtered without telling her, Norm, who knew how Lauren felt, shared in the feast.

Hannah, who never forgave Lauren for having a relationship with Norm, never let herself get in a position to be hurt the way Lauren had been. Hannah had no illusions about Norm when she married him. He was a good provider, a good lover, and a man she thought she could torment.

Exactly what happened during Hannah and Norm's marriage was never clear. Years later, when Richard would try to learn of Hannah's past, one story he would hear was that she had been beaten fairly frequently. By then, he had met Hannah, had personal experience with her viciousness, and suspected that the battles were far from one-sided. Those who

knew Hannah suspected that perhaps Norm was goaded into
violence, and the only times Hannah complained were when
she came out on the losing end. Whatever the case, the relationship was intense.

Another story about the relationship between Hannah
and Norm revolved around his gun collection. Hannah gave
him a .44 magnum pistol which he said was a Christmas present. He loved the gun and carried it with him whenever they
went to a cabin they owned near a mountain lake.

It was during the summer or early fall that Hannah
claimed to have been the victim of an assault that led to their
divorce. Norm allegedly pushed her onto the bed, holding
her there while he brought the revolver up to her head.

Hannah later claimed that she stayed immobile, making no effort to resist. She knew the pistol was loaded, could
see the rounds in the chamber. If Norm pulled the trigger, and
any movement might cause his finger to twitch, she would be
dead. Norm quietly cocked the hammer, the gun still pointed
at Hannah's head, and Hannah closed her eyes and waited. At
the last instant, according to the story, Norm turned the barrel
away from her and fired. The noise left her with a permanent
partial hearing loss, but the bullet landed harmlessly in the
bedroom wall.

In the retelling, the incident was never very clear. What
was certain was that the divorce case of Hannah Leigh Graybill
vs. Norm Graybill went to court soon after. Hannah already
had a restraining order against Norm which forced him to leave
their apartment. But Hannah had no money, and Norm
wanted nothing to do with the bills she was running up on her
own. Even worse, she had worked hard to make the down payment for a new red pickup truck Norm wanted. She considered it a shared asset, even though he was the primary driver.

Hannah realized that she had to set up grounds to
divorce this jerk and began seeing a counselor to whom she

described a situation of domestic violence. She would later claim that Norm sat mutely while she talked with the therapist, then drove home in the truck, punching her repeatedly in the side of the head while he maneuvered through the streets. Afterward, when Norm left her, he took the truck she'd given him and left the payment book.

On the morning of the court date of the divorce, September 24, Hannah planned to stop by a friend's home, then see her therapist as preparation for the afternoon appearance before the judge, at which she was angry and determined to get the pickup back. Only after she was on the road did she remember that her friend was working that morning and would be unable to take a break to see her. She made a U-turn and headed back home, unexpectedly spotting her soon-to-be ex-husband's pickup truck ahead of her on the road. When he pulled into a Seven-Eleven convenience store parking lot, she followed.

Inside the store, the couple was civil towards each other, exchanging small talk. They both agreed that a major part of their lives together was over and said that past animosity had no place in their new relationship. Norm mentioned that he still had a suit in the closet of the apartment where Hannah was living that he wanted to wear to court. He asked if he could pick it up later that morning.

Hannah did not want Norm stopping by, but she agreed to take the suit to the job site where he was directing construction that day. She also said that she would return a black powder rifle of his that was also still in the apartment. Norm had left both the black powder weapon and a .22-caliber rifle, though the latter was the least treasured of his weapons and he forgot she still had possession of it.

It was mid-morning when Hannah arrived at Norm's job site. He was sitting in his truck, taking a coffee break. She drove up and signaled him to follow her. He started the truck and drove only about 300 feet down the road when she stopped her car by the curb. As Norm got out of the truck, he saw that Hannah had the .22-caliber rifle leaning against the front passenger seat. The weapon surprised him, and he apparently said something nasty to her when she picked it up and pointed it at him.

There were no witnesses to the words the couple exchanged. Later Hannah would allege that he said, "You bitch! Don't threaten me. The whores down on Williamson Road are better than you are!"

A woman standing outside her house watering her lawn saw the rising argument but could not tell what it was about. She saw Hannah get out of the car and slap some keys into Norm's hand. She saw him go back to the trunk of Hannah's car, open it, and remove the black powder rifle wrapped in a blanket to keep it clean.

As Norm straightened up, cradling the weapon, he realized that Hannah was now standing in the street, aiming the .22 directly at him. "Oh my God!" he cried as a smiling Hannah fired the first round at Norm's head. Instantly, the woman watering her lawn dropped the hose and crouched in her flowerbed, hoping the plants would hide her from view. She did not realize she was safe. Hannah was totally focused on Norm as she fired round after round until she emptied the clip of thirteen bullets and continued to dry-fire, oblivious to the fact that she was out of ammunition.

Later, the woman across the street would tell of her horror at seeing the delighted smile on Hannah's face. Later it would be found that five rounds hit their mark, while nine other bullets flew wildly through the neighborhood.

Hannah calmly walked over to her fallen husband's side. Norm was unconscious. She and the witness were certain he was dead.

Next, Hannah grabbed her car keys from Norm's

hand. Then she calmly cleaned up the brass, making certain she did not litter the street by leaving the shell casings. Finally, she got in her car, sat behind the wheel, and studied her ex-husband in the sideview mirror for a while. She slowly drove away and calmly reported for her appointment at the medical clinic with the therapist she was supposed to see prior to her court appearance.

"Good morning. May I help you?" asked the therapist's receptionist, looking up at her.

Hannah stared at the woman, then replied, "I shot my husband."

"What? What did you say?" the receptionist asked in disbelief.

Hannah smiled at her. "I just shot my husband. I think I killed him."

To her surprise, Hannah hadn't killed Norm, but she had come very close. He recovered after major surgery and months of prolonged convalescence. To add insult to injury, Hannah found herself in jail for the attack. But there was a silver lining in this cloud; Hannah met the only man she would ever really love while locked up. This love would sustain her through the years following her release, years in which her hatred for Lauren for having had a relationship with Norm, her anger towards anyone who dared to love Lauren, and her desire to impress her future love—a convicted career bank robber—would lead to Richard Goetzke's life becoming a nightmare even Norm Graybill could not imagine.

— CHAPTER 3 —

Men and Swine

Hannah's disgust and contempt for Richard and Lauren's perfect little romance grew each day. Not only were these two slobbering idiots together, but she was separated by bars and razor wire fence from her true love. The more joy Richard brought to Lauren, the more Hannah came to think of him as "the Swine," a term she used when writing to her boyfriend in prison.

That was a fact of life that burned her butt. So long as Lauren and Richard were together, there was no way for John Anthony Taylor, the man she loved, to call her. A post office box enabled her to get letters from him without anyone stumbling across their declarations of love. However, the only way they could speak was via the telephone if he could reach her, something only possible *if* she were ever around to receive the collect call. A five-minute delay getting through a checkout line in a grocery store and some other poor son of a bitch in the prison would be hogging the telephone.

Maybe things would have been okay, Hannah thought, had Lauren stayed as stupid as she had been before she married Richard. She was one of those women who wimped out the moment the preacher said, "I now pronounce you man and wife." Stay home, have kids, wear an apron, dab a little flour behind each ear, and put out whenever the bastard wants sex. Little Suzy Homemaker. Little Suzy Whore was more like it. She had never had the balls to stand on her own two feet, to become independent, so when the bastards had started knocking her around, little Lauren had borne the pain as if it was her due, until they had kicked her out of their lives.

Hannah was different. She had become an entrepreneur with a business of her own. She was earning hundreds a day, more than she had ever earned in those menial jobs she had had when her earlier husbands tossed her out on her ass.

For the first time Lauren was earning money too. Not that she and Richard needed money. Richard Goetzke was the vice president and director of security for branches of a large bank all along the east coast. The Swine spent his time traveling from bank to bank, an expert at foiling criminals. He told Lauren about the ways he investigated check fraud, credit card fraud, embezzlement, and all the other problems banks had. He was also the one who went after professionals who made a career out of making withdrawals from banks in which they never deposited money and catching bank robbers like John.

Of course, Hannah had never meant to fall in love. She had always seen men the way she saw Norm Graybill, as either play toys or violent bastards you had to hurt before they hurt you. Romance was for suckers, and commitment meant you had to believe his bullshit when he came back from getting a newspaper and some smokes and couldn't understand where or how he might have gotten lipstick and perfume on his collar.

However, the one man that changed her view of the male gender was John Anthony Taylor, the man she met while she was serving time for shooting Norm. John was different. He understood loyalty. He understood monogamy.

Hell, being in the penitentiary, he couldn't cheat on her if he wanted to, though she had a gut instinct that he would never want to, and that instinct of hers had kept her alive in some tight places in the past. Besides, he was a professional in his field the way Michael Jordan had been a professional in basketball. He was the man others fantasized being, a natural, and only a self-righteous prick like Goetzke could feel the country was a better place with John locked away for life.

John Taylor had been born to rob banks the way other boys are born to be dancers, gymnasts, writers, or painters. He studied bank use, bank security, and the ways a professional might slip up. Then he did his best to never make the mistakes that caused the less dedicated, the foolishly opportunistic, or the amateur to get caught. And if he did get caught, his resolve was not to change his career but his method until he perfected it.

Hannah had learned that Taylor had enlisted in the Air Force when he was barely out of his teens. It was then that he decided to put his studying to best use by robbing the banks that clustered around the base. Banks know that the military payroll for both GI's and civilian employees working at the base can bring in millions of dollars each year. That is why they open branches to take advantage of the potential business, and that was why Taylor was able, after studying their operations, to pick and choose which ones he wanted to rob.

Taylor developed his style while still young. First there was the matter of deadly force. Most bank robbers claim to have a gun, but few do. Guns are expensive, dangerous, and can add to your sentence when caught. Besides, the fear of a weapon can be as intimidating for most people as the weapon itself. However, in a crisis, if a robber is confronted by an armed security officer, a handgun may be his only chance to escape. That was why Taylor always planned for the worst, tucking a weapon in his waistband, then hiding it under a jacket, sweater, or shirt. When he ordered the tellers to hand over their cash, he would raise whatever covered the weapon just enough so the teller could see he truly was armed. The added fear enabled him to leave the bank before anyone had the courage to sound the alarm.

Taylor also liked to rob banks on Tuesday, another sign of his professionalism. There are three days when banks have larger than normal sums of money on hand, Hannah had learned when deliberately listening in on the Swine's conversations with Lauren. The most obvious day is Friday. This is when people get their paychecks and need them cashed. Depending upon the location of a branch, several hundred thousand dollars more money might be on hand Friday compared with the rest of the week. However, since everyone knows this, security is likely to be more intense, and the bank staff is more on the alert.

Monday and Tuesday are days of high merchant deposits. Monday is the day when many merchants deposit their weekend cash. Tuesday is similar, many other merchants using Monday to count the cash and compare it with the receipts, holding it in safes until their second business day. Because the public is generally unaware of this high influx of weekend business cash, security is usually normal on the first two days of the week. In addition, the staff is frequently lax, still more focused on the weekend just past than the work they are paid to do.

John Taylor also recognized that if he could mask key features of his face, he would look like a thousand other men. He wore a brimmed hat that both hid the shape of his head and added shadows to his face from overhead lights. He wore sunglasses, a common sight in banks in the sunny southeastern cities where he did his work, and he wore a bandage on his chin. He looked as though he might have badly nicked himself shaving or perhaps sustained an injury in a fall. He certainly didn't look like a man who was going to rob the bank, nor would the cameras record a face anyone could recognize. As a result, it took him ten years before his first arrest, and though his conviction was for a string of eleven robberies, Hannah was certain he had gotten away with dozens more.

John Taylor had served ten years for his crimes, causing no trouble in prison and spending all his spare time planning the rest of his robbery career so he would not return to jail. That was another reason Hannah had come to respect him. Bank robbery was his profession. He was proud of his accomplishments and proud of the potential for the future. Prison was a setback, but it was also an opportunity to plan capers so he would not be caught again. He didn't waste his time getting involved in the perverted sex and violence which take place in prisons. He remained dedicated to what he considered his calling. He was more together than Hannah had ever been in her own life, could ever imagine being. If truth be told, there were many times when Hannah was so scattered, people would tell her she had done things she couldn't remember. Most of them were lying, she was sure. But not all of them, and that was what was so troubling.

She consoled herself: at least Lauren was as scattered, albeit for different reasons, as she was. The two were so much alike in so many ways, they might have been mirror twins. Except that Lauren had Richard, the Swine, while Hannah had the love of a real man—John Taylor.

It was back in the '80s that John Taylor was released from prison. He had used the time well for a career criminal, cops and bank officials like Goetzke seeing him as arrogant and cocky, with renewed self-confidence. For example, after robbing one bank, the staff had immediately introduced new security measures. Unfortunately, a bank executive who spoke with the news media that evening announced that the new measures would prevent a future robbery of the type that occurred earlier that day. It was a statement John watched on the evening news, laughing at an arrogance even greater than his own. The next day he put on his hat, his glasses, and his bandage, entered the bank, walked up to the teller he had robbed the day before, and calmly said, "Okay, Honey, you know the routine!" He smiled as she gave him the money.

Hannah knew from both listening in on Goetzke's conversations and talking about bank robberies with John that there was little that could be done to stop someone from robbing a bank. There are cameras, of course, and many banks have armed security guards. Yet with all the dangers of violence in a building filled with innocent people, banks spend most of their security resources on apprehending the robbers after the crime is committed. They hope to deter a robbery by making it a crime where the perpetrator feels certain he will be quickly caught.

Hannah had no idea what the bank John Taylor robbed might have added to better assure apprehension, and, of course, she didn't care. Admiration, not prevention, was her rationale. The Swine, on the other hand, was an expert in loss prevention, training the employees of the bank branches for which he was responsible, as well as speaking to national organizations of security professionals. He taught bank personnel how to reduce the bank's vulnerability and how to make it easier to catch the rare individual who went ahead with such robberies anyway. From listening to some of his conversations with Lauren, Hannah thought it most likely that the bank teller John had robbed that unfortunate day had placed activating dye packs in the teller cages. These were extremely effective against amateurs, but the professionals knew the secret. They realized that it was sensors in the doors of the bank that activated the dye packs, and back then, the packs were easy to spot. While there were legitimate bills at the top and bottom of a wrapped pack of money, the bills in between were phoney and hollowed out to hold the dye pack. Just fanning the bills to see if they were all genuine would reveal the pack. The experienced robber would throw it on the floor rather than pass with it through the activator located in the exit door. He or she would escape, confident that all the other money was genuine.

Taylor was great, but he was still a man. Hannah had seen the inside of a jail or two in her own day so she couldn't claim to be that much better, but she knew that he might never have been caught had he followed the pattern that made him a success. John Taylor's robberies at that time were earning him between $250,000 and $300,000 per year. He bought a home in Fredericksburg, Virginia and moved in with a cocktail waitress at least twenty years his junior.

Taylor's girlfriend at that time, Tina Marie Julian, probably was unaware of how he earned his money. She also did not care about their age difference, despite her being twenty-two and him being in his forties. She loved him, loved the way he treated her, and would do literally anything for him.

At about that time, John met Robert Tindle III, a troubled young man from Groton, Connecticut who moved to Fredericksburg after his marriage fell apart. Tindle found a job, then began going to bars after work. It was in one of them that he had met Taylor, who decided to use the lonely young man.

Taylor introduced Tindle to cocaine, something John could readily afford and which he used in moderation. Tindle, by contrast, became hooked on the drug. Soon the expense of Tindle's habit was greater than his income, at which time he agreed to become Taylor's partner in a string of bank robberies.

Tindle was not a career criminal. Had he not been desperate for large sums of money, it is doubtful he ever would have committed a crime in his life. In order to satisfy his drug habit, though, Tindle was willing to do anything for cash.

The partnership was a mistake. John was accustomed to working alone and was not ready for any problems involving the judgment of a second person.

At first, Tindle was effective. The new partners successfully robbed Old National Bank in Inwood, West Virginia on May 7, 1987, then returned on June 29 to rob it again. Their total take was $23,579, money that paid the bills until July 20 when they struck the Williamson Road branch of United Virginia Bank, in Roanoke, Virginia.

Robert was the wheelman for the United Virginia Bank robbery. Taylor handled the robbery inside the bank on his own, confident in his sunglasses, hat, and chin bandage, while Robert waited outside ready to drive them to nearby Interstate 81 from which escape would be easy.

As John entered the bank, Robert sat in the car by the curb of the street adjoining the bank's parking lot. The location assured that no matter how crowded the bank became, he would still be able to swiftly blend with the morning traffic as they made their getaway.

Entering the bank, John told the teller, "You know what to do!" He slid a paper bag across the counter, then raised his shirt enough for her to see the handgun stuck into the waistband of his trousers.

The teller panicked. She moved more slowly than Taylor wanted, her hands shaking so intensely it was hard for her to get the money from the two cash drawers she maintained. Knowing that the risk of getting caught rose with the number of minutes he was inside the bank, John softly hissed, "That's it! Give me the bag!" There was no sense in staying any longer. He would settle for less in order to make a clean escape.

He didn't count on the fact that, though scared, the teller was also a professional. She slipped a dye pack in with the rest of the currency. There had been changes in the dye pack design over the years, and with the pressures of the heat of the moment, John overlooked it. He passed through the triggering device imbedded in the front door. First the timer went off, and twenty seconds later he was enveloped in a fog of powder, pepper spray, and dye. Whatever dye touched his skin would remain there through several days of washing, a constant beacon alerting anyone seeing John to his crime.

At the same time that the dye pack activated, a Wells Fargo armored truck entered the parking lot and stopped at the front entrance. Flustered, John moved past the truck, frightened that one of the two armed guards sitting in the cabin would open the door and stop him. The fear was groundless. Armored car guards owe their first allegiance to the large sums of money they transport. During a robbery in progress, they were required to stay inside the truck and radio for assistance, rather than put themselves at risk. John probably knew this, but in the confusion of the red smoke enveloping him, burning his eyes, making him feel as though he could not breathe, he was no longer rational. He lurched towards the getaway car, stumbling, tears streaming down his face, his heart racing rapidly.

Robert Tindle was not an experienced criminal. He had never studied banks or bank security. He was once a decent man who had become addicted to a drug more meaningful to him than life itself. All he understood was that the robbery had gone wrong and John was in trouble. There were two armed men watching the escape, and there was a good chance Robert would go to jail if he waited around. When he saw Taylor drop the sack of money in the parking lot, he started the car's engine. By the time Taylor reached the passenger side, the panicked Tindle was starting to pull away from the curb. Unable to open the door, Taylor pulled his automatic and ran alongside the slowly accelerating vehicle. Pointing the barrel through the window, he screamed, "Stop, you chicken shit bastard!" Tindle, suddenly realizing no one was in pursuit, hit the brakes so John could pull open the passenger side door and leap inside. With great feelings of relief, the two men made their escape.

During the next ten days, Taylor and Tindle robbed two more banks, this time without problems. Feeling as though he was getting back in the groove, Taylor, who had to carefully cover any skin stained by the dye pack ink with makeup, took his friend to the Citizen State Bank in Kingsland, Georgia, walking out with $5,287. From there they went south on Interstate 95, moving on to Daytona, Florida for their next robbery.

Then John's luck ran out. He was arrested, placed under federal jurisdiction, and returned to the Roanoke County Jail in Salem, Virginia. Because the crime spree had covered seven states from New York to Florida, John knew he was looking at a minimum of twenty years in prison.

There was little news about John Taylor's activities throughout the fall and winter of 1987 as he sat in the Roanoke County Jail awaiting trial on federal charges relating to the string of bank robberies. The focus of the prosecutors was the United Virginia Bank robbery. This was their strongest case and the one they felt certain to win. They had eyewitnesses, bank surveillance photos, and the FBI laboratory reports showing that the chemical dye used in the rigged money pack was the same as they found still staining Taylor's clothes. In addition, as Hannah learned later, Robert Tindle III had agreed to testify against his former partner after John told him he would not mind. John told Tindle that he shouldn't have to pay a high penalty for crimes that were primarily Taylor's. As it turned out, Taylor encouraged Tindle to testify because he felt his manipulated partner deserved a better shot at the future.

What Taylor never said was that the main reason for his generosity and the encouragement of his friend was that Taylor was certain he would not be going to prison. Instead, he was planning to manipulate his girlfriend to help him escape.

The Roanoke County Jail where Taylor was being held was as close to a maximum-security facility as could be found. New, modern, and with many high security features, no one had ever escaped and it was doubtful anyone could. The windows were narrow slits too small for anyone to squeeze through. There were closed-circuit television cameras, special mantraps created by synchronized doors, and numerous other devices impossible to defeat. It was also a high-rise structure with the exercise yard located on the roof where county correctional officers kept a close eye on inmates stretching their legs in the fresh air.

Taylor decided that the answer to his need to escape would come only if he could leave the jail. After coordinating an escape plan with Tina Julian during her visits to see him, he pretended to develop severe chest pains requiring him to see a doctor.

The procedure for handling a prisoner needing medical care involved having him transported to a private facility after he was restrained with handcuffs and leg irons. The latter were essentially hobbles that made walking extremely difficult and running impossible. The United States Deputy Federal Marshals, an elite federal protection service, would escort him.

Marshals are expert shots who are skilled at keeping people safe from even the most expert killers. They are assigned to protect witnesses involved in the prosecution of powerful mob figures, for example. They are assigned to help people obtain new identities and a fresh start. And they are assigned to escort federal prisoners, including those at high risk of escaping or becoming violent.

When Taylor's chest pains seemed severe, he was taken to the Roanoke Medical Clinic in downtown Roanoke for examination by Dr. Thomas Walker. The doctor found nothing obviously wrong with Taylor, but when someone claims to have chest pains, there are many underlying causes that can be diagnosed only after specialized tests. As a precaution, the hospital scheduled Taylor for two follow-up appointments, the first being for February 25 and the second for March 9.

Taylor thought his best chance to escape would be during one of his visits to the Roanoke Medical Clinic. He figured that if the escape attempt did not occur until the third visit, there was a chance the deputy marshals would be somewhat lax. All Taylor needed was his girlfriend Tina to coordinate matters for him, and he was certain he could flee the country successfully.

Tina Julian was a woman with mixed feelings about John Robert Taylor. It is uncertain if she believed him to be guilty of the bank robberies for which he had been sent to jail, because she had never probed the source of his money. She loved him, loved what she perceived as his caring attitude and respect for her as a person. If she did think he was a criminal, she was probably like Hannah, who refused to look upon bank robbery as a serious crime. Besides, if she helped him escape, they would be able to travel on his savings, starting fresh in a new location where they could have the life she always desired. The past would be over for both of them.

The problem was that she was scared. She was not a criminal. She had been kept away from John's business life. Even if she understood that he was doing something dishonest, she never felt his actions could affect her. Yet suddenly she needed to be a participant in a crime in order to set him free.

It was not that anyone would get hurt. The threat of violence in a public place would undoubtedly prevent anyone from actually using a weapon. Too many people could get hurt. Tina would just scare the guards, freeing John, leaving the guards bound and helpless, then fleeing to where they could start a new life together.

Tina was certain that it would work, yet to be on her own, without John.... She was hesitant and frightened, but John was at his most persuasive.

There were many visits, love letters, and telephone calls between them in which he cajoled, pleaded, and intrigued her. When they were certain they would not be monitored, their talk was of the escape plan. When Taylor thought the guards might read or overhear their conversations, their talk was of their love.

Not that Tina truly understood all the risks. So far as can be determined, she focused on Taylor's declarations of undying love. She would adore him whether he was in or out of jail, but she could not stand the idea of never again being able to hold him in her arms, to know the intimacy of their love-making, to spend the nights sleeping by his side and the days sharing the joys and sorrows of life. She agreed to help free him.

Taylor taught Tina how to do the type of reconnaissance at the medical clinic that he had used when successfully robbing banks. On February 25, she arrived at the medical clinic well before he was brought there for his appointment. She sat in her parked car watching his arrival, making mental notes of everything that was done. She saw how the deputy marshals checked the area, where they parked, the procedures they used taking Taylor into and out of the building and where they were most likely to be distracted. Over the next two weeks, during her visits to the county jail, John reviewed with her the final plans for his escape.

By March 9, the day of Taylor's third medical
appointment, Tina knew what her future would be. She and
John would go to Hawaii, get married, and live the good life.
There would be no more crime, no more hard work, and no
more loneliness. She was assured of his love, a love she
seemed to believe was as sincere and complete as her own
for John. That was why she was willing to call a friend of
John's, a man named Barry Dotson who lived in
Fredericksburg and would do just about anything for a price.

On the appointed day, Tina Julian and Barry Dotson
drove to the clinic far enough in advance of Taylor's appointment that they would be able to surprise the deputy marshals. They carried with them two handguns, a rifle, canisters
of tear gas, a bolt cutter, and duct tape. So far as could be
determined, they planned to bind the marshals, cut Taylor's
chains, and escape.

As Tina and Barry waited, John Taylor was riding
toward them in an unmarked government van, his hands
cuffed, his legs shackled. His escorts were two marshals—relative rookie Julia Webber who had just completed her second
year with the service and sixteen-year-veteran David Hopkins
who was four years from retirement. Despite their differences,
both were well trained and ready for any confrontation.

Marshal Webber drove, parking the van in front of
the clinic entrance. She exited the driver's side, then walked
around the front of the van to establish cover for her partner.
Once she reached the passenger side, Marshal Hopkins began
removing John Taylor from the van. It was at that moment that
they were most distracted, and it was at that moment that Barry
Dotson placed the muzzle of his pistol against Julia Webber's
face. "Get your gun out," he yelled to his accomplice, glancing
over at her. Tina Julian stood mesmerized next to him, her
handgun tucked in the waistband of her jeans. She was too
scared to move. Taylor knew he had only seconds to act. With
his cuffed hands he pushed Tina aside to get to Hopkins.

In law enforcement, the difference between life and death is often a matter of training under pressure. Deputy Marshal Hopkins saw Barry Dotson's eyes look away from Julia for just an instant. Taking advantage of his prisoner's limited mobility, Hopkins slammed into Taylor, knocking him to the ground at the same time drawing his pistol from his shoulder holster. He kept himself controlled enough to fire two rounds in rapid succession, assuring that if he missed the first time, he would have a chance with his second shot before the gunman could shoot his own weapon.

Practice had given Hopkins the skill he needed. Barry Dotson's head jerked back from the first shot. As he fell, the second shot slammed into his body. He was dead before he hit the ground, never able to use the gun that had threatened the life of Marshal Webber.

Two more rounds struck Tina Julian. A look of astonishment crossed her face as she struck the asphalt of the parking lot, bleeding profusely. She was dead within seconds.

John Taylor showed the only emotion he would be witnessed experiencing over the death of his lover and his friend, who had uselessly sacrificed their lives for him. He raised himself to his knees, weeping at the sight of the two bodies, though no one could tell if he was crying over the loss of his love or because he knew there would be no further chance to escape. His dreams of freedom were unquestionably over.

Marshal Hopkins hauled Taylor back into the van as Marshal Webber radioed law enforcement's standard call for help: "Shots fired!" Within minutes, several marked police units of the Roanoke City Police Department were on the scene, followed by television camera crews, newspaper reporters, and radio journalists.

The story of the escape attempt was major news for the next several days, and it was a story that fascinated

Hannah. She saw John Taylor as a man who dared to live on the edge. He thumbed his nose at conventional morality. He defied authority. His life was his own, and others be damned. She could love a man like that.

After their relationship began, Hannah never did ask John why he had decided to change his pattern. It was the kind of question the Swine might have wanted answered so he could talk like he knew something about everything, but what did she care? John was behind bars again when Hannah met him. If he was on the streets, she would have had a stake in keeping the guy away from the joint. But he wasn't. She was in the free world and had no intention of seeing bars and fences and razor wire again. So who the hell cared what made a great guy momentarily act like a jerk?

Hannah had never been someone to look upon bank robbery as a serious crime. Banks were rich. Who cared if a guy like John took a piece of the action? No matter how much he stole, there was always a hell of a lot more left. Robbing banks must be exciting. A man who would rob a bank was a man Hannah knew she could love, unlike the straight and upright pricks Lauren was drawn to.

Not that Hannah's thinking was so far removed from the mind-set of the likes of John Taylor. She had a boldness of her own, and it went beyond stalking Lauren. She had gone to jail long before she met the Swine, and there was seemingly nothing she would not do, no matter how violent, to satisfy her lust for power.

Strangely enough, Hannah and Lauren came from the same type of background, though their personalities developed in very different ways. Lauren had once thought that the role of a woman was to be a housewife, to have the children, to be the primary care giver, and to please her husband in any way he desired. What she had not anticipated was that "happily ever after" requires two people working together, and while she was willing to do her part, her husband became uncaring and abusive. She suddenly found herself faced with the necessity of a divorce she had not anticipated and responsibilities for which she was not prepared. Reconciliation was impossible. Counseling proved a waste of time. She had to leave her husband, and he refused to pay her alimony. That was when she discovered that being out of the job market for a while left her unprepared for many of the available jobs. She had to take any work she could find, no matter how menial or low paid, just to keep a roof over her head and feed her children, and so she began cleaning houses. She vowed no matter what she had to do, she'd never be dependent on anyone else again.

Soon she formed her own cleaning maintenance company, serving as president, marketer, receptionist, and sole employee, doing everything that had to be done. By the time she'd met Richard Goetzke, the business warranted hiring others to work for her. More importantly, she knew she would never again have to depend on anyone for survival and was her own boss.

If Lauren was gratified by being self-employed, Richard was the ideal, hardworking employee. He had always worked for someone else, first as a police officer who rose swiftly through the ranks, and then as a high level bank executive. He loved the fact that Lauren, who'd had such a difficult life, was trying so hard to be independent, though it caused her to spend long hours on the job. He wanted to change her life, to bring her love, to protect and support all her endeavors.

It would have been easy for Richard and Lauren to fall into a routine that focused on work, spending less and less time together. They could have told themselves that each was being supportive of the other by tolerating the long hours apart and the need for rest when they were together. Instead, they determined that their marriage was more important than their jobs because the jobs would end with retirement, but

marriage was for life. That was why they began taking every
weekend to get away together.

Every Friday night they put their jobs behind them,
packed their bags, and drove to the historic Chamberlyn
Hotel located in the Phoebus area, not far from Norfolk.
This was the "new" Chamberlyn Hotel, not the old one built
in 1816, in which Edgar Allan Poe read poetry in the 1830s
and which later served the needs of people traveling to Fort
Monroe just down the road. The fort was used to house
Confederacy President Jefferson Davis after the Civil War,
and the hotel served visiting government officials and those
dealing either with Davis or others at the fort. Following a
devastating fire in 1890, the second Chamberlyn rose from
the ashes. This "new" one only dated back to 1928, but it
maintained the appearance and the atmosphere of those earlier days. Stepping inside was like going back in time to an era
of opulence and optimism, a period when everything seemed
possible, when the stock market was making millionaires of
savvy laborers, and the Great Depression was still months
away. Richard and Lauren could relax, enjoy excellent meals,
walk the nearby beach, attend concerts in a park directly
across the street, and make love, knowing their tomorrows
would be even brighter than the joyous days they were living.

Hannah knew about the idyllic weekends at the
Chamberlyn Hotel, of course. She made sure she saw the
place for herself and watched the happy couple on these getaways. She was jealous not to have getaway weekends with
her own lover, but consoled herself with the knowledge that
Lauren and the Swine's time together would be very short,
and that she would be the one to bring it to an end.

Thoughts swirled through her mind. "Richard
Goetzke, I hate you," she hissed from her hiding place.
"How did you worm your way into our lives?"

CHAPTER 4

Goochland

Goochland, Virginia is a small community to the west of Richmond with a name that was hard for me to take seriously. It sounded like a town that might be used for a sequel to *The Wizard of Oz*, I had thought when my boss Arnie Walters first told me of the town.

I could just picture the movie. Dorothy and Toto would once again leave Kansas, this time encountering elflike creatures tiptoeing through cow pastures, dancing among the trees, and cavorting with colorful butterflies. In reality, it might be said that Goochland had the equivalent of the wicked witches who had caused Oz so many problems. The real Goochland was home not only to farmers and commuters, but also to many truly bad women housed in the sprawling complex of brick buildings, high fences, razor wire, and armed guards that constituted the Commonwealth of Virginia's State Correctional Facility for Women.

The area was a pleasant enough place to call home if you weren't primarily a city boy like myself. There were locals—Goochlanders they called themselves—who made a daily fifty-minute trip to Richmond so they could live in the midst of my imaginary elves. The almost two hours of driving each day assured that during the winter months they had to leave their idea of paradise before sunrise and not return home till after sunset. These residents ignored the presence of the prison, focusing instead on their town's closeness to nature.

It had been a cool December when my boss and long-time friend, Arnie Walters, called me at the office and said, "Dump the suit and tie and get out here to Goochland. I want you to look like a native and blend in with the locals."

"Okay, Arnie, but what does a Goochlander look like?" I asked, jokingly. Instead of an answer, Arnie hung up.

I drove to my apartment at the west end of Richmond, unaware that my life was about to change forever. At home, I changed into undercover clothes I thought suited the job— jeans, boots, a sweater, and a vest. As much as I wanted to tease Arnie, I knew what the call was all about, I knew why I needed to blend in with the locals. The trial of Susan Gabriel was taking place.

Susan Gabriel had been the talk of the Corporate Security Department when I was hired at the Virginia bank six months earlier. She had been a school teacher who had traded the classroom for a real estate office. She sold houses, a business she came to love and in which she excelled.

Among Susan's clients was a woman named Ann Croft who was going through difficult times with her marriage. Ann and her husband decided to buy a house in an upscale area apparently for much the same reason that some couples decide to have a baby when their marriage is in crisis. They thought it might bring them together. Instead, they decided to get a divorce before any decisions about property could be made. Susan had been extremely compassionate when she learned that Ann would no longer need her real estate expertise because her marriage was coming to an end. Susan even shared her home with Ann until she could get on her feet and find an apartment.

As the staff told me, Ann Croft began putting her life together by getting a job as an executive secretary in the bank for which I worked. At the bank Ann met our president and CEO, Harrison Bradford, a tall, handsome, extremely intelligent bachelor who was as lonely as Ann. When they eventually began dating, neither expected anything from the relationship.

I never did find out how Susan became angry with Ann. There was a suspicion that Susan might have fallen in love with her, but if that were true there was no evidence of a relationship that we ever discovered. More likely Susan was a disturbed individual who created a fantasy about Ann that was shattered when the woman began dating Harrison Bradford and found her own apartment.

The dating apparently came as a surprise to Susan. Susan had been happy for her friend when Ann was able to get a good job at the bank. She had not expected Ann to begin dating, and she certainly had not anticipated that the new relationship would be serious.

The courtship between my bank's CEO and Ann had been an intense one. They were both lonely people who needed a committed relationship. Harrison had money, renown, and power, but they were inadequate to satisfy his emotional needs. Ann was rebuilding her life, enjoying her job, comfortable in her new apartment, yet longing for the love she once thought she was going to find in her marriage. Lonely myself, I could well understand their needs.

Ann and Harrison spent every spare moment together and before long, got married. Other friendships were temporarily ignored, including Ann's relationship with Susan, not because anyone was being rejected but because the new situation was so all-consuming.

Susan apparently became livid over this. She seemed to feel as though she were deliberately being abandoned and believed that the couple had a conspiracy against her. When Harrison and Ann started looking to buy property in the same area that Susan had shown Ann during her first marriage, Susan felt her suspicions were confirmed. She was outraged to learn the Bradfords were using a different real estate agent, and when they purchased a house, Susan decided to strike back.

First came harassing telephone calls, one of the reasons my department became involved. The calls went to the Bradford home and the bank. Then Susan began visiting the couple in their new home, returning repeatedly even though she was regularly asked to leave. Finally, Susan waited for Ann in the parking lot of one of our banks in downtown Roanoke, physically and verbally attacking her former friend. She was arrested, charged with assault and battery, then released on bail with a trial date set for six months later.

With the physical assault, the bank's Corporate Security Department initiated protective actions for the Bradfords. Among other measures, ongoing surveillance of the Bradfords' cars was ordered when either or both were parked in any of the bank lots. Surveillance cameras were put in place to film any problems.

It was in June, approximately one year before I would join the bank's corporate security division and a month before Susan's scheduled court appearance, that she was spotted in the bank parking lot. As the videotape recorded the incident, Susan approached Ann's luxury car, took a key, and slowly scratched the paint. Before she could be stopped, she had done extensive damage to the finish of the car. The police came and arrested her, but bail was posted, and Susan was freed the same day.

Frustrated at being caught, Susan decided to find someone who could help her do serious harm to the Bradfords. She mentioned her troubles to a local house painter known for having less than reputable friends, and through him she was introduced to Jim Sanders, apparently a thug who would do anything for money.

Sanders met with Susan and obviously wanted nothing to do with the reasons she hated the Bradfords. He didn't care about motive. He cared about the job and how much he would be paid. "So what is it that you want done?" Sanders asked.

"I want to send a severe and extreme message to Harrison Bradford and his wife, Ann," Susan told Sanders.

"Like what?" he asked. "You want me to beat him up or something?"

"More than that," Susan told him. "Something like throwing acid in their faces, or maybe firebombing their house." She paused, thinking about what would please her most, then said, "Yes, that's it! Firebomb their house!"

"I could do that," Sanders replied. "It will cost you five grand."

"Five thousand? No way! I could have somebody killed for five thousand dollars!" Susan complained. Her assertion was probably not true. It was doubtful that she had ever even spoken to anyone who sold his skills at violence until she was put in touch with Sanders. However, he seemed to want the job because he said, "All right, what is it worth to you?"

"I'll give you five hundred now and fifteen hundred later. But it has to be finished before my trial on the fifteenth," Sanders told him calmly.

"If I have to, I'll kill the Bradfords or anyone else that gets in my way. Would that bother you?" Sanders asked Susan.

"Just do what you have to do!" Susan replied eagerly. She then wrote out a personal check for $500.

The problem for Susan was that Jim Sanders wasn't

a thug, nor was he an arsonist for hire or a hit man. And the supposed painter had no intention of using any connections he had so someone could be hurt. Instead, he went to the Roanoke Police Department and told them about his meeting with Susan. Sanders was a special agent with the Virginia State Police. His job was to protect people from individuals such as Susan, and he was gratified that she had found him and that he was able to bring the case to justice. With her check in his hand he had airtight evidence against the vindictive woman. On July 9, a thwarted Susan was arrested and charged with two counts of soliciting an undercover officer to commit bodily harm on the Bradfords. This time she would not go free.

At about the same time as Susan was jailed, Hannah entered pod 3B of the Roanoke County Jail in Salem, Virginia. She was livid. The bitch who worked for her therapist had made certain the police put her in jail, and for what? So she shot the bastard. Big deal! He hadn't even died—a fact that had ruined her whole day. Her rage and hate was as strong as Susan's. As luck would have it, the two women met at the county jail and were instantly drawn to one another.

As soon as Susan saw Hannah ferociously working out at exercise time, she trusted her. They exchanged stories, and Susan felt she had finally found a soul mate as comfortable with venting rage through violence as herself.

Like Hannah, a thwarted Susan was a deadly Susan. She wanted Ann and Harrison dead. "I'm going to lay back. I'll do my time and then lay low for a year," Susan told Hannah. "Then I'll take care of the Bradfords."

Hannah understood rage. She was equally determined to murder her ex-husband. "Susan, I should have run over that son of a bitch with my car," Hannah admitted. "Finished him off once and for all!" She scowled. "Hey, I put five bullets in him! You'd think that would have been enough to kill him! I've got to kill that son of a bitch."

The two like-minded inmates spent hours planning how they could kill the Bradfords. The Bradford home was on a lake, and Hannah came up with a plan. "We'll get a high-powered rifle and wait until they come outside. We'll kill both of them. After they're dead, we'll find Norm Graybill and kill him too!" Susan liked the idea, and they laughed together and slapped the tabletop gleefully. They were sisters in hate, and they delighted in their plans.

But they were careless and held their conversations where other inmates could overhear them. Neither Susan nor Hannah was wise about the ways of life in jail and did not realize the small advantages with the prison staff one inmate could create for herself by squealing on others. Other inmates heard the two women plotting against the Bradfords, and several reported the threats to Captain Stephen Huff, the officer in charge of the Roanoke County Jail. Being a responsible officer, Captain Huff wrote a letter to the judge in charge of Susan's case expressing his concerns about her actions.

The two women were also unrealistic about their timing. Neither would be leaving the jail for some time. In fact, in October Susan's attorney filed notice with the court that he would be seeking an insanity defense for his client. This led to a psychiatric evaluation that showed that Susan was sane and competent to stand trial. With this diagnosis, she chose to enter a guilty plea.

Susan got lucky. She was given two years' probation, ordered to make restitution for the damage to Ann Bradford's car, told to undergo psychiatric counseling in a closed facility, and to stay away from the Bradfords. The Commonwealth Attorney told the press, "By what has happened on the misdemeanor counts, we have ensured that she will receive psychiatric counseling. That was one of my main concerns."

Harrison Bradford issued his own statement, saying, "We're pleased she will receive psychiatric treatment. We earnestly hope this settles the matter. I suppose none of us will ever know how she became so obsessed and focused on doing us harm. They were terrible things she was contemplating. If` she were released immediately, we would be uneasy."

Susan realized that ultimately she would draw some jail time. She also knew she had been facing up to ten years in prison. But for the moment, she was going to be sent to Charter Westbrook Hospital in Richmond for a month of testing and observation. A psychiatrist had already told the court that Susan suffered from a "paranoid personality disorder that makes her believe she is being persecuted." However, that did not justify her vicious plotting against the Bradfords.

Susan posted a $75,000 bond and was sent to the hospital's Ward E. This was the high security wing which housed criminally insane patients as well as those patients who potentially were too dangerous to be in the general population. Ironically, Hannah would eventually be sent to the same ward.

It was in ward E that Susan met Randy Gladstone, a man who had not been charged with any crime and would soon be released. Since he was in a ward for violent individuals, Susan decided to ask him if he would help her kill the Bradfords. He enthusiastically agreed.

Susan stayed in touch with Randy after her month's hospital stay ended and she was returned to the county jail. This time she was cautious about how she handled herself. She never put anything in writing that might come back to haunt her. They both knew that when the time was right, she would give Randy the go-ahead.

While Susan had been in the hospital, Hannah had been dealing with her own psychiatric issues. A sentence-reduction hearing had been scheduled. She was taken to the transportation pod of the Roanoke County Jail where she waited with her escort for an elevator that would take her to a lower floor. The jail had secure sections to assure that no matter where a prisoner might be, he or she could be locked in, in case of an emergency. The pod was a mini-holding facility, and the elevator itself could be locked solidly by the outside guards if need be.

When the elevator reached the transportation pod level, a heavily shackled prisoner shuffled from the car surrounded by four county corrections officers. Hannah recognized him immediately. You could not read the local newspapers or watch the news on television without knowing who John Anthony Taylor was. She knew about his career as a bank robber. She knew of the escape attempt that had cost the lives of two people. And here was the man in the flesh.

Hannah liked what she saw.

"Hello, pretty lady!" said Taylor, smiling.

"Hello, John Taylor," said Hannah, also smiling. The attraction was obvious to them both. Had they been in a bar, they would have moved to a table for some quiet drinking, talking, and physical foreplay. But this was the county jail, and John Taylor was in handcuffs and chains.

"Pretty lady, you have me at a disadvantage. I don't know your name," said Taylor.

"Hannah. Hannah Graybill."

There was little time to say more. Taylor was moved to the back of the pod, away from the elevator. Hannah was escorted into the car that would take her downstairs and outside where a van was waiting. As she entered the elevator, John called, "Good luck, pretty lady!"

"Thanks!" called Hannah as the door was closing. "Stay in touch!"

The hearing went reasonably well for Hannah. She

had her supporters, including a report from a doctor who had been visiting Hannah in jail, counseling her on behalf of the court. "Based on my findings during the treatment of Mrs. Graybill, I do not believe that she is a threat to the safety of Norm Graybill."

There was further testimony from Hannah's mother explaining that she would provide a place for her daughter to live if she were released from jail. However, the judge was not fully convinced. He wanted Hannah to stay in the county jail with the exception of a temporary, two-week transfer to the extremely unpleasant county jail in Harrisonburg, Virginia. It had been built around the turn of the century from quarried granite and had an almost medieval appearance.

The Harrisonburg stay gave Hannah a chance to vent her anger. She spent hours being interviewed and tested by a forensic psychiatrist, then used her free time to write about all the abuse she had suffered at the hands of men over the years. Day after day she filled the pages of a legal pad, detailing the horrors that allegedly drove her to shoot Norm Graybill. When the psychiatrist studied the writing, he felt Hannah was telling the truth. He believed she was suffering from "battered wife syndrome," and felt this justified her shooting Norm.

Susan was not as fortunate as Hannah. Her month of testing resulted in a determination that she needed further treatment within a psychiatric facility. According to one of`the doctors, "Susan Gabriel suffers from an extremely rare paranoid delusional disorder, a developmental dysfunction that causes seemingly well-adjusted people to feel persecuted. I treated Ms. Gabriel for a month, and she believes Harrison Bradford orchestrated an elaborate scheme to break up her friendship with Mrs. Bradford. Without treatment, it is my opinion that Ms. Gabriel will continue to be a threat to the Bradfords if she were released."

There would be no psychiatric facility for Susan. She was "Goochland Bound" when the judge sentenced her to five years in prison on each count, the terms to run consecutively, and another ten years of supervised probation after her release.

Susan's psychiatric evaluation did not matter to Hannah. Susan had become her ally. If Susan wanted to hurt the Bradfords, Hannah would help her as promised.

Hannah's trial in June led her to plead guilty to malicious wounding by a firearm charge. There was nothing else she could do. There was no question that she had committed the crime. The only issue was why she had done it, and that was taken up in the sentencing hearing.

The "battered wife syndrome" defense was introduced but it had little impact. Hannah was sentenced to eight years in the Women's Correctional Facility. However, her defense attorney convinced the judge that she should see mental health professionals while staying in the county jail, then have a new sentencing hearing. This was done, and the experts decided that Hannah no longer hated Norm and she was no longer a danger to him or others. Her sentence was reduced to jail time served, plus seven-and-a-half years' probation.

But, although Hannah had fooled the experts, inside her a caldron of hate simmered. And into it she poured her desire for violence, for vengeance. And it was to Hannah who was stirring that pot that Susan wrote on a regular basis, enclosing letters to be relayed to Randy through the one friend who understood her obsession with the Bradfords.

In an ironic twist of fate, three of Susan's letters to Randy went astray and fell into the hands of Lauren. She opened them, curious, and discovered they were detailed plans to eliminate Harrison and Ann Bradford.

Lauren was as gentle as Hannah was violent. She could not imagine allowing one human being to hurt another.

Lauren immediately contacted the Commonwealth Attorney's office and gave them the letters. Little did she know that she would become an important witness who would have to testify later.

Susan did not realize what was happening, because no crime had been committed and no charges were filed. Instead, thinking Randy would murder the Bradfords on her behalf, she turned her hate towards the staff of the Goochland jail. This included filing an assault charge against prison nurse Jane Elmsford, whom Susan claimed had bruised her arm while forcibly taking away her medicine. Susan's problem was that there were numerous witnesses to the non-incident. Both inmates and staff sided against Susan, and the judge was livid.

"The prison nurse is presumed innocent," said the judge. "Every witness I heard made her more than innocent, if that's possible. Every witness that I heard made it sound that Jane Elmsford was trying to protect you."

"Crooked court!" Susan screamed at the judge.

"You've got ten days in jail," the judge told her and found her in contempt.

Between the false claim against the nurse and the letters misdelivered and turned over to the Commonwealth Attorney, the Virginia Parole Board's files were growing almost as large as the files my office at the bank was also keeping on Susan. On June 2, the parole board told the judge, "Ms. Gabriel is considered a poor parole risk because of the serious nature and circumstances of her crime."

Susan refused to take personal responsibility for her actions. She insisted that the only reason she wasn't being freed was because of the Bradfords' influence and the notoriety of her case.

The anger festered uncontrollably. Susan had only to wait until the second week of June in order to be given a mandatory release from prison. The bank security personnel were reviewing her files and planning how to protect the Bradfords, certain that Susan would not be so foolish as to jeopardize her release. What they did not count on was the depth of Susan's hate and her lack of awareness that others might interfere with her plans.

Susan had been indicted on nineteen charges including two counts of conspiracy to kill Harrison and Ann Bradford. Even the other inmates at the jail had become frightened of her rage. One of them wrote to the warden, saying that Susan told her, "I will get the people here who are responsible for getting my good time revoked. I will get them! Ask Harrison Bradford how well he sleeps. I will get Bradford for what he has done to me and my family."

At the end of September the charges against Susan were still pending. She had already served three months beyond what had been her mandatory release date. However, with so many charges pending against her, the judge ruled she had to stay in the prison until they were resolved.

The judge brought Carol Conrad, one of the prison counselors, into court to discuss what she had been told by Susan. "'I'll take care of the Bradfords when I'm out of prison,' Susan had said," the counselor related. "'The next time I go to jail, I won't be coming out.'"

Susan's words and attitude were chilling. The prison counselor was not another inmate who could be expected to remain silent. The counselor was an employee of the prison, a person responsible for the safety and well-being of the public. What was told to her in session was not private and could be used either for the benefit of the prisoner or to the prisoner's detriment. The judge asked Carol Conrad her professional opinion of how she saw Susan's statement.

"To me," said Conrad, "it meant that the next time Susan Gabriel did time, it would be for murder."

Susan was returned to prison to await a formal trial a year later. By then, as head of security for the Eastern region, I was treating the file on Susan Gabriel as must reading. I just did not expect getting the call telling me that I would have to go to Goochland for her trial. But I knew that the trial was a big deal to my CEO and the corporate security division, so I unquestioningly left Richmond for Goochland. As I pulled out of my apartment complex, I had no idea that I would soon be meeting my future bride.

CHAPTER 5

The Woman in the White Shawl

I entered the courtroom, looked around for a moment, and then went to the rear where I said hello to my CEO and his wife. Harrison and Ann Bradford were sitting with Arnie Walters. Then I took a seat to the right of the defense table so I could get a good look at the defendant. Though I had seen her before, I wanted to be doubly certain I could spot her anywhere.

Susan's appearance surprised me. She had gained considerable weight in jail and looked rather matronly. Her expression was unreadable, but as the Commonwealth Attorney began his opening remarks, she sat taking notes on a pad of paper. If it could be proven that she conspired with others to commit murder, she would be looking at more time. If not, she would be a free woman, someone the files indicated would continue to be a danger to the Bradfords.

I glanced around the courtroom, curious about how the people in the gallery fit into the case. There were reporters present, and the usual court watchers—retirees, the unemployed, and people whose work schedules allowed them the freedom to attend trials. These regular court watchers moved from courtroom to courtroom, sitting in on cases and listening to soap operas far more dramatic than anything on television. The most experienced of them could read a jury at least as well as the opposing attorneys. They knew when telling points were being made and when the case was going against the person speaking.

Finally there were people who were somehow connected with this particular trial. Usually these were not witnesses. In most cases a witness might have his or her testimony tainted by hearing the give and take between the attorneys and whoever was on the stand, so the witness was seated in another room, out of hearing range. The people in the courtroom were family members, friends, victims, or others who felt they had a stake in what was taking place.

My eyes settled on a woman seated two rows to the rear. Her face, though worn and tired, was beautiful. She had dark brown hair and a heart-shaped face setting off doe-like brown eyes. I had no idea who she was or what her connection with the case might be. I just knew I wanted to meet her.

The morning proceeded as these things always do. The prosecuting attorney laid out the state's case against Susan Gabriel, explaining the crimes for which she was charged, then discussing how the charges would be proven. Next, the defense counsel attempted to place a more desirable spin on the case. The defense wanted the jury to see Susan Gabriel as the victim of an overzealous criminal justice system. Perhaps a mistake was made. Perhaps words and actions were misinterpreted. "Whatever the case," Susan's attorney, Bill Marks, said, "it is a travesty that this case is in court."

In Susan Gabriel's case, Bill Marks added, "My client is innocent of all charges. Susan Gabriel has paid her debt to society for her previous failings. These latest charges are an effort to keep Susan Gabriel incarcerated for the convenience of a prominent citizen."

And then I understood why I was there. In this mostly blue collar, rural community where clothes were meant to get dirty and not be worn to cocktail parties, the influence of a wealthy and prominent big city resident was going to be examined. The defense was going to try to prove that the only reason Susan was in jail was because Harrison Bradford wanted her there. It was a class struggle, the hard-working woman who had made a mistake, just as any one of the members of the jury might have done, was now being denied a new chance to lead a good life.

I didn't know if the opening remarks and the way I saw the case proceeding would be effective. However, given what I had learned from reading Susan's file in the bank's security department, I was certain that if she was released, she would be an even greater risk.

As it turned out, despite the usual practice, there were witnesses in the courtroom. Apparently the judge had asked them to be present to hear the opening remarks from the attorneys and himself. When the defense counsel finished his presentation, the judge asked all the witnesses to leave the courtroom. That was when I saw the woman who had caught my eye wrap her shoulders with her white shawl and rise and walk out to the hall. Unable to help myself, I followed after her, but was stopped.

"Hey, Richard, I see you made it!" laughed Arnie. He had also gone into the hall to speak with a former deputy sheriff who now worked as a member of the bank's Roanoke-based security detail. The Bradfords were safe in the courtroom. There was enough official security there so that none of us from the bank needed to be present. And since we all knew how Susan had harassed and assaulted Harrison and Ann in the past, the only question we had was whether or not she would again be on the streets.

Arnie looked at my vest and joked, "We're going to have to chip in and buy you a coat with sleeves!"

I always enjoyed Arnie. We had first met ten years earlier at a security conference in Orlando, Florida. We were both speaking to the group, a situation that would repeat itself over the years, and our professional affiliation had led to a strong friendship.

Our career paths had gradually brought us together. I went from Miami, Florida to southwestern Virginia while he went from Phoenix, Arizona, to Roanoke. It was as if destiny had determined that we would work together. That was why, when Arnie accepted the position of Corporate Security Director for the bank's sixty branches he had offered me the position of Regional Security Manager for the Eastern District. I didn't hesitate to accept the job.

The conversation turned serious as Arnie outlined what he thought would be the outcome of the trial. "It won't be good if they cut her loose," said Arnie, concerned. "'They've got her doped up on anti-depressant now, but God only knows what she will do when she hits the street."

The former deputy, Fred Townsend, now part of our security detail from the bank, looked worried. He would be one of the people directly responsible for keeping the Bradfords safe. Seeing his concern, I joked, "Fred, if Susan walks, you are not going to be spending much time at home."

"Yeah, Richard." Fred laughed. "Well, you won't either if she goes to live with her family in Danville. Let's see, in whose district is Danville, Arnie?"

"I believe it's in his," said Arnie, pointing at me.

Then he said, "Seriously, Dick, one of the reasons I asked you to come here was to get a good look at her. She's changed her appearance quite a bit in the past year. I wanted to make sure you'd recognize her if you saw her out on the street." Arnie's voice was serious. We were all former cops. We all had seen the results of not taking someone's threat to do harm seriously. We all knew Susan was determined to find a way to kill the Bradfords. Until that changed, it would be our jobs to keep them out of danger while assuring that they could live as normal a life as possible.

As we talked, I kept noticing the beautiful woman in the shawl. At first she was pacing quietly, obviously trying to calm her nerves. Then she walked to the fire door exit, opened it, took a cigarette from her purse, lit it, and inhaled deeply. By the time she had started her second cigarette, I was finished talking with Fred and Arnie. Since I wasn't needed in the courtroom, I walked over to the door. To my surprise she smiled, held out a small ivory hand, and said, "Hello. I'm Lauren Wexler. You're with the bank, aren't you?"

I took her hand. The skin was cool to the touch. "Yes," I said, smiling. "My name is Richard. How do you do?"

"Are you from Roanoke?" she asked.

I began explaining that I was from Richmond, when I noticed she had become distracted, a look of concern spreading over her face. I realized she had momentarily stopped listening to me, her soft brown eyes fixed on something behind me. I turned and saw that a television news cameraman had entered the building, his camera at the ready on his shoulder. It was also obvious that Lauren did not want to be on the evening news.

"Allow me," I said, moving between Lauren and the cameraman in such a way as to block his view. I didn't know why she might be of interest to the media, and I didn't care. She was so soft, so helpless, like a deer caught in the headlights of a car. I just knew I wanted to protect her from anything that might cause her concern.

"Thank you so much," said Lauren, smiling warmly as she snuffed out her cigarette in the ashtray. She left me then and walked to a bench where she sat down between two other witnesses, obviously trying to disappear from view without leaving the area from which she might be called to testify.

At eleven o'clock the hallway began to fill with people from the courtroom. The judge had called a recess. The Bradfords emerged. They immediately walked to a small conference room at the other end of the main hallway. With them were both the prosecution and defense attorneys, a situation Arnie and I both recognized. He looked at me, rolled his eyes, and I could almost read his thoughts. He said, "It's let's make a deal time."

Arnie shook his head. I shrugged my shoulders.

We waited for an hour with nothing happening, then decided to have lunch. As Arnie, Fred, and I left the building and walked across the parking lot, I turned and saw Lauren Wexler close behind me. We were all heading towards the car the bank had rented for the use of employees and others involved with the case. For the first time I realized that Lauren must be some sort of witness who flew over with Harrison's group in the company aircraft. We reached the car, and when I opened the rear door, Lauren slid onto the back seat. My day was looking brighter by the moment.

There was no argument about where to go for lunch. The Goochland Diner was the only place in town. It was small, with booths along the windows and a few tables in the middle of the floor. Locals occupied some of the tables so we sat in a booth. I made certain I sat next to Lauren. I was surprised by my sudden and intense attraction to her, an attraction that seemed to be reciprocated when she smiled warmly at me. I just knew I needed to learn more about this woman, and the fact that she was somehow connected with the Bradfords made it easier.

Lunch was one of those magic moments that are foolishly meaningless to anyone not in the first stages of falling in love. Everything Lauren did delighted me, though she did nothing special. She only ordered potato salad. Desperate for something to say, I teased her about her lunch. "I like potato salad," she laughed, and it was the most marvelous laugh I had ever heard.

Arnie watched me with the same bemused expression he probably normally used when watching a puppy at that awkward stage of development when he falls over his own feet, forgets to close his mouth after drinking water, and generally looks foolish every waking moment. I should have cared, I suppose, but I didn't.

Lauren finished her lunch and began chain-smoking cigarettes. When her pack was empty, she went to the counter to purchase another. Her nerves were causing her to lose her health, I suppose, but all I saw was the type of sensual sophistication women seemed to have in the old movies that were shown on late night television. Like the ones from the 1940s when smoking, drinking, and witty conversation were considered the high point of adult savoir-faire. Arnie saw a nut lusting after a woman he didn't know, a woman who was a witness in an attempted murder case and who was once a friend of the defendant, a defendant that doctors said was not in her right mind. But no one ever said you had to be rational when you fell in love.

We returned to the courthouse and were told what we already suspected. The attorneys and the judge were negotiating for probation in lieu of more jail time. There was nothing to do but wait.

Lauren sensed my interest in her, and in the hours we had to wait in the hall, we talked and talked. We discussed everything and nothing, though mostly we talked about travel. "Have you ever been to Hawaii?" she asked me.

"No," I said. "But I'd like to see it some day."

"Oh, it's beautiful," she said. I was entranced by the way her face came alive as she spoke, her eyes seemingly dancing with delight. She was a woman filled with life despite her exhaustion. The words did not matter. We were together on what amounted to a first date, and I couldn't have been happier.

Finally, we received the news that Susan Gabriel was

going to plead guilty to two of the charges of soliciting Randy Gladstone to murder the Bradfords. The other seventeen charges against her were to be dropped. She was to be released on supervised probation that included prohibitions banning her from the waterfront area where the Bradfords lived.

"I just want to get on with my life," Susan told the judge, and he believed her.

Shortly after six in the evening, the deal was struck. Susan would be released on parole and placed on supervised probation.

Fred Townsend rolled his eyes. He, Arnie, and I knew the woman had not repented of her attitude, and with parole, she remained a free killer waiting to strike. The idea that she would stop harassing the Bradfords was ridiculous. We all knew that we would have to keep the Bradfords safe from Susan Gabriel, and it was going to be a Herculean task.

Due to the lateness of the hour, the entire party from Roanoke was to stay at the Hyatt in Richmond. Ann Bradford informed us that the company aircraft had not arrived at the airport but would be in Richmond the following day. It was news that delighted me. I could finally relax.

While we prepared to leave for the hotel, we saw the press gather on the sidewalk like vultures. There were television news videographers, still photographers from the newspapers, reporters with their notebooks, and radio personnel with tape recorders and microphones at the ready. Lauren, again, was obviously troubled by all this, and since we would be providing security, Arnie, Fred, and I were not anxious to have our pictures plastered all over the print and television news either.

Fred suggested that he and I go out the side door to get to the car in which Lauren would be riding while Arnie stayed with the Bradfords. In that way we could protect her, a woman whose involvement with all this I still did not know, and avoid the press. This we did, being shocked as we stepped outside by how cold the early December air had become.

Lauren had no coat, only the white lace shawl she had been carrying. She put it on and pulled it up over her face, though I suspected that the action was to keep her face hidden, not protect herself against the cold air.

When we arrived at the car, Fred exclaimed, "Ah, shit! Arnie has the keys." He looked at Lauren, who was shaking from the cold, uncertain what to do. Fortunately I also had a company car which I would be taking back to the hotel. It would have been inappropriate for me to suggest Lauren drive with me instead of the Bradfords, but at least I could keep her warm until Fred got the key.

"Okay, go get 'em, Fred," I said. "We'll wait in my car."

I took Lauren to the car, opened the door, and let her in. Then I got in behind the wheel and turned on the heater while she reclined her seat, leaned back, and let out a long sigh of relief. Whatever ordeal she had anticipated on the witness stand would no longer take place. She would not have to testify, to be cross-examined, to meet whatever fears were in her heart.

Calmer and warmer just from being in a closed vehicle out of the night wind, Lauren lit another cigarette, inhaled deeply, and exhaled slowly.

"It's over now," I told her, wanting to put my arm around her, to protect her from the bad people of the world and the demons that haunted her. There was something about her that made me feel intensely protective. The instinct was almost primal, as though I was staking out my woman in the midst of a hostile world. I knew instantly she was someone to love, to nurture, and to keep from harm. I also knew all these feelings were totally inappropriate. I knew nothing of this woman except her name, that she liked potato salad, and whatever inanities I had gleaned from our small talk that had filled the afternoon.

"Relax. Now you can go back to Roanoke and forget about the whole thing," I reassured her. The words were meaningless if I bothered to think about them. I didn't know who this woman might be. I just knew she was one of the witnesses whom the attorneys had planned to use to try and keep Susan Gabriel in jail. Who she was, what her role had been, what her role could be—these were all mysteries.

"Susan used to be a friend of mine. I found some letters from Susan threatening the Bradfords," she suddenly blurted out. "I knew I had to give them to the police, but I never thought I'd be caught up in this. I just got divorced, and I have to work to support myself and my two kids—I can't get this kind of publicity; it will ruin my business."

After the words tumbled out, she just sat quietly, an angel resting on the passenger seat of my car. I felt like a schoolboy with his first serious crush on a girl in his English class, a girl whom he watches constantly yet to whom he fears talking.

After a few minutes, Fred pulled along side us in the Bradford's Cadillac, and signaling to me, he quietly pulled the car onto the street and parked in front of the courthouse. The Bradfords had agreed to meet with the reporters so they were still all inside the building. Arnie had returned with Fred and jumped out of the front seat to open the back door. No one was looking for our stray witness, so we were able to get Lauren into the car without a hassle.

"Thanks for everything!" Lauren said, rolling down the window and smiling.

"Good luck," I said, smiling back.

I got out of my car and stood near the door of the Cadillac. Professionally, I was waiting for the Bradfords so I could act as back-up security to be certain they safely got into their car. Personally, I wanted to be near Lauren as long as I could. I think she sensed my interest because she leaned out the window again and said, "Hey, if you ever decide to go to Hawaii, give me a call."

"That's a promise," I said, laughing. And suddenly there was no question in my mind that I was going to have another opportunity to see her.

Ann Bradford left the press conference and stood at the front door of the courthouse beckoning to Arnie. After a brief discussion, she disappeared back inside the courthouse and Arnie walked over to where I was standing. "There's been a change in plans," he announced. From the look on his face, he was obviously noticing my interest in Lauren, a woman who would be leaving town sooner than I originally anticipated.

"We'll be going direct to the airport," Arnie informed me. "They were able to get the company aircraft into Richmond International Airport a few minutes ago. Stay with us for a few exits after we hit the interstate, and then you can head on home. Thanks for coming out. Stay out of trouble, Richard. I'll call you tomorrow."

Arnie opened the back door once again as the Bradfords came hurrying down the courthouse steps. They got into the back seat of the Cadillac, Arnie got into the front, I got into my car, and within minutes we were rolling east on Interstate 64. I followed the Cadillac to exit 167, made one last check in my mirrors to be certain no one was following us, then left the interstate to return to Richmond. On my way home I stopped by Applebee's, a restaurant nearby, for a drink and dinner. All I could think about was the beautiful, fragile woman in the white shawl. I had to see her again.

— CHAPTER 6 —

Searching for Dreams

I suppose it was odd that Friday the thirteenth proved to be a lucky day for me. However, I have never been superstitious. When I refuse to walk under a ladder, it is because I know that one slip by the worker up top and I will be crowned by a bucket of paint. I give the right of way to black cats in the same manner that I give the right of way to Siamese, calicoes, and all other breeds. I hate being responsible for more road kill. In fact, I was not even aware that this particular Friday was the thirteenth until my secretary pointed it out to me. My mind was still mostly on the recent Goochland trip and the woman in the white shawl. To my embarrassment, I was not certain I remembered her name correctly. Yet I could recall every detail of the face that had so captivated me.

The telephone rang shortly after I reached my desk. It was a jubilant Arnie who didn't even bother to identify himself. He just said, "Susan is back inside!"

I was half-delighted, half-wary. This was either good news or something more had happened to the Bradfords. "What happened, Arnie? Did she go nuts again?"

"No. The Commonwealth finally figured out that conspiring with fellow prison inmates to murder someone

69

just might be a violation of probation." I could hear the smile in his voice. He was delighting in the ending of a very troubled period for him and his staff.

"Do you have any idea how long they can keep her in this time?" I asked.

"Nope, but Fred is taking some time off while he can. We'll keep you advised."

We discussed some of the ongoing investigations with which we were both concerned and a few of the planning tasks that were needed for the department. I turned the conversation to lighter subjects, then gradually got around to what really mattered to me, the woman I had met at the courthouse. Assisting the DA, Arnie had coordinated the appearances of the witnesses at the trial. He knew who she was, why she was there, and how to reach her.

"Hey, Arnie, how about letting me have that lady's telephone number?" I asked.

"Lauren Wexler. Yeah, sure, that's just what you need, Dick," Arnie laughed. "She claimed she was a battered wife with a violent husband, but there was a lot of gossip about her and a really messy divorce," he said.

I could tell by the tone in his voice that Arnie obviously felt I didn't need the hassle with someone of this background. When I pushed the issue of her phone number, he just changed the subject.

In my mind's eye as we talked, all I could picture was the beautiful woman in the shawl, her face tired, her body slightly bent against the cold and the fear of the courtroom appearance. I had spent years dealing with violent men and women as a police officer. I had arrested people who killed. I had arrested people who were capable of great violence. And I had comforted many of the victims and family members who had lived in the horror of shootings, stabbings, and vicious beatings. The woman in the shawl, I was absolutely sure, was the type I had comforted.

Rather than pushing the issue, I steered the conversation back to bank topics, then hung up the telephone.

The week was a busy one. I was scheduled to start my Christmas vacation in twelve days, and that meant my department had to be ready to handle the workload in my absence. Still, I could not stop thinking about the woman in the shawl, Lauren Wexler. When I had a moment, I stopped by the library and searched through the Roanoke telephone directory, finding a single listing for that last name with a different first initial. So I tried calling information but there was no listing for a Wexler with the first name Lauren.

By Saturday I was wrestling with all matter of concerns. I kept thinking about all the work I had to finish at the bank, the vacation ahead of me, and Lauren.

Arnie said that Lauren had been an abused spouse, and she certainly had the look of someone who had seen some hard times, had been the victim of physical or emotional violence. If anything, that knowledge seemed to make the occasional smile that electrified her face, smoothed out the lines about her mouth and around her eyes, and radiated gentleness all the more remarkable.

And what about Lauren? What had the gentle, hurting woman whose smile could warm the December snow endured?

On Monday I returned to my office and placed a call to Fred Townsend. "Hi, Fred," I said when he got on the telephone. "Hey, do you remember that woman from Goochland?"

"Yeah, sure do. Why, what's going on?" asked Fred.

"Well, she left something in my car that day," I lied. "Would you happen to have her telephone number or address?"

"No, I don't, but I'm sure Arnie does. He had to have had her number because he was the one who set up the trip to Richmond last week. Hey, hold on a minute!"

He put me on hold, and my stomach began churning from nervousness. I knew Fred was right now dialing Arnie and that Arnie would get on the line and ream me out. Instead he was curt. "I am only going to say this one time!" said Arnie harshly. I grabbed a pen from the top of my desk as he recited a seven-digit number, then hung up the telephone. You could almost hear his frustration with me in the way he put down the receiver. I didn't care, though. I folded the piece of paper on which I had written Lauren's telephone number and placed it in my wallet. Then, feeling as though my life was about to change for the better, I returned to the job I was paid to do.

I didn't call Lauren that night, nor did I try her on Tuesday. I tried to tell myself that since I had her number, I was back in some semblance of control. I was fairly certain she'd want to talk with me again, maybe have dinner or something, so I wasn't afraid of being rejected. And I genuinely did have a lot of work to complete before my time off. Still, there was something else. Arnie's obvious displeasure rankled me. I considered calling him to find out why he was so against my contacting Lauren, but deep down I didn't want to hear that there was any reason why I shouldn't get to know her. Instead I rationalized that Arnie was just concerned about a friend, a lonely friend, getting involved with a woman who just ended an abusive marriage with a bitter divorce. Certainly, such a woman would bring a lot of baggage to a new relationship. But I felt prepared for anything. Loneliness may have played a part in my desire to get to know Lauren better, but I felt confident that I was levelheaded enough not to allow a little loneliness to cloud my judgment or land me in a messy relationship.

I finally came up with a plan that would allow me to see Lauren. I reasoned that since part of my vacation was going to be spent in the southern part of the state where I would be visiting my two children before driving on to Florida, *I'll call her and meet her for dinner when I pass through Roanoke.*

No big deal! We'll just go to dinner and talk. But I couldn't help wondering if I'd feel the same about her as when we met or if I'd see things differently and stop thinking about her. What if my interest was just fueled by the mystery? *There's only one way to find out,* I told myself.

I took the paper from my wallet and carefully dialed the number Arnie had reluctantly given me. I felt like a schoolboy who had just gotten up the nerve to ask the most popular girl in class for a date.

"Hello," she said, her voice as soft, gentle, and sensual as I remembered. It was a voice I could listen to for the rest of my life.

"Hi! This is the man from Goochland," I said, trying to keep my voice from cracking with nervousness. "Do you remember me?"

"Yes, I remember." I knew she was smiling.

"You're a pretty difficult person to find! Your name isn't Wexler, is it?" I asked, serious enough to get an answer. I don't know why I said it. Certainly Arnie had given me no hint that this might be the case.

"No, not originally, but I'm divorced and I didn't want to keep his name so I took a new one," said Lauren. This time she was the one who sounded nervous. "You see, all that business with Susan was years ago. I had to give those letters to the DA but I didn't want to be a star witness and have my name all over the newspapers. Oh, by the way, thanks for running interference with the press back there. You did a great job."

"Hey, no big deal. So let's start from scratch. What's your name?" I asked her seriously, but we both laughed. We might have been two high school kids on a first date we expected to be one of many to come.

We both relaxed and talked for a while. Eventually I asked her to meet me for dinner the next evening at *Le*

Jardin, a plush, romantic restaurant in Roanoke. She agreed, and a few minutes later we said goodbye.

To understand what happened next, you have to understand how lonely I was. So many things had happened in recent years. First, there was the estrangement and divorce from my first wife and separation from our two children. She and I had taken our vows very seriously when we were married. However, it is one thing to intellectually accept the idea of a relationship lasting forever and quite another to seriously work at what should be the reality of those vows. Our lives had moved in two different directions without either of us making the effort necessary to keep our paths intertwined. And though our children were vitally important to us, it was a marriage of strangers without passion that eventually ended.

But my desolate life had just begun. I went from having a familiar companion, someone with whom I could at least engage in small talk with whenever I wished, to living within the cold walls of a bachelor's luxurious but impersonal apartment. I went from the delightful chaos of children constantly underfoot to experiencing only the sounds I created by turning on the radio or television. I went from eating meals with my family to spending most evenings at the local restaurant.

Not that Applebee's was all bad. The food was good, and more important, I was one of a number of lonely single adults who made the restaurant a substitute for family. We each instinctively understood the other's pain, the isolation of living alone after years with others.

I suppose my low point had been Thanksgiving. Thanksgiving is the start of the warmest, most festive holiday season of the year, or the start of the loneliest and most depressing, depending on the circumstances of your life.

Advertisements, television shows, the photos displayed in magazines and newspapers all stress the joy of being with loved ones. This might mean a couple celebrating together by candlelight on a makeshift table in an efficiency apartment or it might mean a gathering of dozens of aunts, uncles, grandparents, parents, and cousins all clamoring about a large old house. Neither the ads nor the programs, nor even the traditional food, lend themselves to celebration by a single person. And after Thanksgiving come such other festive events as Hanukkah, Christmas, Kwanzaa, and New Year's Eve. All cultures and many religions within the United States have special family celebrations within this period. I would not.

There was no family for me that Thanksgiving. I had been with the bank for just six months. I had made friends at work, of course. I had close friends in the industry, such as Arnie. But there was no one to share a family holiday with. So I spent the day and early evening in my office calling my children and catching up on work. Eventually I went home to the same empty apartment.

I suppose I could have microwaved a frozen turkey dinner, opened a can of cranberry sauce, bought a frozen apple pie, and told myself I was a modern Pilgrim. Instead I went to Applebee's where, though it was after hours, I dined on turkey and French fries while talking with the cook and the bartender who doubled as a server. That was it. There were just the three of us in the restaurant, everyone else having long gone home.

A few nights later at dinner, I was talking with a woman named Isabel Morgan, another single Applebee's goer. We had become friends in the many days that we had been in the restaurant at the same time. We had talked extensively and honestly, recognizing that we enjoyed each other's company, that we were intensely lonely, and that there would never be more to the relationship. We were friends who would never be lovers. We were friends shoring up each other's loneliness while each of us sought a life partner.

After the pain of that Thanksgiving, a pain Isabel had experienced elsewhere, we began talking about our feelings and the approaching Christmas holiday. I told her I would be alone in Florida and she said she would also be alone. I suggested that she might want to drive down there with me. We could have separate bedrooms in the hotel, meeting for meals, for sightseeing, and whatever else we chose. We could go our separate ways when we wanted and have a companion when that seemed appropriate. To my delight, she agreed, though a few days later she had to cancel for business reasons.

As I packed for my trip, I thought about Isabel and the reason I had asked her. I told myself that I would not be lonely in Florida. I told myself that the companionship would have been nice, but the important thing had been to not let another person feel the emotions I had experienced sitting alone at Applebee's at Thanksgiving, eating my turkey and fries.

The next evening, before my date with Lauren, I packed my car for the trip to Florida, then drove to Roanoke, reaching the restaurant before Lauren was due to arrive. I was standing on the sidewalk, looking down the street for her, when I heard a too-familiar voice shout, "Hey, Dick!" It was Fred Townsend. He was standing in the restaurant doorway, grinning at me. *Of all the luck....*

Go figure the odds! I thought, annoyed. Now the whole damned Corporate Security Department was going to know who I was out with that night!

Fred introduced me to his wife and another couple they were with and invited me to join the four of them inside. Since it was early, I accepted, sitting at their table for a few minutes while watching the entrance. When he asked me for whom I was waiting, I told him, "The woman I befriended at the trial."

Fred seemed genuinely startled, but he said nothing.

Nervous about missing Lauren, I excused myself, wished Fred and his dinner companions a merry Christmas, and returned to the sidewalk in front of the restaurant.

Lauren drove into the parking lot, and I walked over to meet her. We both laughed as I opened her car door and she got out, the laugh of two nervous people uncertain what was happening with each other or their futures.

Lauren was everything I remembered her to be, except the stress was gone from her face. In a pale blue silk dress which showed off her lovely body, she seemed taller, relaxed, her complexion smooth, totally at ease with herself and her surroundings. Whatever demons had haunted her when she was scheduled to testify were gone. She was one beautiful woman.

I suppose the staff hated us by the time we left the restaurant. We had drinks and dinner, and I left a good tip, but we had lingered for hours until the place was closing. We talked about everything imaginable, including our respective families and our plans for Christmas. Lauren said, "I'll be alone for the holidays. My children are staying with their father for Christmas," she added wistfully. I instantly remembered my feelings of her fragility that day of the trial when we'd had lunch together.

"No one should be alone at Christmas," I said. "Why don't you pack a bag and come spend Christmas with me in Florida?"

I don't think I was serious when I said that. I'm no longer sure what I was thinking or feeling. It just seemed the right thing to say.

Lauren looked at me, smiling. It was as though my invitation was the most natural one in the world, an invitation that made perfect sense to her. "Okay," she responded.

We left the restaurant, and I walked Lauren to her car, kissing her good night. From there I went to a motel in

Blacksburg for the night. The next day I spent with my children. We went to an amusement park where a day of their laughing voices and calls of "Dad" lightened my heart and momentarily eased my loneliness for them. I returned to Roanoke the following morning to pick up Lauren.

I began laughing as I approached her friend's house where she told me she'd been staying since her divorce. There was Lauren struggling with the largest suitcase I had ever seen. I could have sworn it was the modern equivalent of the steamer trunks the wealthy used to pack with clothing, jewels, fine china, and their best silver, when they and two or three servants headed off to take an around-the-world voyage.

I put her mammoth suitcase in my trunk and then we headed off to the south, driving throughout the day and night. We stopped to eat. We stopped for coffee. We stopped to stretch our legs. Most importantly though, we talked all the way of our feelings, future desires, and past hurts. Although Lauren said we should not dwell on the past, I could see that she had experienced great pain. The trip became a journey of discovery, of learning so much about each other that the attraction we felt the day of the aborted trial had a basis of reality to it. The more we found out, the more we liked each other.

I got off I-95 in the predawn hours, heading my automobile into Saint Augustine. From there we went to Annacostia Beach, leaving the car, walking along the water, then standing together to watch the sunrise. I stood behind her as we looked across the horizon, my arms encircling her body, my head against hers, my senses intoxicated by the subtle aroma of her perfume. I needed a shave and we both could have used a shower. She was tired, and if I was truthful, I could have used a few hours of sleep myself. But none of that mattered. "Look, Lauren," I whispered into her ear as the first rays of light erupted across the darkened sky, turning the black of night into an array of red, purple, blue, and yellow.

"God is trying to tell you something. He is saying that you'll never hurt again. He is telling you that this is the first day of the rest of your life."

And so we stood there, holding each other while the sunrise turned from the first tiny fingerlike probing to an explosion of light that chased away the night and brought us to full morning.

Finally, we walked back to the hotel on the beach, checked in, and the porter carried our bags to the room. This was no longer about two lonely people staying together through the Christmas holiday. I loved Lauren, and she loved me. Of that I was certain. We stripped off our clothes, kissing, touching, and eventually exploding in the intensity of our embrace before falling asleep entangled in each other's arms.

Neither of us spoke of the magic of that morning when we finally awakened in the afternoon. It was only that evening, as we were walking over a footbridge that spanned a pond separating the motel rooms from the main building where the restaurant was located and stopped to look at the reflection of the pink and orange setting sun in the peaceful water, that Lauren turned to me and said, "Someday I'm going to be your wife."

The words startled me. *Things are moving too fast,* I told myself. Yet I knew her words were true.

The idyllic holiday passed too quickly. When it was time to leave, neither of us wanted to. We were driving over the bridge, listening to Barbra Streisand sing "Evergreen." I glanced over at Lauren and saw tears rolling down her cheeks. It wasn't the song; it was the time together, the happiness, and the fact that we were leaving. The time had been so special for her, and she didn't want it to end.

I pulled off the road and into a gas station. "Lauren," I said, absolutely certain that I would never regret my words, "Will you marry me?"

The answer was as direct and surprising as when I had suggested we share the holidays together. "Yes, my true love."

I took Lauren in my arms, kissing her and holding her. We stayed like that for several minutes before I again pulled onto the road, heading back north.

Back in Roanoke, Lauren's father stopped by to help us pack as much of her things as we could fit into both our cars. She planned to come back to Roanoke periodically to take care of her business, so she knew she could pick up the rest of her things later. Before we left, he turned to his daughter and said, "Be good to him."

It was an odd comment to make. I expected such a comment to be directed toward me, not toward his daughter. "Be good to him." It was partially a warning; partially an awareness of something to which I had not yet been exposed. I didn't think too much about the comment at the time, though there would come a day when those words would haunt me.

The trip north from Roanoke was during one of those bitter cold winter days the tourism bureau never tells vacationers about. The weather in Roanoke was far better than up north in Richmond, but Roanoke was not southern Florida or Arizona. It was cold, and the heater in Lauren's mustang was on the blitz. I was worried it would not hold out for the 184-mile trip to Richmond.

As I suspected, when we stopped at a truck stop halfway to Richmond, Lauren was shivering with cold. The heater had failed. "Lauren, you look like you're frozen to the bone!" I exclaimed.

"I'm okay, it's not that bad." Lauren said through trembling lips.

"Let's go inside and warm up. And when we get back on the road, we'll switch cars."

I put my arm around her and led her inside the rest stop. We got a table in the restaurant and ordered steaming hot coffee. Despite her obvious discomfort as she slowly began to thaw her body, Lauren's smile radiated warmth throughout the room. She was obviously happy with her decision, with me, with moving to Richmond, with the radical change in both our lives.

When we finally rolled into Richmond that night, I was happier than I had been in a long time. I had found someone with whom to share a life. I had found the most intimate of friends, the most delightful of lovers. She had interests in areas I had never considered. We each were fascinated by the other, and as snippets of her past life gradually were offered during our conversations, I felt nothing but compassion.

"In our life, we'll turn all the negative you have experienced into something positive for ourselves and all the others we love," I told her, and through her tears, Lauren smiled lovingly at me.

CHAPTER 7

Head of Security

B ank security is not a career choice I'd suggest for just anyone, and particularly not for those who are faint of heart. It is like working in a pressure cooker, the stress enough to drive even the most dedicated and tough security executives to the breaking point. But for me, it was also a rewarding and interesting field in which every day was different from the last. Even in the intense environment, we sometimes got a moment of comic relief, thanks to some of the unusual and amusing characters we encountered.

One morning, I stepped into the imposing bank lobby where I was an executive and ran a professional eye over the sixteen-foot ceilings, eight teller windows, and velvet ropes draped through the center to keep the line orderly during the early morning and midday rush periods. Everything looked quiet. There were waist-high writing tables with marble surfaces and teller windows that were open to look customer friendly. Any customer could reach over and steal money if so inclined, which was one of the reasons we used a two-drawer system. Robberies were extremely rare, but when they occurred we wanted to be certain we limited the potential take. That was why the top drawer, the one the public could see, never had more than $2200 to $2500 in it. The lower drawer, the one John Taylor and other professionals knew about, might have considerably more money in them.

As head of security for this and other branches in the Eastern region, my office as well as the administrative offices and the proof room were upstairs on the second floor. The proof room was the place where an employee handled the encoding of checks which had to be computerized on magnetic tape, then sent to the regional Federal Reserve bank by 8:00 P.M. of each working day. From up there, none of us could see or hear what was taking place on the floor below, which was the reason I frequently stayed downstairs visiting with the employees who were most directly involved with handling the public.

I went over and took a chair in one of the six raised desk areas. The assistant manager with whom I was speaking, the loan officers, and other officials all had desks resting on platforms, elevating them a little above the rest of the floor. It was a system that allowed them both to watch the floor and be accessible to the public.

We didn't have security guards in the bank. I don't believe in them, a sentiment shared by about half the bankers in the United States. Even the best security guard is not trained for the days, weeks, or months of boring sitting and standing around, then seconds of life-or-death decision-making. Does the guard draw a weapon when a robber appears? Does the guard's presence encourage a robber to use a weapon? Will a stray bullet strike a bank customer or employee? The risks are so great, the benefits so limited, that I prefer devices such as cameras, silent alarms monitored by law enforcement, and specialized equipment such as dye packs which can lead to an arrest after the robber is safely away from the crowded bank.

It was some time between 10:45 and 11:15 in the

morning, a quiet time for the bank. The merchants and business people had come and gone and would not return until after noon. The only customers were an elderly couple and a few office workers on a coffee break. The presence of a rather unkempt-looking bearded man in line, whom I later nicknamed "Scruffy," carrying a folded newspaper and wearing sneakers with three white stripes across the front, did not arouse suspicion.

As I sat talking with the assistant manager about some security issues, Scruffy waited calmly for his turn, his demeanor no different from that of those in line with him. He did not look around. He was not sweating or tense. He was just another customer, perhaps a laborer getting some cash to spend at a construction site lunch wagon or in one of the nearby coffee shops.

I paid no attention to Scruffy as he reached one of the open teller windows. I never saw him pass the note that said he was armed. I never saw the teller hand him the money he placed in his newspaper. I never saw her hit the alarm button as he quietly walked out the back door and into the parking lot. It was only after he was gone that I was alerted to what had just happened, and by then his fate had been sealed. The quick-thinking teller had activated the videotape cameras, and we would soon have an excellent photograph of him. Other than wearing a beard, something he apparently just enjoyed having, he had made no effort to disguise his appearance. Unfortunately, though we immediately knew what he looked like, it was too late to catch him today. A second man who earned a relatively small fee for serving as his driver had quietly waited for him in the back lot, then pulled onto the street and inconspicuously driven away.

Later when I learned about Scruffy, I was incensed. Here I was, responsible for all security measures for scores of bank branches, a respected leader in the security field, on all manner of state committees, and a robbery took place just eighty feet from where I was sitting. I wanted to apprehend this guy!

Scruffy had none of the professionalism of John Taylor. He was, I soon discovered, a creature of habit. Scruffy not only dressed the same each time, as though he considered his appearance a good luck charm, he followed such a distinct pattern of bank robbery that we soon could predict where and when he would strike.

Unlike John Taylor, Scruffy did not know that tellers keep two drawers. Scruffy's average take was from $2200 to $2400, and we soon calculated that he was spending the money at the rate of $220 per day. That meant the money ran out, on average, every ten days, when he would strike again. This happened with such frequency that I soon put together a pattern that identified his method of operation.

Scruffy liked to rob banks with large lobbies and at least two easy exits, one of which would lead directly to a parking lot from which he always made his escape. He only worked between 10:45 A.M. and 11:15 A.M., and he worked in a rotation of three areas. I tracked his robberies and quickly saw a pattern. He would hit a bank in a particular city, then move on to a second town. Finally, he'd hit a third town and then start all over again in the first city. Once I knew the city in which he had taken money and the exact amount stolen, I knew what day and in which city he would strike next.

It took a while for the various police departments to believe my warnings once Scruffy's pattern had been determined. In one town, there were only two banks that matched Scruffy's pattern. On the day of the expected robbery, I called the watch commander for the local police, suggesting they increase their patrols. He thought I was nuts and ignored my request to watch the banks.

I staked out the parking lot of the bank that was part of the chain for which I was responsible. I did not have a return visit from Scruffy, though. Instead he struck the other bank, a fact that led an embarrassed watch commander to call me back, asking for help in the future.

I felt certain I knew which branch was the most likely to be Scruffy's next target for robbery. Based on his previous take, he would be out of money, and based on the locations of the previous robberies, I knew which town he would strike next.

Scruffy was no exception to the rule that most bank robbers never carry a gun. But when someone claims to carry a weapon, as Scruffy's hold-up notes to the tellers indicated, the presumption has to be that he or she has a gun. As a result, we arranged for armed plainclothes police officers to be inside the bank I thought would be targeted. Other officers in unmarked cars were positioned around the perimeter in a way that would attract no attention but which would assure that they could move swiftly into place, blocking off an escape. I was in the parking lot, and both helicopters and small planes were in the sky, ready to coordinate any chase.

We were ready to move as 10:45 approached then passed with nothing happening. 10:50 came and went. Then 10:55.

At 11:00 A.M. a female proof operator left the bank to begin her lunch hour. As she reached the parking lot she began searching for her car keys in her purse and was momentarily distracted. A twelve-year-old boy who had been nervously hanging around the lot looking for such an opportunity raced over, snatched her purse, and began to run across the street, only to find himself surrounded by police cars, officers on motorcycles, and a police helicopter hovering overhead. Startled, terrified, and not certain what else to do, the boy raised his head towards the sky and shouted,

"Hey, man, it's only a purse!" We didn't get Scruffy that day, but hopefully we turned a truly startled kid away from a life of crime.

In addition to my position as Eastern Region Security Manager for the bank, I was also involved with a state banking association. The group decided to offer a $5000 reward for Scruffy's conviction. The money was aimed at the driver of Scruffy's getaway car and was enough of an incentive, because the man quickly called us with information we double-checked and found to be accurate. The money he earned from Scruffy was enough so he had no problem with driving Scruffy to and from banks, but it was such a small amount that the $5000 convinced him to talk. Although Scruffy would eventually have to serve approximately twenty years, the driver who helped us was given no jail time.

Despite all the knowledge we had, we still kept missing Scruffy. Even though he wasn't as professional as John Taylor, he was slippery; we needed all the help we could get. We circulated Scruffy's picture to all applicable law enforcement agencies as well as the news media. Meanwhile, Scruffy was becoming so frustrated by his notoriety that he planned to move to Baltimore, Maryland to continue his career.

While this was happening, the eccentrics and the crazies began calling us. One of these was a man I called Abner the Seer. Abner claimed to be a psychic, a man who could predict the next robbery just by running his hand across the photograph of our robber.

There are all manner of people who call the police with information. Some have a dream in which they see the identity of some bad guy who has been in the media. Some turn in a family member or co-worker because they are convinced that person is inherently evil. Some are nut cases who blame everything on aliens. And some are psychics, men and women who claim to know certain hidden facts about robbery, murder, carjackings, and other crimes in the news.

As a detective, I often talked with such individuals. I took them seriously because that was my job. After all, even crazy people can witness crimes.

When I moved on to an executive position in the banking business, I thought my days of dealing with the eccentrics were over, but Abner, the local seer, insisted that he could help us solve the serial robberies. As I had done while a police officer, I made certain that I talked with him.

Abner asked for a copy of Scruffy's photo, passed his fingers over it, and then announced, "I see a white male standing in a bank on the Causeway. He is holding a sawed-off shotgun."

The area picked by Abner was one where no robberies had occurred. It did have a bank with the right layout for Scruffy, one point in Abner's favor. However, I knew that Scruffy never carried a sawed-off shotgun or any other kind of gun for that matter.

I dismissed the psychic in a way that was not meant to win a lasting friend, nor did I care. However, when three days after our meeting, a man with a sawed-off shotgun robbed a bank on the Causeway, I asked the seer to return to my office. To be right about half of what happened at the bank was impressive enough for me to listen further.

This time the psychic, rather arrogant to my way of thinking, announced, "He's planning to leave town."

"Do you know where we can find him?" I asked.

You'll find him at the airport," he replied.

What the hell else is he going to do? I thought. *Ride a bicycle to get out of town? Of course he'll go to the airport if he leaves town.*

There was no other information from the psychic.

He could not give a day when Scruffy might try to run. He could not give a time, destination, or anything else. Just, "You'll find him at the airport."

Scruffy might flee tonight. He might wait ten years. It was all the same to the psychic. He had given me the answer he seemed to feel I needed or deserved. There would be no further information forthcoming. We parted civilly, though it was obvious neither of us respected the other.

Scruffy's last attempt to rob a bank occurred a few days later. As he walked up to the bank, the employees spotted his distinct appearance through the window. "Hi, Scruffy," they called to him. They waved like the audience of a circus clown prancing along in a parade. He was an object of amusement to the staff who alerted the police to his presence.

Scruffy fled successfully, returning home to shave and, probably, change at least some of his clothes. Then he prepared to leave for Baltimore, his hometown and a place where he presumably was not known as a robber of twenty-three banks.

It was the Fourth of July, and an agent with the United States Immigration and Naturalization Service arrived at the airport with a man from the Middle East who was being deported. The agent and the man to be deported stopped by the bar for a few minutes, then proceeded to the gate for check-in. Because the INS agent was carrying a gun, he had to report to the sheriff's post at the security checkpoint. This was a podium on which Scruffy's photograph had been taped in case he came through airport security on his way to a plane.

The INS agent handed his gun to the deputy on duty to be checked for him while he made the flight with his prisoner. Then he glanced at the photograph, did a double take, and said, "What do you want him for?"

"Bank robbery," replied the deputy.

The INS agent studied the photograph for another minute, then motioned with his head in the direction of the main terminal. "He's down in the bar," he said matter-of-factly.

The call went out, and deputies converged on the bar. Sure enough, there was a clean Scruffy. He did not resist as they arrested him. When he got to court, the judge saw no reason he couldn't return home to Baltimore—in twenty-one years. Meanwhile, he would be the guest of the Federal Corrections System.

Characters like Scruffy made my job even more interesting than usual and, because no employees were physically hurt, rather amusing. I shared my amusement with Lauren when discussing my job and characters like Scruffy whom I worked to put behind bars, for Lauren was a true crime buff. She loved to read psychological true crime books and rent movies on similar subjects. One of her favorites—though fiction—was *Basic Instinct.* "I like to see justice triumph," she said the night we rented it, smiling as she planted a kiss on my nose just before we went to sleep.

My work was my life, a fact that caused the demise of my first marriage. Although I wanted to find a better balance between work and family with Lauren, she still encouraged my passion for my job. It was wonderful to not only do something stimulating, but to be able to share the daily trials and rewards with the woman I loved, a woman who was always interested in my work and eager to hear about the ups and downs.

One weekend shortly after we were married, we were discussing our various work problems over dinner at the Chamberlyn. I told Lauren, "We're having problems with altered twenties."

"What's an altered twenty?" she asked.

"Somebody takes a twenty dollar bill and cuts off the number twenty on all four corners," I explained. "Then they take a one dollar bill and paste a twenty on each corner. If they then pass it in a dark place like a bar or nightclub, especially during a rush period when the employees are a little frantic, it's usually accepted. The next day the perpetrators take the twenty to the bank, and because there is so little damage to the bill, it's still legal tender. The teller accepts it and gives them a new twenty, and the bank sends it to the Federal Reserve for shredding."

"And it works?" she asked, amazed.

"Better than counterfeiting. The person's using a genuine bill. They've just altered it so, if they're lucky, they'll get change. You can probably pick up a hundred bucks a night or more bar hopping on a Friday or Saturday when the joints are jammed."

Lauren shared my moral outrage. That was one of the things I loved about Lauren, her strong sense of right and wrong. Not like some of the crazies I sometimes had to handle in my profession.

PART II

Living With the Demons

— CHAPTER 8 —

Meeting Hannah

The first few months of our marriage were idyllic. We talked so much that there seemed no joy not enhanced by our union, no secret so dark, so terrible that we could not share it. Lauren knew I loved her unconditionally, and I was confident of her love as well.

It was during one weekend that my life with Lauren began to change in ways I could not comprehend. It had started out innocently enough. On Friday night I met Cindy and Gordon, a couple who were Lauren's first clients in Richmond and who had quickly become her friends. Lauren and I had dinner at Cindy and Gordon's home. After dinner they gave us a tour of their beautiful house. Upon learning of my law enforcement past, Gordon proudly showed off the gun collection he kept under lock and key in a gun case. We had an enjoyable evening, but I was happy to have Lauren all to myself the following night.

Saturday night had been wonderful, an evening spent relaxing, enjoying television, playing with our cat, listening to the parakeet sing, and just being together. We had made love, drifting off to sleep in each other's arms, awakening late the next morning, and enjoying a leisurely Sunday brunch filled with talk about the many things we were each doing, the things we planned to do together. Then, shortly after we finished cleaning the dishes, Lauren's body stiffened slightly, and she looked at me in strange way. "Richard," she said coldly, "I think we should go see a marriage counselor to work out our problems."

"Work out what problems?" I said, dismayed by her words. "What are you talking about, Lauren?"

"Richard, I saw an advertisement on television for Charter Westbrook. They were talking to us. They are the place that can help us. We should go there and talk to them," Lauren answered.

"Talk to them about what, Lauren?" I was totally confused. I started searching my mind for whatever problems Lauren might think were creating a crisis less than two months after our wedding. I knew Lauren's business in Roanoke was suffering in her absence, despite weekly trips down there. She was trying to establish her business in Richmond and had been under stress, but she was slowly building a clientele and could now even count her first clients as good friends. I felt sure that her business could not be the source of any marital crisis. Was there something she had said that I had not taken seriously enough? Was there a crisis brewing which I had ignored? Had I failed Lauren in some way? Had I missed some signal, dismissed a remark made lightheartedly, yet meant to get my attention? Try as I might, I could not think of anything.

"Talk to them about what? What is going on here?" I asked again.

Lauren kept insisting we had problems, though never giving me any details. Finally I decided that there must indeed be something wrong, a problem she had made clear to me which I had somehow overlooked. I had made enough mistakes in my life in the past. I was determined that this time I was going to do everything in my power to make my marriage work. I found Charter Westbrook's number in the telephone book and called for an appointment.

To my surprise, we were given an appointment at Charter Westbrook Hospital on the north side of Richmond that very afternoon. They must have assumed that even non-emergency calls could be masking a real crisis. Certainly it made sense not to assume anything about what was taking place until they could talk in person with the people calling.

We met with a caseworker on the hospital staff. She was the one person there with whom I was not impressed. She asked questions that I found totally irrelevant, such as, "Do you resent the fact that since you have married, your electric bill is higher?"

My God, I had not even given that a thought. My electric bill? Higher? Was it? And who cared? The electric bill was of no importance to me or my relationship with Lauren. Could Lauren be upset about something so trivial and mundane? I doubted it.

Assuring themselves that we were in no danger to ourselves or each other, we were referred to a counselor in private practice. I made an appointment for later that week.

The first two sessions passed uneventfully. Lauren was relaxed, in control. She wore a long-hemmed denim dress with a round white collar and flat-heeled shoes. She was self-confident and quite different from the person I had been with when we went to the hospital on Sunday.

I did little talking during those first two sessions. I wasn't avoiding questions. It was just that Lauren needed to dominate, and the therapist encouraged her to talk. "I'm tired of the lies," Lauren said. "I'm tired of the abuse I have to take from him. Lies and abuse, that's what this marriage is all about, and I'm sick of it."

Ted Carter, the therapist, was gentle with Lauren,

probing little, letting her talk. I stayed silent most of the time, speaking only when Lauren gave me an opening, then hoping to find some answer.

"Where do you feel I have been lying to you?" I asked gently. "Please, Lauren, tell me the lies that are bothering you."

"It's the lies, Richard. All the lies. I'm tired of the lies."

"I understand that, Lauren, and I want to make things right. But I can't change if I don't know how you think I have been lying." I began to get frustrated but I remained as calm as I could. She was obviously very upset and I didn't see the point in turning the session into an unproductive yelling match.

"The lies. All the lies. That's what's got to stop. A marriage should be based on trust, not lies, and all I hear are lies."

I searched my mind. Had I not been totally open and honest with her? Was there something she found out that I never told her? I couldn't think of a thing, so I said, "One lie. Please, Lauren, tell me one lie. I've bared my soul to you."

"All the lies and the abuse," she repeated.

"What abuse, Lauren? You're with the therapist. We've agreed to be open and honest here. I promised I would cooperate. Just tell me one instance of abuse, one lie."

"Lies and abuse," she ranted. "That's what my life has become."

Round and round we went, Lauren never naming one specific incident. It was as though she could gain sympathy by speaking in generalities, yet this was not counseling. This was not therapy. This was being in the midst of an out-of-control stranger whose anger seemed to have no basis in reality. I was confused and angry and tired of listening to a broken record of groundless accusations that the therapist seemed to believe without any proof. My presence meant nothing because nothing of substance was being discussed despite probing by both the therapist and myself. In fact, by the third session I had become a nonentity.

It was at the third session that Dr. Carter looked at me and quietly said, "Richard, would you have any objection if I saw Lauren alone from now on?"

We were there for marital counseling, and a marriage takes two people, not one. Did his request mean that I was all right? Did Lauren have the problem? Did he recognize some hidden meaning in her ramblings that I had overlooked? Or perhaps he was concerned that she wouldn't open up with me sitting there.

I waited for a moment, expecting Dr. Carter to explain his request. When he did not, I said, "No. I suppose that would be all right. Does that mean you want to see me in another session?"

"No, not unless you want to see me. Do you want to?"

"Not really. Okay, if you think that is best, then we'll do it your way," I agreed.

I left Dr. Carter's consulting room and went to the outer office to wait for Lauren. Our "marriage counseling" ended. In its place was the start of a complex journey into the world of mental health professionals, though I did not realize that at the time. All I could do was wait until the session ended. As Lauren was putting her coat on, I asked Dr. Carter, "What is wrong with my wife?"

Neither at that session nor the next would he give me an answer. Doctor-patient confidentiality took precedence over the committed relationship between a husband and wife. Lauren would have to sign a waiver before the therapist could speak to me, and I knew she was not going to do that. I felt like a drowning man who was being shown life preservers available only by signing triplicate forms and getting the approval of a committee which was safely on dry land several miles away.

As I drove Lauren home from Dr. Carter's office, we said little. Our drives home from the counseling sessions had been filled with tension. I turned onto Broad Street and looked out of the corner of my eye at her. Lauren had been watching me and saw my sideward glance. She placed her hand on my knee and smiled, erasing the tense air between us. She leaned over and began talking lovingly in my ear, giggling and delighting as she got closer to me. Her behavior created an abrupt change of mood in the car, and I can't say I was upset about that. It was nice to have the sweet, loving Lauren by my side again, to take a break from our relationship which was only becoming more confused and tense with time.

However, I was not prepared for her next move. Before I knew it, her hand was slowly sliding up the inside of my thigh.

"Lauren, stop it. I'm trying to drive and this is not the time or the place for that," I scolded. Instead of stopping though, she burst into wild laughter. "For God's sake, Lauren, I mean it. Stop!"

Then, as if she realized I was really serious, she suddenly stopped. She didn't remove her hand, but she didn't continue either. My relief was momentary. I felt an intense jolt of pain that almost caused me to sideswipe a parked car. Lauren had taken my testicles in her hand and squeezed with all her might.

I screamed, jerking the steering wheel, almost causing an accident. I pulled the car over, gripping the steering wheel so tightly my knuckles were white. I kept my hands glued there in an effort to fight the intense urge to raise my clenched fists at her. Lauren had let go and sat back in her seat, staring straight ahead. I shouted a bunch of foul words, at her, at myself, at the pain. But Lauren continued staring straight ahead, defiantly, angrily. As confused and enraged as

I was for the unprovoked attack, I realized with shock that there was a moment when I wanted nothing more than to strike the woman that was inflicting the pain.

I was confused by all that was happening. First, my wife demanded marital counseling for problems which I was not aware and did not understand. Then, our counselor asked me not to be part of the sessions. Finally, Lauren turns from sweet and loving to violent and brutal in the span of a few seconds, pretending afterward that nothing happened. What could possibly occur next?

A few nights later, I would have my answer. As Lauren and I were relaxing in the living room of our apartment watching television, I met someone I never knew existed. I met Hannah.

I was seated on the couch, absorbed with the evening news. Lauren was sitting across the room, rocking slowly back and forth in an upholstered rocking chair. Suddenly the gentle rocking became a harsh, highly concentrated movement, an extension of her stiffened, angry body. Then I heard a voice so deep, so ominous, that I thought it was a voice-over on the television promoting some upcoming horror movie.

"Look at me!" the voice commanded. "Look at me now! Listen to me! Listen to me now!"

There was an electrical charge in the room. I felt the hairs on my neck stand up the way they do when you are too close to an electrical storm while outside on a rainy day. I realized that the voice was coming not from the television but from Lauren. I stared at her in disbelief.

"Lauren, what's wrong?" I asked.

"Look at me!" Lauren repeated. "Look at me, now!" Lauren rocked slowly in the chair, back and forth, back and forth. Then, in a deep voice that seemed to come from the pit of some tormented soul, she growled, "Listen to me now, you motherfucker!"

Jesus, Lord God, what is going on? I thought as Lauren turned to me, a smile on her face. It was a smile so transparent, I felt as if I were looking straight through her.

"Lauren, what is wrong?" I asked, frightened. *My God*, I thought again, *what is happening?*

"Shut the fuck up!" Lauren said softly, almost in a whisper as she stood up and walked to the fireplace.

But it wasn't Lauren. Not the voice. Not the language. Not the way her body moved. Even from the side I could tell this woman's face sagged where Lauren's flesh was tight. Her breasts drooped. Her eyes seemed half-dead, what little life they held was the life of hatred, not joy. I could have sworn a strange woman had somehow spirited away my wife, then put on her clothing and sat in her chair. Had I seen this woman walking down the street, I would not have spoken to her. It was not my wife, yet it was my wife.

This Lauren who was not Lauren reached up to the mantel and pulled our framed wedding picture off the shelf. Her actions were so smooth, so deliberate that it took me a minute before I realized what she was doing. I rose from the couch, moving to stop her, but was too late. She had slipped the photograph from the frame and dropped it on the burning logs of the fireplace. The edge of the photograph was in flames as I moved across the room. The entire image was engulfed by the time I reached the poker.

Lauren turned towards me, facing me full on for the first time. Her jowls sagged deeply, and a crease resembling a scar appeared on her right cheek. The scar extended three inches, ending just above her upper lip. To my horror, I realized that this was my wife, yet I had never seen her before in my life. I did not yet know that the Lauren I knew had left and in her place stood the woman whose name was Hannah.

"I need to talk about John," she said abruptly.

"John? Who is John, Lauren?"

"John Anthony Taylor. Have you ever heard of him?" Hannah responded coldly.

I was not thinking of work, of criminals, when she said the name. My mind was only on the woman I loved, not some criminal who had been working his way through the banks of the southern part of the United States.

"No," I said. "Who is he? A former boyfriend or something?"

She didn't respond. Then she said, "I met him when I was in jail in Salem. We're good friends."

I shook my head baffled. "You were in jail? Oh my God, why?" I could scarcely get my mind around the fact that the woman I had married had been in prison and that she seemed to know this man. "And who is this man? Is he on the staff of the jail, a counselor or something?"

"No! Don't be ridiculous," this new Lauren said with a sneer. "He's in jail for bank robbery." She paused, studying my face for a reaction.

Suddenly, I recognized Taylor's name. I remembered his many crimes. I was shocked, but I tried to keep my cool telling her, "Lauren, I'm sorry. You have to realize that under the circumstances you can't have any contact with him any longer. You're the wife of the bank security executive. It's not appropriate for you to maintain this relationship. Can you understand why you have to break off your friendship with this person?" I beseeched her.

"Like hell I will," she retorted.

She began moving through the apartment, gathering up all of our wedding photographs. I stayed by the fireplace, positioning myself to stop her before she could burn them. As she approached with them, I took her arm, and an intense expression of hate and anger was on her face.

In all my years in law enforcement, dealing with people who were violent or psychologically damaged, I had never witnessed anything like the expression I saw on my wife's face. I had arrested men and women whose murderous rages led them to try to destroy other human beings. I had faced their wrath when they felt I had stopped them from destroying someone they felt had no right to live. I had worked with mentally ill individuals who were protecting themselves from demons with whatever weapons were handy. And never had I seen the expression that came across the face of the woman before me, the woman I loved.

"Lauren, please tell me what's wrong," I said as gently as I could through my confusion.

She laughed. "Why the hell do you keep calling me Lauren? My name is Hannah."

Hannah pushed me away with a strength that surprised me. Lauren could not have moved me the way Hannah did, sending me stumbling towards the doorway to the balcony.

I stared at her. The old Lauren, the Lauren I knew and loved, had vanished. Of that I was certain. In her place was a demon determined to destroy everything that reminded Lauren and me of our special happiness.

I fought to regain my balance as Hannah began to rip more photographs, this time of my children, into pieces, tossing them into the fire. She watched me with scorn, her look telling me that she was certain she could counter any move I might dare to make. Knowing I was defeated, I sat down on the rocker and stared at the fire rising with the fuel of the photographs. I was in shock, sitting motionless, uncertain what to do.

Still wanting to think the woman in front of me was Lauren, unable to accept someone else had taken her place, I watched as her venom propelled her into the bedroom.

She returned with the lingerie Lauren had worn on our honeymoon. She sat on the couch, close to the fireplace, and began ripping the garments and throwing them in shreds into the flames.

Then suddenly the woman who called herself Hannah pulled the engagement and wedding rings from her fingers. "Lauren! For God's sake, stop it!" I pleaded with her. Stopping her was futile. I still talked to her as if she were my wife, but this other woman, this creature from Hell, seemed to feed off my horror.

The destruction of the rings was followed by the rending of our marriage license. Soon everything we had in the apartment that was a celebration of our marriage or my children was in ashes.

Then, just as suddenly as the mood had come on, the room seemed to grow still as Lauren's body softened. She still sat on the couch, but her face became relaxed, the skin taut, the scar having vanished.

"Lauren," I said hoarsely, "are you all right?"

Lauren turned toward me, her face loving and gentle. "Yes, Richard," she said. "What's the matter?"

"Nothing, Lauren," I said.

Then Lauren looked around the room and saw the path of destruction that included shreds of photographs and lingerie satin. "Richard, what happened? Where did this mess come from?"

Oh my God, I thought, she didn't even seem to realize what had just taken place. How could I tell her? How could I say that her face had twisted into something grotesque, that she had deliberately destroyed pictures and documents we valued, that she had told me she'd been in jail. I would call her therapist in the morning and try to make sense of what had happened. In the meantime, I cleaned up and assured Lauren that I had made the mess while looking through some old documents. I felt I could let go of what happened momentarily, but I had to know why she was in jail. I quietly asked her about the past.

Lauren told me about some hidden memories and the events I had learned from Hannah, but now they sounded very different. Lauren told me about how she had been married to her high school sweetheart right after graduation. But after two children in as many years, she and her husband—practically children themselves—realized their high school romance was not a foundation for a solid marriage. There was a quick divorce and Lauren was back home. A few years later she married a man who seemed sweet, but soon became merciless in his treatment of her. "Richard, I endured beating after beating before I got out of the relationship," she told me, her voice shaking. She was obviously deeply scarred by what must have been a traumatic and turbulent time in her life, and she hesitated to tell me any more of the brutal details. My heart ached for this delicate, fragile woman. Yet I knew she must be strong to have endured all that she had.

Tears began flowing down her cheeks. "It's okay. You don't have to be afraid of him now. You're here with me, I'll protect you." I said softly, putting my arms around her.

"Richard," she sniffed, "There's more, Richard. I didn't tell you everything..."

I pulled away and looked at the face of this scared, hurt woman that I loved so much. "Lauren, don't be scared. I love you with all my heart. You can tell me anything."

Lauren stared down at her hands, then looked into the fire. She couldn't bring herself to look me in the eyes. "Richard, what I'm about to tell you may make you feel differently about me." Lauren breathed deeply.

I squeezed her hand, a gesture of assurance, of comfort. "Go on," I said.

In a torrent of emotion, her words came tumbling

out as if she couldn't unburden herself fast enough. "Richard, he beat me up so badly, so many times. I couldn't take it anymore. I knew if I didn't do something, I wouldn't live to see a divorce, see my children, see tomorrow. I just couldn't take any more punches, kicks. I just snapped. I don't know how—I mean, it's all kind of a blur—but I fought back." She drew in a deep breath, the hot tears having subsided for the moment.

"I was arrested and put in jail for attacking him," she continued. "It was awful. But I got out pretty quickly because the court recognized that I had been battered. Still, it was horrible." Her voice cracked and she began sobbing. I felt sick thinking about that bastard. He had beaten her for God knew how long before she finally stood up to him and they threw *her* in jail? It was ludicrous. And what if she hadn't stood up to him? She'd probably be dead.

"It's okay, it's okay. You're safe now. I love you so much," I said soothingly as I stroked her hair.

This revelation only made me love her more, only made me want to protect her and make her happy, to help her get rid of the demons that haunted her, to fix our problems. Right then and there I promised myself I would do everything possible to give us both a fresh start. Holding her close, I vowed silently to protect this fragile woman from ever being hurt again.

Later that night, I sat before the fireplace in our living room, staring at the crackling flames, trying to sort out truth from fantasy. Lauren had been napping, drained from the intensity of the events from earlier in the evening. I heard the bedroom door open, and like a frightened child, Lauren came to me, needing me to hold her in my arms. She looked at me with the fear of someone who was being torn from her loved ones by forces beyond her control. She clung to me as someone cast outside might cling to a tree trunk in the midst of a tornado's harsh winds. "Richard, I love you!" she cried out. "Do you hear me? Do you hear me?"

"Yes, Lauren," I said softly. "I hear you." And I held her tightly, as if I was holding her back from the storm threatening to hurl her over the edge of an abyss.

"I need to tell you something. I mean,..." said Lauren. Tears streamed down her face, her voice broken. Suddenly, her body grew rigid in my arms. Her voice became clear, stronger. "I need to tell you about shooting my ex-husband."

"You what?" I asked, startled by yet another confession.

There had been a number of cases of spouses shooting their husbands in which the facts resulted in great sympathy for the shooter. The women had been kept emotionally and physically isolated by their spouses. Even if they worked or had friends, their fear of their husbands' hair-trigger violence was so great that they felt they dare not tell anyone what was happening to them. Perhaps they knew help was available. Perhaps there was an escape. But they also realized that if there wasn't, if they made a failed effort to get help and their husbands learned about it, they would be battered horribly. When the relationship became intolerable, the women who knew no alternative picked up the nearest weapon and used it on the abusive brute. Sometimes this was a knife. Sometimes it was a frying pan, a hammer, or some other household weapon. And sometimes it was a gun.

"Battered wife syndrome," psychologists called it. Defense lawyers used it as a strategy during court trials. Sometimes the women went free, sometimes they did time. But a look at some of the women made you understand that these were individuals who were pushed to a breaking point to act as they had. More important, your gut level knew they would never act out violently again. They were loving, gentle people who had stayed in a relationship well past when they should have left, paying an unbelievable price for their mistake.

I was not thinking of Lauren as a criminal when she said it. My mind was on the woman I loved. She was silent, so I said, "Come on, Lauren. I love you. You can talk to me."

Lauren turned toward the fire, her face bathed in its warm glow. She remained silent for a few minutes, and I did not press her. One of the things I learned as a police detective is that silence can be an effective tool for helping someone to talk. Most of us are uncomfortable with silence when we are with another person. We will say something, anything, just to fill the space. Many a detective has gained a confession just by waiting quietly when a suspect has paused in the midst of a partially incriminating statement. He or she will say a little, then feel the need to say more just because you are being quiet. Eventually the person tells you everything you need to know.

I wasn't trying to trick Lauren. She wasn't a suspect in a criminal case. But she obviously was having difficulty speaking, and my silence was likely to help her find the words to go on. Finally, she looked back at me and said, "He was rotten. He hit and abused me one time too many, and I shot him. That was why they put me in jail."

Lauren's voice was different as she spoke, though I blamed the change in tone on hoarseness from the tears she had shed. I could see the light of the fire reflected on the tears that still dampened her face. I wanted to reassure her that I was there for her now, would always be there for her. How bad could what she was telling me be?

"There's more, Richard. I may be out of jail but I'm on probation and I skipped town to go to Florida with you for a few days. Does that make me a criminal?" She hurried on without waiting for an answer, as if she desperately needed to unload the weight of the terrible things she'd been carrying around for so long. "You know how I've been going down to Roanoke every week to take care of my business? Well, I've also been seeing a court appointed psychiatrist and checking in with my probation officer. He thinks I'm still living down there with my friend."

I sat in silence for a few minutes trying to absorb it all. What was it she had just said? Did I hear it right? I suddenly felt foolish. What had I gotten myself into? Did I really know my own wife? My mind raced. *I still have friends on the force. I can get a copy of her criminal record...* No. I couldn't do that. I had to trust Lauren. I had to believe in her words, believe in her, believe in us. She needed me now more than ever, and I was determined to be there for her. I took her in my arms. "Oh my God, Lauren. You poor thing. It's all over now. You're mine now. I'll protect you forever. We can get your probation transferred up here. We can also request that the court allow you to see a local psychiatrist. You have nothing to be worried about."

Lauren turned her back towards me and shook her head. She remained like that for another minute or two, then her body seemed to relax as she returned to my arms. Her voice was normal, and as she touched her cheek, she seemed a little surprised by the tears on her face, by the wetness of my shirt where she had cried against my shoulder. She looked at me, as though about to ask a question, then fell into silence as I held her close.

Finally, Lauren relaxed and began to drift off to sleep. I gently picked her up and carried her down the darkened hallway to our bedroom. I eased her onto the bed and rested by her side in the dark, listening to the sounds of her breathing as she fell into a deep sleep. The woman I loved was there, but so was the demon inside her. I could only wonder which one would be the first to awaken.

— CHAPTER 9 —

The Dark Rider

Heavy black and gray clouds gather inside the dark abyss, swirling counterclockwise like brew in a witch's caldron. The gathering storm clouds rise to the top of the abyss obscuring everything from view. From deep within the chasm, lightning strikes illuminate the rising mist with a red-colored hue. The sound of thunderclaps, heard in the distance come closer, like a rolling tide. With each strike of threatening fire, the sound of the thunder grows more intense until it becomes the sound of thundering hoof beats.

Out of the darkness, a huge black stallion rides forth, flanks sweating and nostrils flaring. A female rider sits astride the steed, her gown flows in the wind and brushes the steed's sweating flanks as she lifts a silver bladed broad sword above her head. Slowly, the rider lowers the point of the sword towards me. The rider's eyes glow as two red dots on a blurred, featureless face. She lowers her head and I look the demon in the eyes. It is like looking straight through the gates of hell. Then the apparition speaks to me. In deep resonating tones, I hear her words, "Look at me! Look at me now! Listen to me! Listen to me now! The truth shall be known! The truth shall be known!" The rider's final words become lost in the thunder of hooves as dark swirling clouds overtake both horse and rider. They turn away. I watch as they ride back into the darkness of hell!

I awoke with a start and found myself soaked with sweat. *It was a dream!* I thought about the dream and what it could mean. The dream ended with the mysterious rider speaking her final words, words that I could neither hear, nor understand. *What did it mean?*

Lauren was sleeping peacefully beside me; her breathing easy and unlabored. I looked at her, thinking about the events of the previous evening. What was happening to her? What would happen to us? I quietly rose and went into the kitchen to make the morning coffee, my mind swirling with worried thoughts. A few minutes later, Lauren passed by the kitchen doorway, heading straight for the living room. "Good morning!" I called out to her, trying to sound cheerful. I hoped we could have a good start after the intense night we had just gone through. There was no response. I walked to the doorway and looked into the living room where Lauren sat in the upholstered rocking chair. She silently rocked back and forth with a vacant stare fixed on the fireplace. Perhaps she was remembering what happened, remembering burning our photos and marriage license.

"Honey, are you okay?" I called. Again, no response.

I nervously went back to the coffeepot. Although I wanted to help her, I realized that whatever was going on with Lauren, whatever was upsetting her, was too big for me to handle alone. I hurried through my morning routine, dressing as quickly as possible. I was most concerned with giving her some space, but I also wanted to avoid a confrontation that would be a repeat of last night. That episode drained me; I was exhausted both physically and emotionally. I did not know how to help her on my own, but I hoped her therapist would know what to do. I decided that I would call Dr. Carter from work to see what should be done.

When I left the apartment, Lauren was still sitting in the rocker. Her response to my goodbye was a silent glare; and the look in her eyes a forecast of what was to follow.

I arrived at the Richmond office early, long before the rest of my staff. Just as I reached for the phone to call Dr. Carter, it rang. It was Lauren. She rambled for a few minutes then hung up. I managed to put two calls in to her doctor, but he was busy with patients. I decided against leaving any message. What would I even say in a message? How could I explain what had happened to a receptionist? No, I would just keep trying until I reached him. But I would not get much of an opportunity to place anymore calls to his office. Over the next hour, Lauren called fifteen or twenty times, each call more rambling and pointless than the previous one. *She's upset about last night,* I told myself. I tried to remain as calm as possible hoping that if I let her vent, the calls would stop and she would feel better. But as the hours passed, I became more anxious and worried. What was going on? I decided to turn on the tape recording equipment in my office to document these phone calls. I didn't really expect to need the recordings, but I was so shocked by what I was hearing that I felt no one, not even her therapist, would believe me without proof. Not that I had any intention of telling anyone except her therapist about the calls, but who knew what might happen? As soon as I set up the recording equipment, I felt a twinge of guilt. *What kind of person would you be if you taped your wife's phone calls?* I asked myself. Before I had a chance to disconnect the tape recorder from the telephone, the calls started coming again. Now, Lauren turned from meandering to abusive.

"Richard, I am tired of your shit, Richard!" Lauren's voice was full of authority.

"What are you talking about, Lauren?" I asked.

"All of it, Richard. I am tired of them!" I finally recognized the voice; it belonged to the woman I met last night; it belonged to Hannah.

"Lauren, tell me please, what is this all about?" I asked again. I was afraid of the answer I might get, but all I heard was silence. I felt like I was back in the apartment the previous night, watching a stranger burn everything that symbolized my marriage.

"Lauren, please stop calling. I am trying to work. I've been trying to call Dr. Carter, but he's been with patients. Maybe you should give him a call."

"Do you want me to come down there?" Her voice became shrill. "I am coming down there! Do you hear me? Do you hear me?" I looked at the clock on the wall. It was almost noon; I had spent the entire morning taking phone calls from Lauren.

"Please Lauren," I begged, my voice choking. "Please, call Dr. Carter."

"I am coming down there..." Lauren's voice was softer now, a taunting whisper.

"No, Lauren. I think that's not a good idea. You know what? I'll leave a little early. I'll come home soon. Just please, please calm down." I felt like I was talking to a child, but I didn't know how to react to this person my wife had become.

"I am calm, Richard." Lauren said, her voice changing to an almost singsong mode.

The conversation continued for a few more minutes before Lauren seemed assuaged by my words. She hung up and there was an hour of quiet before the telephone began ringing again. Around two o'clock in the afternoon, I realized

I was not going to accomplish anything. Even without the steady phone calls, I couldn't stop thinking about Lauren's bizarre behavior. I was over the initial shock that I felt the previous night, but I still didn't know what to make of it all. I knew that I had to attempt to get a measure of control over the situation. I tried to reach Dr. Carter once more, but to no avail. I made a few business calls and then advised my office staff I was going home for the rest of the day.

In the time it took me to drive home, I reflected on our past relationship. Despite the angry words she flung at me in Dr. Carter's office, I felt that our marriage was good, that we were good together. I felt happy. And up until yesterday, I thought Lauren was happy, too. But in less than twenty-four hours, things seemed to be falling apart. I turned on the radio trying to drown out my own thoughts. I have to calm down, I told myself. Things would be okay. We would weather this storm. I hoped.

I arrived at the apartment, my stomach churning. "Lauren, I'm home," I called out. No answer. I looked down the hall and saw the bathroom door shut, the sound of running water faintly emanating. I poured a glass of juice and sat down on the sofa in the living room to wait. I began nervously tapping my fingers on the coffee table, then my foot on the floor, than my hand on my knee. What was she doing in there? Several minutes passed. I was about to get up to see what was going on when I heard the water stop. After a minute, the bathroom door creaked open.

Lauren entered the living room, dressed in a miniskirt and high heels—clothes I had never seen before—looking much like one of the streetwalkers down on Broad Street. She wore the same cold look I had seen Hannah wear. It was a combination of a blank stare and a smile void of feeling.

"I'm going out!" she announced, walking towards the front door. I sat in stunned silence while she slammed the door behind her. I felt glued to my seat, helpless to stop her. Then I heard the distinct sound of her Mustang's engine outside in the parking lot. As if snapped from a trance, I was suddenly freed from the sofa; I raced to the window. I watched as Lauren backed out of her space and then began driving around the apartment complex parking lot. She went in circles, faster and faster. I watched from the window as she did several laps. Imagining the neighbors on the phone to the police with reports of a mad woman in the parking lot, I decided to head outside and try to do something to make her stop. Just as I opened the front door, debating what I could possibly do, she slowed, then parked. She got out of the car and dug around in the back seat before finding a bottle of wine. As she sauntered towards our front door, I ran back to the living room like a frightened child watching a horror movie. I didn't know what to do but just sit and wait to see what would happen next.

Lauren strode through the front door, the bottle of wine in hand. She grabbed a glass from the china cabinet and sank into the upholstered rocker opposite the couch. She clutched the glass and the bottle, rocking slowly back and forth. The look of the demon was on her face. I hadn't noticed it as much when she came out of the bathroom, but now the change in her appearance was distinct. Her eyes were wide, her jowls drooped, and the scar-like crease had formed on her cheek ending at her quivering upper lip. I sat in silence looking into her dark eyes. I could see nothing of Lauren in that face, in that body. I could hardly believe it myself, but another woman sat before me.

I felt the knot in my stomach tighten. *My God! Who is this woman? Where is Lauren? Is this going to go on all day and into the night? What would tomorrow bring?* My thoughts tormented me.

Suddenly, Lauren threw the bottle and the glass to

the floor, sending shattered glass in every direction. Her momentary quiet was replaced with loud, hateful rage.

"Look at me, you son of a bitch! Listen to me! Listen to me now!" It was Hannah. I knew that now. Her eyes burned into me. These same words, spoken somewhere else in time, spoken by someone else, would have seemed absurd; almost to the point of being crude comedy, but what I saw before me was neither an apparition nor comedy. It was all very real.

"Lauren, how much longer is this going to go on tonight? What's wrong with you?" I asked out of pure frustration. I knew that there wouldn't be an intelligent answer forthcoming. There was no rationale to anything that was happening.

"Do you love me, Richard?" She asked almost coyly. I stood up and tried to leave the room. I had to get out of there. It was all too much. Hannah jumped up and blocked my path, smiling. I looked defiantly into her eyes and saw a person I didn't even know. I felt this person could wreak havoc and would probably enjoy it, so I turned around and went back into the living room, defeated. Hannah followed close at my heels.

We both sat down again, me on the couch, Hannah in the rocking chair. The demon was raging, both reason and understanding were absent. The absurdity of her question struck me. It was pure madness, but whatever this demon said or did seemed to have no rationale.

"Tell me! Tell me!" she screamed again. I answered her with silence, realizing that whether or not I answered the question, the demon would invoke the same question again, and again. I began to see a pattern in the madness; the demon tried to torture me with repetition. She would ask them same questions over and over and no matter what answer I gave, it was wrong.

Suddenly, her body seemed to transform. Lauren stretched her arms over her head and yawned. She turned to look at me and smiled. I was looking into the eyes of the woman I fell in love with.

"I am so tired, Richard. I think I'm going to take a bath and go to bed early." She stood up and headed toward the bathroom, unaware of the shattered glass and puddle of wine a few feet away from where she was just sitting.

With that, I heaved a sigh of relief. Just looking at her face, into her eyes, I felt a glimmer of hope. *It will turn out all right, everything will be all right,* I told myself. And in that moment I believed it. I had to believe it. I didn't want to admit to my friends, to my family, and most of all, to myself, that maybe, just maybe, I had rushed into a marriage with someone who was turning out to be a complete stranger. I pushed the thought from my mind. No matter what was happening, Lauren needed my help and support, not doubt and weakness. I had to believe in Lauren, in myself, in us.

Lauren's counseling sessions with Ted Carter continued. I was never able to reach him the day Lauren made all the phone calls to my office, so I never told him about what happened. I was actually relieved not to have to tell him. After all, I barely believed what I witnessed. What would a professional like Ted think? What would anyone think? Even though I had tapes of some of the phone calls, I couldn't bear the thought of actually playing them for anyone. I knew they would humiliate Lauren. Instead I clung to the hope that Lauren's sessions with Dr. Carter would produce some sort of miracle cure and I would never need to tell him or anyone about Hannah.

But Lauren's behavior became more erratic. There were visits to my office from her over the next several weeks. Each time the craziness became more difficult to hide from those around me. Life on the job became a nightmare filled with Lauren's incessant and repetitive telephone calls. Life at home became a series of inconsistencies, good times followed by bad, then good times again. One Thursday evening in early May, Lauren became violent. Around ten o'clock that night she stormed from the apartment in a rage. I followed her outside and watched helpless from the sidewalk as she drove her Mustang in circles around the parking lot again. I could hear her laughing. Luckily, most of our neighbors were in for the night. I went back inside, sat down on the couch, and waited.

Later when Lauren came back into the apartment, it was after midnight. She headed straight for the bedroom and slammed the door. Within moments, a new woman appeared, dressed in black leather. *What now?* I thought. "I'm Peg," she said in a vile tone. Her eyes were dark, narrowed slits. She walked slowly, deliberately, as if carrying out some great plan, to a utility closet next to the kitchen and returned brandishing a hammer. Before I could move, she stood over me, the hammer raised above her head. I looked into her eyes and sat there frozen. I watched her carefully, searching for a signal that she would strike or retreat. Her eyes taunted me while her lips formed a thin smile. I don't know how long we stayed like that, frozen in place. I decided to take my chances. In the blink of any eye, I reached up and grabbed her wrists. I felt strength rise within her and a struggle began. She tried to thrust downward with the hammer while I tried to wrest it away. Finally, the hammer fell to the floor. Peg broke away and ran to the bedroom.

I stared dumbfounded at the hallway through which the woman I would come to call Lucifer's Daughter had just disappeared. With my heart racing and my knees feeling weak, I practically fell backwards onto the couch. I sat there wondering what to do next. Over the past several weeks I had endured a lot of angry, irrational, even abusive episodes with Lauren, but I had never felt that my life was in danger until now. Was the act I had just witnessed a serious threat? Given the chance, would Lauren have used the hammer on me? No, I pushed those thoughts out of my mind. I decided I would call her therapist in the morning and tell him the whole story regardless of how unbelievable it was. I sat there for a while in the semi-darkness, praying I would find a way out of the situation.

I went out around the apartment turning off the few lights that were on and locking the doors and windows. When I went into the bedroom, Lauren was already asleep. I lay down beside her, listening to her breathing. Finally, when I was convinced she would not awaken till morning, I found an uneasy respite and fell asleep.

— CHAPTER 10 —

Life in Wonderland

In May, my mind was not on Hannah, Lucifer's Daughter or John Taylor, but on the Lauren I'd married, the Lauren about whom I was learning more, much of which I did not want to know. That month, an investigator from the Henrico County Probation Office visited our apartment. His visit was related to the transfer of Lauren's supervised probation from Roanoke County to Richmond.

Several weeks later we met Lauren's new probation officer. It was obvious from the beginning that Lauren did not like the new arrangements. Apparently Roanoke was somewhat less restrictive, with fewer requirements for supervision.

I felt relieved. The rather lax supervision was proof to me that my early judgment had been right—that whatever had happened between Lauren and her ex-husband was provoked by brutality. I did not know the details of the case and did not want to know. I was aware that Lauren had been a battered spouse. I felt that she had been abused beyond her limits. I knew now that after she tried to commit that terrible act and failed, she had paid the price. The Lauren I knew, the woman I first met in the courthouse in Goochland, was incapable of violence or hate.

121

But her new probation officer made it clear that he would be following restrictive procedures, including monitoring her business and any other types of jobs she might hold. He seemed to think her violent. I assumed that both he and her previous probation officer were looking at the same case file and that the Roanoke officer was using better judgment.

My feelings were reinforced by the fact that Lauren's probation would end the moment she paid off her court costs of more than $5000. She couldn't have done anything so terrible, I reasoned, if such a sum of money would free her from all further obligations. I paid off her bill, freeing her from the stress of the probation requirements.

Meanwhile, Lauren continued in therapy with Ted Carter and was required to occasionally see her court appointed psychiatrist as well. However, since Dr. Carter had asked me not to come, I was not a part of the sessions, a fact that still made no sense to me. I still did not understand what was happening. My wife was mentally ill, yet there was no information for the man who loved her, who had taken an oath to see her through whatever hell she was enduring.

"What is wrong with my wife?" I asked one day after a counseling session. "Could she have a brain tumor?"

"I don't believe it's physical. I'm sure the court appointed psychiatrist has had the requisite tests performed."

"Then what is it?" I asked, anguished.

"It's confidential," the therapist told me. "I can't comment any further."

I tried to tell him what was happening at home but he stopped me. "Lauren is my patient and I can not discuss her therapy with you," he said firmly.

Only once did Dr. Carter give me a direct answer. That was when I asked, "Do you think that Lauren is focusing all the wrongs she perceives to have been done to her on me? Is it possible that she is blaming me for everything bad that has happened in her life?"

Carter looked at me in a way that convinced me I had hit upon something. "Yes," he said, slowly. "That's possible."

It also apparently did not matter. Whatever was taking place in the therapy sessions with Dr. Carter and with the other psychiatrist was not helping any. Things were getting worse.

The telephone calls to my office increased some time later that month. Angry calls. Senseless calls. One time there was swearing at me. Another time there was a verbal attack against my secretary. Yet another time there was maniacal laughter.

The calls had to be answered. That was part of the secretary's job. There was no way to screen calls, and even if we could, it was not one of the employee's responsibilities to make a judgment about the importance of a personal call.

I didn't tell anyone about the troubles I was having in my marriage. I didn't want to betray Lauren's trust and I was ashamed to say anything to those who had warned me not to get involved with her. To others, we were still in the newlywed stage when, under normal circumstances, friends joke about sex, about learning to adjust to cooking skills, about getting used to keeping the toilet seat down and remembering to put the cap back on the toothpaste tube. It was not a time when someone might receive as many as eighty-five calls in a single day, not one of them having to do with work or romance.

I knew I had to get control of the situation, but I did not know how. Each time I talked with Lauren about it, she seemed genuinely shocked. I realized I couldn't dare play the tape recordings I made of these phone calls for fear of how they would affect her. She had not made such calls. She would never make such calls. Lauren loved me, respected me and the work I did. She would never harass me. "I love you so much, Richard. I can't understand how someone could do this to you. We'll find out who it is. We'll stop them. Together we can do it and we'll learn the truth about this horrible woman. You'll see."

Oddly, I believed Lauren. Not that I failed to recognize the voice that harassed me, but rather that she knew nothing about what was taking place. It was like living in a Lewis Carroll children's story. I had become Alice and Lauren was the Mad Hatter, and who knew how many other characters.

It was a warm evening, summer just around the corner. Lauren was cooking in the kitchen when I came home a little late. I knew I would be delayed so I called first to let her know.

"Hurry," she had said. "It's so lonely without you. I miss you so much." Her voice was as soft as a caress, her words like a kiss. It was the Lauren with whom I had fallen in love; the Lauren I had married.

Dinner was pleasant, the conversation covering both our workdays. She was genuinely interested in what I was doing and did not mention the telephone calls. I ignored them as well. Lauren was still the most beautiful, exciting, intelligent, and sensual woman I had ever known, and moments such as we were enjoying were to be savored under any circumstance.

It was around ten o'clock in the evening when Lauren left me. I don't mean she walked out of the apartment. Rather there was a definite change in her body. Her shoulders seemed to slump slightly, and her arms, face, and hands became tense. Her breasts seemed to noticeably sag. The scar-like mark developed on her right cheek, the flesh drooping. "Fuck you, Richard Goetzke!" she shouted. "You think you're so damned special to that bitch? You're nothing but shit, and I'm going to have your ass. Why don't you beat the bitch? Hurt her? The way you talk to her makes me want to puke all over your 'I'm-more-important-than-you-are' three-piece suit."

The language grew increasingly foul until she could no longer contain her rage in the apartment. She fumbled about Lauren's purse, looking for the car keys Lauren always knew instantly where to locate. Finally, emerging triumphant, she stormed out the door, went down to the parking lot, and started the red Mustang. From the window I watched as she began driving around the lot, accelerating more and more. Faster and faster she drove. Round and round. She was playing chicken with parked cars, seeing how close she could get without smashing into them, all the time laughing so wildly that I could hear her as I walked out to the sidewalk, watching, knowing no safe way to stop her. At least there were no people outside or their lives would have been endangered. Besides that, how would I explain Lauren's bizarre behavior to our neighbors?

Finally I returned to our apartment, sat on the couch and waited.

The return confirmed my worse fears. The scar was firmly set in Lauren's cheek. Her eyes had wildness to them. She looked like a cornered animal, her body tensed to spring in a last desperate effort to escape an enemy that existed only in her mind.

Lauren walked into the kitchen, returning moments later with a butcher knife in her hand. I did not move. "Remember me? I'm Hannah," she sneered, raising the knife.

Police officers fear knifers more than they fear people with guns. Getting cut with a knife creates a dirty wound that is often difficult to stitch, easily gets infected, and is intensely painful. Recovery is slow, and the risk of permanent muscle and/or nerve damage is great.

At the same time, we are taught in the Police Academy that using deadly force against a knifer is a problem. The public expects us to be skilled in the martial arts or some other physical ability that will enable us to disarm a knifer with a minimum of effort. Yet the truth is that we are not, and many of the tricks we were taught, such as shoving a chair into the knifer so the legs of the chair act as a defense against the swinging and thrusting blade, require being in the right place at the right time.

I was sitting on the couch, unable to move in either direction without risking having her strike. Instead, I sat poised, staring into those wild eyes, searching for any hint that she might strike when she raised the knife above her head, then seemed to freeze in time and place.

There was a smile on Lauren's lips that never reached her eyes. Her smile might have been painted on a child's doll, so rigid and unfeeling did it look.

I said nothing. I just focused on the upheld arm, tensed to react to any movement she might make.

I'm not sure how long I sat there, willing myself to breathe normally, willing myself to show neither fear nor anger. She seemed frozen in place, and I wanted to do nothing that might lead to one of us getting hurt.

Finally, realizing the woman before me was not going to suddenly thrust the butcher knife into my chest, I reached up and took her wrist in my hand. My grip was firm but not obviously defensive. It was more like the grip a parent keeps on a small child's hand when trying to walk across a busy roadway.

At first, there was no reaction, but before I could move to the side, away from the poised blade, Lauren began to push downward. The movement was slow, yet her strength seemed to increase second by second. It felt as though I was holding a barbell on which unseen forces were adding small weights, one after another, until holding the barbell required exhausting effort.

I tried twisting Lauren's arm to the side without letting her growing strength thrust it into my chest. She kept the knife aimed at my chest, her strength growing, her body seemingly able to anticipate every shift of my body, adjusting to assure she remained in control.

We were both silent in the growing struggle. I reached up with my other hand, grasping her wrist with both hands. I wanted to kick out, to lean back against the couch and use my foot to propel her backwards. That was the kind of combat training I had had in the military and in the police academy, but I could not think of Lauren, even Lauren trying to stab me, as I would a violent street thug.

This was my wife. At least I still thought she was my wife. This was certainly a troubled woman I loved, a woman who, from the first day we met, was someone I instinctively wanted to protect from harm. There was no way I could do otherwise even though I was the one in danger.

Using whatever strength was still in me, I managed to force the knife from Lauren's hand. She stared at me for a moment as I relaxed my grip on her wrist, then she turned and ran into the bedroom.

I put the butcher knife back in the kitchen. I was breathing hard, my heart beating rapidly. I had no doubt that if I hadn't forced Lauren to drop the knife, I would have been stabbed, perhaps killed. I also had no doubt that the woman holding the knife was not Lauren; that she was someone else. Once again I instinctively knew that if I had seen the woman who had been holding the knife on the street, I would not have recognized her. The face, the bearing of her body, so many subtle details were all wrong. It was only when she seemed to be like something out of one of those horror shows where one person morphs into another that I knew this woman was both Lauren and not Lauren.

A few minutes passed. Not knowing what else to do, I sat on the couch, watching the bedroom door. Suddenly, the door opened and a woman I had never seen before came into the room. It was not Lauren. It was not Hannah. And it was definitely not Lucifer's Daughter. She was in Lauren's clothes, and this time the body was definitely that of Lauren, yet there was something else. Her face was smooth, like a child/woman on the cusp of adolescence. It was also wide-eyed and fearful, the look of someone feeling scared, lost, and alone in the midst of strangers, someone looking for that one familiar face whose presence can take away the fear, take away the pain.

"Where has my grandmother gone?" this child/ woman asked. Her voice was higher than Lauren's was. It was the voice of a little girl growing into womanhood, the richness and depth not yet achieved. If I saw her on the street and listened to her words in passing, I would have said she was a twelve-year-old playing dress-up.

"Where has my grandmother gone? Why did she leave me?"

"Who are you?" I asked gently.

"I'm Jenny, of course." Lauren sat on the couch next to me. She looked into my eyes, seeking answers she seemed to hope were there. I had become a safe friend, someone with whom she could share her concerns. Then, knowing I had no answers yet seeking my comfort, she buried her head in my shoulder, sobbing deeply, clinging to me in desperation, saying, "Where has she gone? Where has she gone?"

In one of her rare moments talking of her childhood, Lauren had told me about being born in a small Virginia town to a young woman and her husband, a Korean War veteran. When Lauren was six years old, someone poured scalding hot water over her hands. When she returned from the hospital, Lauren went to live with her grandmother. Her grandmother died shortly after Lauren's twelfth birthday and she returned to her mother's home.

Lauren rarely spoke of her childhood or about what happened to her during her early years. Once, when I asked her about her earliest childhood memory, she responded, "When I was about two and a half years old, I can remember laying under my bed with a knife in my hands. My father came and took it away from me."

I looked searchingly at the woman I loved. What childhood memories were tormenting her? I held this person, questioning her, questioning myself, questioning a world that had seemed so perfect three months ago suddenly going mad all around me. I stroked her hair, her back, kissing her gently on the forehead as one might when comforting a child.

Suddenly Lauren sat up. She stood, walked over to the upholstered rocking chair near the television set, and sat down. Her face was again that of Lauren's, and as she rocked calmly, warmly smiling at me when I looked her way, I realized she had no awareness of anything that had just happened between us that evening.

I kept watching Lauren, wondering what I should do next. She had approached me with a butcher knife, but had she attacked me? She stood over me, holding the knife, smiling. That's menacing, not a very serious charge when a cop makes an arrest, yet a terrifying experience for the person being menaced.

And then I had taken Lauren's wrist...

I had never felt such an escalation of strength. It was as though she was willing herself to become ever more powerful. Was she hoping I would be unable to resist her, letting her plunge the knife into my chest? Or had she been playing some sort of sick game, not realizing that one slip and I would be seriously hurt or dead?

And who was Jenny, the little girl I had just comforted? Was it Lauren as a child? I knew there was only one

person, Lauren, and yet I also knew what I had seen and
held. There were three women in my living room that night,
three distinctly different people of different ages and physical
appearances. If someone had taken pictures of their faces,
then placed them side by side, you would swear that they
were sisters of different ages and temperaments. You would
know they were from the same family, but you would never
say they were the same woman.

It was crazy. A nightmare.

I wanted to tell someone, to discuss what had happened, to find someone who could make sense of it. Yet
whom could I tell? Even after my previous experiences with
Hannah, what happened today sounded insane even to me
and I had just lived through it.

Lauren was quiet, relaxed. The last time she had
been like this, once the violence was over, nothing else
occurred. I realized that this was different, yet I hoped it
would prove to be similar enough that it was over. "Lauren,
it's getting late. I think we should go to bed," I said quietly.

Without a word, Lauren got up from the chair and
walked to the bedroom. I went about the apartment, locking
doors, checking windows, and turning off lights. By the time
I reached the bedroom, Lauren was already under the cov-
ers. Carefully I lay down, listening as I did each night now
before giving in to my own exhaustion to the quiet night
sounds and Lauren's slow, steady breathing. I could tell she
had finally fallen asleep.

Hours passed as I listened. I was afraid to fall asleep,
afraid that whatever demon lurked inside her would take
advantage of her exhaustion to regain control of her body.

Eventually my own tiredness overwhelmed me. I fell
into a fitful sleep, rising early and getting to the office where
I called her therapist. I explained what had happened, realizing as I talked how absurd it all seemed. Worse, I could tell

from his voice that he did not believe me. However, since Lauren would be in for a session later in the day, he promised to find out what he could. By the time I hung up, I knew the call had been a waste of time. I had had trouble believing the attack and its aftermath and I had lived through it. How could I expect a stranger to trust me?

Dr. Carter may have been of little help, but at least the next week passed uneventfully. The first Sunday morning in June, I was feeling relaxed enough to spend some time with Lauren by the free form pool which was located directly below our third floor apartment. After an hour in the sun, I left Lauren to go back to the apartment to prepare lunch and call my children. Although I no longer did this from home, today I felt especially lonely for them. I took the portable telephone and walked out onto the balcony, looking down at Lauren resting on a lounge chair. Once again my heart went out to her. She was so beautiful, all I could think about were the positive memories of our brief life together. I prayed that whatever was affecting her mind could be healed. I loved her too much to let her go.

I said goodbye to my children and returned to the kitchen, unthinkingly locking the door behind me. Ever since I became involved in law enforcement, I've been cautious about the way I live. Doors are always locked, even when I step outside just long enough to dump trash or remove groceries from the car. I had seen too many people lose valuables to an opportunistic thief. I had also been to too many crime scenes where a violent individual took advantage of a tenant's casualness.

Not that our apartment complex was dangerous. Quite the contrary. It was a luxury building with all the amenities one could wish for and was in a safe, quiet setting. I'm sure all the neighbors would have thought I was crazy if they

knew I routinely locked the door. But it was habit borne of
some of the bad things I had seen people do to one another,
and Lauren, who did not share my caution, tolerated my
actions. She understood the reason I did it, and while she saw
no need, she went along with what I was sure she considered
my idiosyncrasy.

Until that moment...

"Open the fucking door!" screamed Lauren, who
again was not Lauren.

I sheepishly unlocked the door, but before I could
apologize, she screamed, "You were talking to *her*, weren't
you?"

"Talking to who, Lauren? Who are you talking
about?" I replied.

"Patsy. You were talking to her, weren't you!" It was
an answer in the form of a question. Patsy was my ex-wife
and Lauren knew full well that the relationship was over. The
only time we talked was when we needed to discuss the children. We each still loved them. We each wanted to help
them achieve their goals in life. But as for Patsy and myself,
the love we once had shared was long gone. Whatever spark
that had seemingly set us on fire was well extinguished.

"I called my kids," I said when she paused long
enough for me to answer. "What's wrong with that?"

I was getting frustrated with what was going on. There
was no reason for Lauren to overreact in the manner she was
doing. There was nothing wrong. She knew I always locked
the door. She knew how lonely I was for my kids, though I
hid the fact that I called them on a regular basis. She knew...

Yet was this Lauren?

Lauren strode into the bedroom, changing into a
blouse and shorts. While she was getting out of her bathing
suit, I checked the refrigerator. The two wine bottles we just
bought were missing, and before I could question what that

meant, Lauren came out carrying her pocketbook. As she walked to the door, I asked, "Where are you going?"

"I'm going for more wine!" she announced. And suddenly, maybe, I had my answer. Lauren and I both enjoyed beer and wine in what I thought was moderation. We always had some chilled at home, enjoying them with lunch or dinner on weekends, when relaxing, or whenever it seemed appropriate. But beer and wine were not a regular part of our diet. So far as I knew, neither one of us ever had more than a couple drinks. It was just not a part of our lifestyle, yet suddenly we were missing two bottles of wine, and without looking or my saying anything, Lauren knew we needed more. Perhaps she was a closet alcoholic. Perhaps that was all that I was facing.

I had seen alcoholics over the years, not just as a police officer but also with friends. I knew people who regularly attended Alcoholics Anonymous meetings, whose lives had been shattered, then were slowly being rebuilt through their efforts within the organization.

Alcohol abuse would account for Lauren's mood changes. Alcohol abuse would account for her unexplained violence. And alcohol abuse was something we could conquer together!

In a rather perverted way, I was happy. This was a problem I could grasp. This was a problem I could fight. This was a place where love could triumph.

"Lauren," I said, quietly, lovingly. "I don't think that's such a good idea. You already have had too much."

"Fuck you!" Lauren said, scowling. "You a cop or something?" She laughed at her joke, but the anger never left her face.

"No, not any more. But if you go out that door, I'm going to call one."

I regretted my words almost the moment I spoke

them. I assumed Lauren was drunk. I assumed she would try to drive her car to the store, in which case I truly would have had her stopped for Driving Under the Influence. There was enough cop left in me to not let her drinking problem endanger others.

Lauren had been holding the doorknob as I walked to the telephone in the dining room and picked up the receiver. Suddenly I felt a sharp pain in my spine and I fell to the floor. Lauren had kicked me, and it was obvious she was trying to hurt me. When she tried to kick me again, I grabbed her leg, pulling her down with me.

There was a smile on Lauren's face as she proceeded to pummel me as best she could. She kicked and struck me with her fists, delighting in inflicting pain. There was no question about her wanting to hurt me, so I instinctively grabbed for her purse, twisting it in a way that caused the straps to wrap around her wrists as we rolled about the floor. If I could just keep the straps tight without their breaking, there was a chance I could get to the cordless phone and call for help. Finally, holding the straps with one hand, staying close enough to her legs so her kicks were relatively ineffectual, I used my free hand to grab the telephone and dial 911.

"911. What is the emergency?" The operator's voice was calm, efficient.

"It's my wife. She's gone crazy!" Lauren struggled against my hold. I could feel her strength increasing as it had the night she tried to stab me. I had no idea how much longer I could hold on.

"What do you mean she's gone crazy? What is she doing?" the operator asked calmly.

"She's been drinking and now I'm trying to keep her from driving, but she attacked me when I told her I was going to call the police. I need help!" I called loudly, having to let go of the telephone long enough to try and hold Lauren. Her strength had grown to where she was rising from the floor no matter how hard I tried to hold her down. She was breathing hard, but it was obvious she would not stop fighting until she got out the door.

"Are you on Sandy Springs Circle?" I heard the operator ask. I confirmed the address and heard the operator say there was a unit on the way.

A few minutes passed, then Lauren stopped struggling. She did not agree to stay home. She did not pause to catch her breath. She just stopped, lying on the floor as though it was the most natural place in the world for her to be. I released my hold on her and she calmly rose, walked to the couch, and sat down.

"What are you doing to me, Richard?" Lauren asked calmly. Her voice had a teasing quality to it, as though we had been playing some new game, perhaps as foreplay for intimacy. There was no hint of the hatred, the violence, even the alcohol I had hoped was fueling her reaction.

"Lauren, what the hell is wrong with you?" I asked. She looked at me quizzically, not understanding my concern.

Rather than embarrassing Lauren and myself by having uniformed patrol officers enter the apartment complex, knocking on our door, preparing to confront domestic violence, I called 911 again. I said that my wife had agreed not to go out while she was drinking.

"I think the crisis is over," I said. I should have looked in her eyes.

"Lauren," I said gently. "We've got to work this out or end our marriage right now," I said out of desperation. The words were painful ones and I hated uttering them. I loved this woman. I cherished the moments early in our relationship when I instinctively knew the happiness that could be ours. Yet there was something terribly, horribly wrong.

"Do you understand what I am saying?" I asked, and

as I looked in her eyes, I realized I had made a mistake. They seemed to enlarge in ways that I once would have thought impossible. A smile came over her now sagging face, and the scar-like mark returned. Lauren was gone, as physically apart from me as if she had left the building. I knew that I was confronting someone else, a different individual entirely. Hannah was back, and she, I was learning, had the strength of a legion of demons.

Smiling, soundless, Hannah grasped the sleeve of my tee shirt in a vise-like grip. Then she jerked me violently from one side of the couch to the other. I felt like I was attached to one of those short bungee cords hardware stores sell as tie-downs for car luggage carriers. She could have flung me from wall to wall without ever taking a breath.

This horrible creature from Hell had me completely at her mercy.

Desperate, I grabbed her wrist with both hands and twisted violently away, moving back across the room. I dared not let her get near me. I dared not let her touch me. Hannah had the strength of several men, and there was no way I could stop her short of using extreme violence.

As quickly as it started, it was over. Lauren, hurting and surprised, sat holding her wrist and staring at me. "Richard," she said, shocked, "My wrist. It must be broken. Did you do this to me?" I was stunned, not only by the display I witnessed, but by the fact that Lauren had no idea what had just gone on. Surely she knew I had had to restrain her. And although I'd been forceful, I had not physically harmed her. However, there were tears in her eyes, and it was obvious that she felt I had somehow betrayed her.

I walked over to the couch and examined her wrist. She held her arm out tentatively, like a small child who had accidentally had her bare toes stepped on by her absent-minded father who failed to notice his daughter playing underfoot. I was the one she wanted to check her hurt, yet she also knew I was the one who had caused it.

I looked at the wrist and gently felt the bone. There was some redness, probably from the strong grip I had used, but there was no indication that anything more serious had happened. "No, Lauren, I don't think it's broken. It's probably just a sprain."

"It feels broken, Richard," Lauren said, looking sadly at her wrist and then at me. She was certain the injury was far worse than it was, but I had the impression that the pain she was in was not from the bruise but rather the shock that I could hurt her. There was no memory of what she had done. All she knew was that her wrist was suddenly sore and only I could have caused the pain.

Although Hannah had confronted me, I was still thinking that Lauren had an alcohol problem. I knew a number of men and women whose spouses were alcoholics. They told me that when the drink took effect, it was like being with a different person. Their lives were ones of living with Dr. Jekyll and Mr. Hyde, the monster coming from a bottle of beer, whiskey, vodka, or some other drink of choice.

I tried to tell myself Lauren's drunken personality was Hannah, the demon from Hell, and that the alcohol was effecting her memory. It was that simple and I still believed counseling, AA, and my support could get her through the crisis.

We talked little during the next hour. Lauren was extremely depressed and non-combative, again a stage typical of alcoholism. I knew that alcohol was a depressant. I knew that the violent period for some drinkers was the result of irritation of the brain lining. I knew that once that had passed, the person would become quiet, perhaps quite sad, and very tired. I also knew that the longer Lauren went without another drink, the more alcohol would leave her system.

However, though she remained docile, at the end of an hour, Lauren announced that she needed to go to the hospital.

I did not think about what the hospital visit would be like. In hindsight, I realize it did not matter. I still loved Lauren and did not want her to suffer, even though I knew that the magnitude of her injury was in her head. All I could question was how so much could go wrong, how two people could go from being total strangers to the closest of intimates, back to being strangers in a matter of months. It was all beyond my experience. It was all beyond my comprehension.

I suppose I should have realized how the Emergency Room staff would view our arrival. The injured wife. The contrite husband. It was a typical domestic violence situation in which I was cast as the aggressor, the unfeeling brute, and the abuser who was out of control.

"Please go to the waiting room," a nurse said to me. "We'll take care of your wife in here."

I sat there, looking across the hall to the treatment area, wondering what Lauren was telling them. Unable to just sit there, I walked outside. As I paced the sidewalk, a uniformed police officer came over to talk with me. He had been asked by the staff to get my story. By the time I was finished explaining what had happened, he seemed to believe me. He just shrugged his shoulders and said that he felt it was the concern of the county in which Lauren was on probation. When he left, I let out a sigh of relief. I had been certain I was going to spend the night in the city jail.

I went back to the waiting room and sat there until a staff member called me over to fill out the medical insurance papers. I will never forget the way the people looked at me. There was barely controlled rage and scorn in their faces. Their bodies were tense, their posture hostile. *My God!* I thought. *They think I'm a wife beater.*

Lauren emerged from the treatment room, a nurse hovering protectively as though I might try to hurt her again.

Lauren's wrist, mildly strained as I suspected, was wrapped in an Ace bandage. We drove back to the apartment in silence, and I was relieved that such an incident was over. I had no idea that during the next year we would return not only to this hospital but also to two others.

When we arrived back at the apartment, Lauren said, "Richard, I'm going to go to a motel. I need some money."

I realized that such a separation was probably a good idea. There was tremendous tension and confusion in the apartment. We both needed a break, and I certainly needed time to think without wondering when the demon called Hannah might return.

Lauren packed a small suitcase, then left in her car. I felt numb. I did not care where she went. Yet to my surprise, a half-hour later, the telephone rang. It was Hannah.

Other than the name of the motel where she had gone, I couldn't make out what she was saying. The calls came repeatedly, one after another, and her words made no sense. She wasn't drunk. There was no slurring of words. Instead, the rantings were even more confusing than when we first went to see the therapist.

Call after call came in. Each time I hung up, there would be another one within minutes. Finally, I unplugged the telephone and went to bed. I needed sleep. I needed to clear my head to try and figure out what to do next.

I was nearly asleep when I heard the key turn in the lock of the front door. Within seconds, Hannah stood over me, an apparition from Hell. She said nothing, her face looking much like it had when she tried to stab me with the butcher knife. It was as though she could sense my fear and thrived on the emotion.

I lay watching her, saying nothing, making no attempt to move. She stared down, also silent. Finally, around four in the morning, Hannah turned away, walked out the door, and returned to the motel. Having slept fitfully, I drank several cups of coffee, then late that morning I went to the motel to see Lauren. She was calm and more relaxed than she had been the day before. We sat in the room talking for about an hour when suddenly she began to cry. She was like a little child overwhelmed by the events taking place all around her. She seemed confused, acting at the direction of others whose words she was uncertain she should believe. "Richard," she said, tears streaming down her cheeks, her voice sounding as though she was seeking approval for her actions. "I went to see the Commonwealth Attorney's office early this morning and swore out a complaint against you."

The news shocked me. I felt my stomach churning. My fear was greater than when she had attacked me with a butcher knife. "Whatever for, Lauren?"

"For...for abusing me," she replied.

"Lauren, you've got to be kidding," I said, but I knew she was not. From her confusion, I had the feeling that the staff of the emergency room had told her to make the complaint. They thought I was a spouse beater, and under those circumstances, it was the right thing to do.

Seeing Lauren's confusion, I had the feeling that she had not wanted to bring the charges, had not been sure even how her wrist got hurt. I certainly realized she had no idea what this might mean. "Lauren, do you have any idea what you have done? Do you know I could lose my job over this, even if the court finds I'm innocent?

Lauren looked at me in shock, then cried all the harder. "I'll tell them to cancel it," she said. She sat on the bed, overwhelmed with emotions she did not know how to handle. Finally, she agreed to come home.

— CHAPTER 11 —

Under Arrest

For a few days, we were almost happy again. There were no visits from the other Laurens and I was spared having to go through hellish nights. There were long conversations between us about our relationship. Lauren related some experiences from her past that she had never told me about. I sat with her listening to her stories of the abuse she had suffered at the hands of her mother when she was young, then by some of the men that came in to her life. I was still in love with Lauren, the vulnerable, gentle Lauren I had first met, and her stories added to the deep compassion I felt for her. A glimmer of hope surfaced. I would help her.

Then the summons arrived. Apparently, Lauren had not cancelled her charges. I had seventy-two hours to report to police headquarters in the Henrico County Public Safety Building for processing.

There is nothing more humiliating for a police officer than to go through the arrest procedure himself. When you read in the paper about a dirty cop, he or she is the exception. Most police officers are dedicated men and women who pride themselves on upholding the law, their own lives not perfect, but at least not disgraceful. They handle the stress of the job without beating their spouses and children. They don't commit crimes. They try to help others in any way they can. A police department is sometimes referred to as a paramilitary operation, but the truth is that it is closer to the Scouting movement in its dedication to others.

No cop likes to see a rogue officer. The police officer who commits a crime, especially under the color of blue (wearing a uniform), is despised. An officer who beats a spouse is considered weak, an object of derision and disgust. For me to be on the same end of the booking procedure as the men and women I arrested during my career was perhaps the worst humiliation I could imagine.

An officer escorted me to the booking area where I was fingerprinted and photographed. I felt humiliated. I wanted to curl up in a fetal position and cry. I had been arrested for assault and battery, and in the eyes of people I saw as my peers, I had become the kind of cop I had always hated.

Even worse, I often worked with Henrico County on various fraud cases. Whenever an external fraud was committed against the bank, I would investigate and then present the case to the local law enforcement agency. Over a period of several years I had become acquainted with many of the detectives. Two detectives I knew walked by as I was being escorted to the Magistrate's office for arraignment. Luckily, the two men spared me the pain of conversation.

I entered my not guilty plea with the Magistrate, was given a June 14 court date, and was released on my own recognizance.

The following days passed without incident. I had begun to think there was a pattern to the violence. It seemed that it occurred every seven to ten days, though as of late, even this seemed to have stopped, at least in my presence. Life continued as normally as it can when you are living with a woman who seems to want to be emotionally and physically intimate one minute and is capable of killing you with a butcher knife the next. When the scheduled court date arrived, Lauren and I drove together to the Juvenile and Domestic Relations Court in Henrico County on the west side of Richmond. The corridor outside courtroom B was crowded, and from reading the court calendar posted on the bulletin board in the hall, it was obviously going to be a long day.

I was becoming desperate, though I dared not let Lauren know that fact. I had no idea what triggered the demon inside her.

I quietly explained to Lauren that a conviction would probably damage or end my career. She knew what happened. At least I hoped she did. Yet I was not certain of what she was thinking.

Lauren rose from the bench where we were sitting and announced to me that she was going in to see the Commonwealth Attorney. I prayed silently as I watched her walk down the hall to his office. When she returned a short time later, she said, "Richard, I spoke with the Commonwealth Attorney. The matter is going to be put on pending for a year, and if you ever touch me again...well...you will go straight to jail. Do you understand that, Richard?"

She spoke forcefully, her words filled with authority. The voice, her physical bearing, everything about her was different from the Lauren I married. Still, the words were comforting even though I knew that Judge Baylor intended to hear our case that morning, something he eventually did at 11:30 A.M.

Despite my experience with the legal system, I was scared as I took the witness stand. Courtrooms are designed to be intimidating places under the best of circumstances. The judge's bench sits high above all others, the robed judge part parent figure, part royalty. He or she is the person who controls the fate of everyone in the courtroom. A judge can not be questioned during a trial. If the judge feels that someone in the courtroom is acting improperly, the judge can legally have the person taken to jail for as long as the trial is taking place.

The witness stand is set lower than the judge's bench so that even the shortest judge can look down upon the tallest juror. The opposing attorneys stand when they question you, making anyone in the witness box feel a little like he or she is back in school being reproached by the teacher and observed by the principal.

Finally there is the jury, when one is used, sitting on banked seats to the side. For the type of hearing I was facing, though, there was only the judge, the prosecuting attorney, and myself, along with any legal counsel I might want to retain.

I did not want to have an attorney. I did not want to have to deal with everything from the expense to the questioning looks when I tried to tell my story. It was bad enough I had to be in court where I already expected to face hostility. What was taking place was so strange, I knew that anyone I asked to represent me would also question my truthfulness.

A deputy placed a waiver form on the defense table. When I signed it, the waiver became proof that I had chosen to not use an attorney. It would be one less reason for appeal if the case went against me.

Next, Judge Baylor asked, "Do you wish to testify?" I did not have to. I could say nothing, listen to the case presented against me, and hope the judge would not believe what was said.

Instead, I said, "Yes, your honor, I do wish to testify."

"Take the stand," said the judge. "But you must be aware that the Commonwealth Attorney has the right to question you on anything pertinent to this case."

"I understand that, your honor. I want to testify.

I walked to the witness stand, then the bailiff approached, had me raise my right hand, and said to me, "Do you solemnly swear to tell the truth, the whole truth, and nothing but the truth, so help you God?"

"I do."

The judge then leaned over the bench and said, "Tell the court what happened."

Slowly, my voice breaking at times, I recounted the details of that Sunday. By the time I was finished, I was fighting back tears. "This is what happened, your honor," I said, my voice barely above a whisper.

The judge's face remained impassive. He turned towards the Commonwealth Attorney and asked, "Does the State wish to cross examine?"

"No, your honor," he replied, sitting quietly at the prosecutor's table.

I exhaled slowly. For the first time I felt a certain amount of relief. I began to believe that things might turn out okay. I was dismissed from the stand and went back to the defense table, glancing over at Lauren. She was sitting with her head down, staring at the table in front of her.

Lauren was called to the stand next. She took the oath, then sat down, carefully smoothing her blue denim skirt across her legs. When she opened her mouth to speak, I saw that once again, her face had changed. The scar was back. Her words caught all of us in the courtroom by surprise.

"I pulled a knife on him," said the woman on the stand with obvious relish. I tried to study her face. I was sure now this was not the woman who had entered the courtroom that morning. The way she appeared and seemed to enjoy the impact of her words told me it was Hannah.

The Commonwealth Attorney buried his head in his hands for a moment, then sat erect.

"You what?" asked the judge, incredulous.

"I pulled a knife on him," Lauren repeated. She looked over at me. "He deserved it." Then she continued with a rambling statement about what happened. Her words were confusing at times, but the sense of what she had to say was clear. It was also accurate.

When the judge dismissed Lauren and she stepped down from the stand, I saw another change. The scar vanished, Hannah was gone. But it was not Lauren either. Whoever this new woman was, she walked back to her seat with an air of arrogance, her demeanor haughty.

The judge asked me to take the stand again. "Please remember that you are still under oath," he reminded me.

I sat down and watched as the judge took off his glasses, glanced at them in the light for a moment, then returned them to their place low on the bridge of his nose. He leaned forward and looked at me. "I have one question for you," he said.

"Yes, your honor?"

"Why?"

"I don't understand. Why what?"

The judge set his glasses on the bench in front of him. He studied me for a moment, then quietly said, "Why are you putting up with this?"

I was stunned. For the first time there were people who had heard my story and discovered it was true. Even Lauren had admitted all that had occurred.

I sat there in silence for a few moments, gathering my thoughts to find the answer. Then I began talking about the problems Lauren and I had been having. I told the court about our efforts in counseling and the treatments by the psychiatrist. I talked like a man who had been isolated from the world for too long and had a desperate need to tell every detail of his recent life. When I finally stopped, the judge looked down from the bench and quietly said, "Why?"

I looked the judge in the eyes and said, "I love her...
and I'm trying..."

Before I could say more, the judge said, "Yes, I understand that. I love guns and I try to handle them properly but
they're dangerous." He paused, then said, "I find you 'not
guilty.' Now you are both dismissed from my courtroom." As
I started to leave the witness stand, the judge added, "Good
luck, sir."

I said nothing. I knew his words were a warning. But
they were a warning which had come too late. I was already
a captive of forces beyond my control.

Lauren and I walked back to the car. I did not look
to see her face. I did not want to know who I was driving
home. Whoever it was had not been in the courtroom on the
witness stand for those last minutes. As she settled down
buckling her seat belt, Lauren said, "I'm so glad we won the
case."

CHAPTER 12

The Queen of Hearts

By July I knew for certain that the woman I married was seriously disturbed in ways I had never before encountered. As a police officer, a detective, and most recently an executive in the security division of a major bank, I had been trained to deal with the mentally ill. I understood schizophrenia and the biochemical problems that could cause someone to believe he or she is communicating with God, aliens from another planet, or even demons that have taken over the body. I had encountered bipolar disorder, a condition most commonly known as manic-depressive illness. I also understood the way someone who was abusing drugs or alcohol might behave. Since neither the counselor nor the psychiatrist would share their suspicions concerning Lauren's problems with me, I began studying her as I might someone I encountered on the job.

I was helped that month because Lauren was facing a long-standing date with a surgeon. She had a serious medical condition that required the removal of a section of her colon to correct. She had known about this condition long before we married, the doctors warning her that there would come a day when it would be so bad they would have to operate. By mid July it had reached that point and Lauren was overwhelmed with fear and pain until one day she left me. In her place was a woman I had met briefly before I came to call Ali, the Queen of Hearts because of her malicious scheming.

Hannah, the woman who was the mirror of Lauren, was all impulsive rage. She hated whomever Lauren loved, whatever Lauren valued. She wanted to cut and maim the flesh Lauren delighted in caressing. She wanted to turn dreams into nightmares. But there was no careful planning on Hannah's part. She reacted to opportunity. Instead of plotting her actions, she let her hatred fester and boil, erupting when she could contain it no more. Peg, Lucifer's Daughter, whose presence was thankfully much less common, was somewhat like Hannah in her desire to inflict pain and act out violently. However, her behavior had a darker twist; unlike Hannah who was reactionary, Lucifer's Daughter thought things through, planned her moves, and executed her plots with premeditated viciousness.

By contrast, Ali, the Queen of Hearts, whose name I chose because of the erratic queen met by Alice in Wonderland, while not physically violent, was a coldly calculating font of evil.

It was easy to recognize the Queen of Hearts once I realized that she always wore a long denim dress with a round white collar and flat-heeled shoes. Now I knew she was the woman who entered the courtroom that day. And although Hannah was the one who testified and relished explaining how she threatened me with a knife, it was the Queen of Hearts who actually went to the courthouse. She was also the woman who kept the appointments with the surgeon who would be correcting the colon problem, and the woman who was to undergo the procedure. Whatever Lauren did not want to endure, the Queen of Hearts could handle.

As I learned to ascertain the differences between them, I realized that the Queen of Hearts did not want to destroy my relationship with Lauren, as Hannah, in her rage, was determined to do. Rather, she delighted in using my emotions to manipulate me. For example, I went to her room shortly after she checked into the hospital and saw her before she changed into her hospital gown. Even if she hadn't worn the denim dress, I would have sensed her presence by the tension that hung in the air. Her voice was sharp, her words demanding. We talked little, my presence meant to be a calming influence for the woman I loved, a woman I realized was somehow not present. Instead, I was to be controlled to see how much I would take.

"Now that they've brought you your dinner tray, Lauren," I said to the Queen of Hearts, "I think I'll go down to the cafeteria and get something to eat."

"What if I need help?" she said. "You can see how little they bother to check on me. Why are you always thinking of yourself? Don't you realize how serious the surgery is?"

"Lauren, you haven't had the surgery yet. They're leaving you alone because you don't need anything. You can eat dinner by yourself. You can go to the bathroom by yourself. You can walk about the hospital if you want to. Now, is there anything you need? It's been a long time since I've eaten, and if you want, I'll bring a carry-out back here."

"How do I know what I'll need? You know the pain I've been having lately. What if that happens again and they don't realize it? What if I fall? All you think about is yourself."

The talk was as meaningless as the day when Lauren first told the counselor that she couldn't stand my lies, all the while never giving even one specific instance. That time the show was meant for Ted Carter or anyone on his staff who would listen. This time it was meant for me, an effort to see how far I could be manipulated.

Hour after hour it was the same. If I wanted to eat. If

I wanted to get some fresh air. Whatever would keep me from being in the room was wrong in the Queen's mind.

On the morning of the surgery I sat in the waiting room with Lauren's parents and teenaged daughter whose father had allowed her to fly in to be with her mother, and tried to learn more of her past. It was a terrible time to probe, yet I knew it might be my only chance. There was nothing any of us could do to help Lauren, so I was hoping they would talk freely. As it turned out, her parents did not, but her teenaged daughter was willing to be candid.

Janet talked to me earnestly. She told me many stories as the hours passed in the waiting room. She had seen and endured all I had experienced, eventually becoming the family chronicler of madness. "There was one time when my mother was married before and she decided that her husband had been looking at another woman."

The truth was uncertain. Most men and women look at members of the opposite sex their entire lives, enjoying someone who is particularly good looking. That does not mean that they want to have an affair. That does not mean they are comparing. Commitment to someone does not mean that you are dead to others, just that you have chosen to be monogamous. However, for Hannah, the woman who had assumed the worst, even looking at another woman was a betrayal. Janet told me that when the couple returned home, she began attacking him and screaming at him.

"'You were looking at her, weren't you? You were looking at her, weren't you?' she yelled over and over.

"Then she hit him, then grabbed him and wrestled him to the floor. I didn't know what to do but I was scared, so I ran upstairs so I would be able to hear what was taking place though I would not be physically in danger. I picked up a pencil and paper and each time my mother shouted, 'You were looking at her, weren't you?' I made a check mark. By the time they were quiet, my mother had said the exact same phrase one hundred and eighty seven times." It was an experience I knew well.

Janet also told me that she was in counseling. I wasn't surprised. She had adapted well to much of her mother's craziness, such as keeping a little in control by carefully noting the number of times her mother had repeated herself. However, she had been extremely troubled by what some therapists call abnormal abuse, something I had not previously considered.

Most abusive parents are consistent in their behavior. They violently overreact to what their children are doing. For example, a child spills some milk and the parent goes into a screaming fit, spanking the child until it is difficult for the child to sit down. Or the child asks the meaning of a swear word heard on television or on the playground and instantly the parent slaps the child's face so violently that the redness lingers for several minutes. "You don't use a word like that in this house!" the parent might scream.

Good behavior might be equally strongly rewarded, or it might be ignored entirely. But the point of "normal" abuse, and I hate to use that word, is that there are known causes and effects. The family rules are clear. Bad behavior is consistently met with the same type of punishment. Good behavior is either positively rewarded or disregarded. The child learns what to expect and when to expect it.

"Abnormal" abuse has no logic to it. One day you spill your milk and receive the punishment just described. Another day you do the same thing and you are told, "Everyone makes mistakes. It's no big deal. You get the sponge and I'll get the cleaning rag and we'll have the mess cleaned in a second. Then I'll get you a fresh glass of milk and a big cookie. Would you like that, my darling?"

Janet was a victim of abnormal abuse. She was a child dearly loved by her mother, Lauren. Yet the greater the joy she brought to Lauren, the more frequently she would be forced to encounter Hannah and the others. Janet, like me, had known the threat of the knife. Janet, like me, had been blamed for bad behavior when she tried to tell her friends' parents, school counselors, and other adults she thought could help. The Queen of Hearts would arrive, presenting herself as the long-suffering parent, a woman in need of sympathy because of the problems with her daughter.

Nevertheless, Janet still loved her mother, just as many abused children do. Just as I loved Lauren, or at least the part of the woman I had met that day in Goochland. I wanted to help her heal. I wanted to know that the part of her that was essentially so good, so kind, and so gentle, could dominate. I felt I had to stay.

My decision was an emotional one. Ali, the Queen of Hearts did not want to physically cause me pain. That was the role of both Hannah, the woman who had come at both her daughter and myself with a butcher knife, and Peg, Lucifer's Daughter, who planned my death so calculatingly. Instead, she wanted to manipulate me, maneuver me, and control me.

Once Lauren was successfully through the operation, I returned home. I worked a normal day, taking time to spend several hours with Lauren before going home to sleep. I wanted her to know I loved her and was pleased with her healing, something that probably would have delighted her. Unfortunately, Lauren was not in the hospital. The Queen of Hearts lay in the bed and she was not about to miss an opportunity for harassment.

"Richard, what are you doing there? And don't lie to me. You always lie to me," one call to our home began. Her voice was a hoarse whisper, so raw from the breathing tube that had been inserted during the surgery, it must have been extremely painful to talk. Yet the Queen began calling the moment the tube was removed, not waiting for any of the healing that would follow.

The calls came to my office. The calls went to our home. If I was en route somewhere, she would place call after call to the apartment until I eventually either showed up by her bedside or returned to our home.

There was never a desire to talk with me. Sometimes she would rant. Sometimes she would say something as brief and superficial as a greeting card insert. Seldom would the calls last longer than a minute. Yet when they were over, when it seemed obvious there was nothing more to say, the telephone would ring again. And again. And again. It would not stop until 1:45 A.M., a time when either the hospital shut down the switchboard for outgoing calls or the nursing staff made certain she went to sleep.

One night, when the calls became unbearable, I called the nursing station responsible for Lauren's care. I told them the problem and explained I was disconnecting my telephone from the jack. In that way they knew I cared, knew I was aware that there was no crisis taking place, and also knew I would be unreachable for the rest of the night. For the first time in days, I had a normal night's sleep, awakening to a beautiful sunrise. Smiling happily, I plugged in the telephone. It rang immediately. The Queen was demanding her due.

It was Hannah I was sure who fell in love with John Taylor, but in hindsight I have come to realize that it was Ali, the Queen of Hearts who began aggressively pursuing the relationship. She did not love the man though; the Queen loved only herself. What she enjoyed was manipulating all those around her, setting up humans in the manner of the living chess game envisioned by Lewis Carroll. She did not care who won. The sport was in the manipulation.

I found out that at least once the Queen wrote to John in prison. One evening, while blindly groping around under the dresser looking for a dropped pen, I discovered the Queen's unfinished letter. When I saw who it was addressed to, I was shocked. Lauren had mentioned John Taylor before, but I had suspected any relationship with him, if real, was in the past. As I read the letter, I learned that she created a life for herself that did not match the world in which we were living.

For example, I found two photographs with the letter that was to be mailed to him. The Queen must have set the camera on a timer then posed in a way that showed her breasts, her clothing obviously ready to be removed for sex. Yet her facial expressions in the photographs had no spontaneity or desire. She appeared to be imitating a high-class prostitute displaying her attributes in a bored and disinterested manner. Again it was the opposite of Lauren whose lust for life made her face glow with the joy of just being alive.

There was no scar with the Queen, yet her face was as angry and lined as Hannah's. The sex appeal was only in the mind of someone desperate who saw a woman for her sexual anatomy and not her personality or feeling. Given the fact that John was in prison, perhaps that was enough. Or perhaps he found her as sexless as I did when I eventually discovered the photos, telling her how erotically charged they made him just to manipulate her.

But it was the Queen's words that were the most fascinating. She told him she hadn't been able to write for a while. Perhaps she was not able to take control of Lauren's body long enough to write. Rather than admitting the truth, she said, "The Slime King [one of her many names for me] was on vacation the week I came home from the hospital. Then he fucked his back up and he's been here ever since!" She also added that she could not get to the post office box because of a lack of a vehicle. "He's not going to get me a car of any kind," she told him, claiming to be a prisoner of the suburbs.

The truth was that I had not had a vacation and certainly had done nothing to my back. I was in excellent physical shape. As for the car, Lauren came into the marriage with her Mustang and it worked just fine. It may have been old, but it was well maintained and only the heater ever gave her any trouble. She could and did go as she pleased, especially for the business she was running. However, the image of the emotionally abusive husband requiring her ministrations fit nicely into the fantasy world she wanted to weave for John.

Although the Queen of Hearts did not realize that I found the letter, she was quite open about knowing him. Lauren had mentioned him early on in our marriage, or at the time I thought it was Lauren. Then I came to believe it was Hannah who talked about John, but it may have been the Queen trying to see if she could make me jealous because, in those days, I would not have noticed the sometimes dramatic, sometimes subtle changes in physical appearance when Hannah, the Queen, or one of the others was around. It was difficult to understand what was happening and who was speaking.

The Queen of Hearts was also delusional. The Queen would make statements that were false, then come to believe them as soon as she said them. For example, one day the Queen came to my office during a lunch hour. "Did you hear on the news that three prisoners have escaped from the Federal Penitentiary in Lewisburg?" she asked.

"No," I said. "I haven't heard the news."

"Well, they did," she replied. "And John Taylor was one of them!"

I looked at her, saying nothing, not certain how to react.

"John Taylor escaped," she repeated, then started dancing around my office like an elated fan celebrating a come-from-behind victory of a beloved football team. "All right! All right!" she sang, joyously. "John Anthony Taylor has escaped! All right!

"All right! All right! John Anthony Taylor has escaped!"

I was not amused by her display of emotion and I worried about what someone might think if they came in the door. How could I tell them that the person who was dancing was the Queen of Hearts, not my beloved Lauren? She just looked like Lauren.

Desperate to get her to stop, but knowing that if I showed my true feelings she would take advantage of them, I said, "Are you sure, Lauren? How can you be sure?"

"Oh, John is out all right!" she said, smiling broadly. At least she stopped singing and dancing.

Finally the Queen left and I immediately telephoned Agent Charlie Brooks, a friend of mine at the FBI, and asked him about any breakout at the Lewisburg, Pennsylvania Federal Prison. He knew nothing about it but said he would check and call me back. Ten minutes later he called me back and said there was no breakout. All prisoners were present and accounted for. John Anthony Taylor was behind bars as he was supposed to be.

Later that evening, the Queen of Hearts was sitting with me in the apartment, so I explained what I had learned. "John Taylor never broke out of prison. No one did."

The Queen refused to believe me. She had announced the escape, and in her mind, that meant it was fact. Reality was whatever she said it should be, nothing more. Finally, frustrated by arguing with me, she looked at me coldly and said, "If I had to, I would gladly give up my life to get John out of prison."

CHAPTER 13

The Dark Rider Returns

The summer had passed, and then Thanksgiving, Christmas, and New Year's. I wasn't alone for those holidays as I'd once been. I had Lauren. I also had Hannah, Ali, the Queen of Hearts, Peg, Lucifer's Daughter, and too many others. If my guess was correct, there were six different women and one child all intertwined, none of them ever knowing what the others said or did.

I had something else, something I had never discovered before. There is the loneliness that comes from being by yourself, a loneliness I thought was a touch of Hell on earth after my divorce. That was why I had been so concerned for friendly acquaintances who were isolated from family and friends over the holidays. That was what had prompted me to ask the beautiful, enchanting, and slightly withdrawn woman in Goochland for a date. And that was what had caused me to revel in her company when we found so many ways we were compatible on that first trip we took together.

There is a second type of loneliness, though. It is a loneliness more intense than anything imaginable in physical isolation. This is the loneliness that comes when you are with another person. To have once shared complete intimacy, to have loved and laughed and talked about everything and nothing, then to discover that you have become strangers wary of one another is the greatest loneliness there could be.

As our first anniversary approached, I was filled with the loneliness of lost love while living with the woman who once meant so much to me.

Perhaps this is a little like what a long married man or woman experiences when the spouse develops Alzheimer's or some other debilitating mental condition. It is the love that sustains the caretaker. It is the memory of what was, the joys of yesterday, that keep the person trying to help as long as possible today. The effort is exhausting. The desire to see a spark from the past becomes an all-consuming passion. And there are just enough moments of remission, just enough moments when the person who had once been so exciting is again present, albeit too briefly, to sustain you.

That was where I was. As short and intense as our relationship had been prior to the marriage, I loved the Lauren I met that day in Goochland with an intensity worth retaining. If I could have her again, all the hell I had endured would be worth the suffering.

Each day I still awakened with hope. Each day I hastened to the side of my beloved as she opened her doelike eyes, watching her body language, listening to her words. Would Lauren be present, dear God? Or would I have to keep my back to the wall because Hannah was on a violent rampage? Would Ali, the Queen of Hearts, start trying to humiliate me? Or...

The nights were also becoming difficult. The nightmare I had early in our marriage returned with a vengeance. Each night I awakened sweating, my heart pounding, my mouth half-opened in a soundless scream.

There was no doubt. It was the same dream again.

Once again the puffy, white clouds floating in the blue sky of a perfect Virginia day slowly darkened, blackening the morning as they blocked out the sun. The wind rose, the clouds moved rapidly, like a gang of toughs barreling down a crowded street, hoping to start a fight with the passers-by.

Soon the day became as dark as night, the air so filled with electricity that the hairs on my arms seemed to stand on end. As I strained to see, there were flashes of lightning from deep within the black abyss. They overwhelmed me with their power, filling me with awe and dread.

Then, just as the last time, thunder began. At first it rumbled in the distance, the tremors rolling through the ground with the force I sometimes felt when standing by a roller coaster as the speeding cars zoom past.

Then the thunder changed to a rhythmic pattern, the pounding growing louder, like the hoof beats of an angry horse racing across the plains. And suddenly it was that horse, the huge black stallion emerging from the darkness, illuminated by the flashes of lightning so my view was that of someone watching a stroboscopic light show.

Closer and closer the giant beast came, flanks sweating, nostrils flaring. When I could finally take my eyes off the approaching behemoth, I saw as I did every time the rider, a woman, sitting astride the steed, her gown flowing in the wind.

Suddenly frozen where I was standing, the climax which had scared me so much when I'd first dreamt it came. The woman raised a silver bladed broad sword above her head, then slowly lowered the point towards me. Her face, so familiar yet ultimately an unrecognizable blur, like a distorted television image, had those two glowing red eyes.

Just as that first night and since, when it had come to me, I was again drawn to those eyes, drawn into those eyes. They were the gateway to Hell, and rather than being engulfed by them, I was to be destroyed. Then, with the blade still coming towards me, I heard her deep, resonating voice shouting, "Look at me! Look at me now! Listen to me! Listen to me now! The truth shall be known! The truth shall be known! I have told you before. This is my last warning!"

I remained rigid, the broad sword coming straight for my chest in the same way that Hannah had wielded the butcher knife. Then, without warning, the horse turned away, racing back into the swirling blackness which I realized was Hell.

As always, the nightmare terrified me. I awakened, breathing hard, sweat pouring down my face. The dream never changed. I then remembered trying to defuse the horror by calling the woman on the horse the Dark Rider. I had tried to make her just another person sharing the body of the woman I loved. But this was something more, something less, something that made me wonder if it was the final loss of my sanity. Would I soon be following the Dark Rider into the swirling blackness, only to be locked away as a hopeless madman?

Each time I awakened, Lauren was sleeping peacefully beside me. Her breathing was easy and unlabored, her face smooth, like soft clay waiting to be molded by whatever forces within were turning her from Lauren to Hannah to....God alone knew what else.

At the end of the winter, Lauren and I returned to Virginia Beach for our first wedding anniversary, but nothing was the same, nothing could ever be the same again. During our first visit there, I had trust in this woman who had so enchanted me. I was open to anything and everything. I lay emotionally naked before her, certain she would never take advantage of my vulnerability, equally certain that she was doing the same.

Now I was wary, like a lover of reptiles obtaining a

pet rattlesnake he had always wanted. Each day I would awaken, speaking to Lauren and waiting for her reply. Then I would watch to see who would answer or if she would go to her rocking chair, sitting in silence, moving back and forth, back and forth, her signal that any intrusion would result in physical or verbal assault. She was the snake, and while I loved her presence, I found myself ever alert to the slightest hint of a rattle warning me of an impending strike.

I was also being manipulated by evil and I realized I did not know how to help myself. My job at the bank was in jeopardy. No one said that to me. Certainly Arnie was kind, though I knew the longer I stayed married, the harder it was for him to understand why. I didn't tell him or anyone the details of what was happening, but I couldn't hide the abusive phone calls and visits to my office.

There were so many factors in what was taking place. The moments when Lauren was in my life were coming with less and less frequency, as though she had become the hated stepsister in Cinderella's family. Instead, the Queen of Hearts, Lucifer's Daughter, and Hannah were dominating. Still, I focused on the love lost, not the demons found.

I desperately wanted to keep my job as well, something the Queen of Hearts understood. She and Lucifer's Daughter called my office repeatedly, sometimes attacking the staff, though more frequently waiting until I came on the telephone to begin their diatribes. The sheer number of calls made my work suffer. But the ultimate problem was due to the occasions when Hannah would show up on a whim, bringing a tornado of violence into my workplace.

Others would come, too. Ali, the Queen of Hearts, wore denim. Peg, Lucifer's Daughter, always wore black with gothic make-up. Hannah wore the clothing of the streetwalkers from the neighborhoods I once patrolled. There was always a mini-skirt, tight blouse, and high heeled shoes worn

with an attitude of defiant sexuality. The minute she walked
into the bank, the staff could sense trouble and I always tried
to avoid her presence there.

On the morning of an unusually warm spring day for
Richmond, I arrived at the office early, partly to avoid problems with Lauren and partly to get extra work done in the
hour I would be alone.

The telephone rang within minutes of my arrival,
and though banks often receive calls at all hours from
throughout the world, I knew instinctively who was going to
be on the line. I looked at the telephone, my stomach tense,
wishing, hoping anyone but her would be on the other end.
Inhaling deeply, then exhaling slowly to calm myself, I
picked up the receiver.

"Richard, I am tired of your lies, Richard!" The
voice was authoritative, like a schoolteacher's stern
demeanor when she needs to instantly take control of a recal-
citrant class.

"What lies?" I said, knowing the Queen of Hearts
was on the line. "Lauren, what are you talking about? What
have I lied to you about?"

"All your lies, Richard. I am tired of them."

I wanted to address her as "your majesty" in defer-
ence to the regal role she was playing, but I dared not so
much as acknowledge that I was aware what was happening.
I was not even certain what it meant, though I did know that
Lauren wasn't the only person in that body. Quietly I said,
"Lauren, tell me please, what lies?"

"Are you going to the police?" she asked. The police?
For what? Had she done something wrong? Her voice was rising an octave or two.

"Look, Lauren, this has got to stop. I am trying to
work here. You have got to stop calling."

"Are you going to call the police?" she repeated.

I was silent. What could I say?

"Do you want me to come down there?" Her voice was high pitched and sharp.

"I am coming down there. Do you hear me? Do you hear me?" And then she hung up.

Lauren arrived before lunch. She walked past my secretary Gail, who was already shell-shocked by these episodes, saying, "You look like hell, bitch. Don't you know how to dress? No wonder you have to work. Only the bastard I married would hire someone like you."

When my secretary was unable to stop the Queen of Hearts, she left the office to get one of the security officers. No one likes to interrupt a domestic problem and this was no exception. The officer did not want to get into the middle of an argument that might be none of his business. On the other hand, the vicious verbal aggressiveness my secretary reported required a response. He telephoned me and asked, "Is everything all right?"

"Yes," I lied, turning away from the Queen and forcing my voice to stay calm. "Everything is fine. No problem."

The moment I replaced the receiver, before I could turn back to look at my wife, the heavy stapler that had been on my desk was hurtling through the air. It struck me on the side of the head, a blow so painful I thought at first she had broken the skin.

I looked up to see Hannah. The thin smile on her face told me there would be more to come if I wasn't careful. I had turned away from Her Majesty, only to receive a visit from one of Satan's other minions.

Eventually I succeeded in convincing Lauren to go home, and she left without further incident. At least no one reported an incident to me. However, I knew that with all that had happened, my career with the bank was going to come to an end. Not only was I being distracted on the job, how could

I be expected to handle delicate personnel matters when my own wife seemed to be an out-of-control harridan?

The Queen's actions were not meant for confrontation. She wanted to establish fear. She knew the impact her presence could have on my job. By putting my career in jeopardy by coming into the office, she only had to threaten coming to the office in the future to make me more pliant.

I tried to take precautions. The men and women who worked at the security desk knew my wife. They had been instructed to not let her into the building unless I was notified. Then I would come down and personally escort her to my office. It was a small step, but it took some of the burden off the other employees, a gesture that hopefully would look good for me when my next job review came along. However, that did not prevent her from getting that far and raising hell.

The Queen did not let me forget her visit. A few days later she called. "I am coming down there." No reason was given. None was needed I suppose.

"No, Lauren," I said more quietly than I felt. "I don't want you to come down here. You know that. Now, why don't you try to calm down and I'll be home soon."

"I am calm, Richard," she said, her voice changing to a musical lilt.

The conversation continued for a few more minutes before she hung up. She would not be coming to see me, but it was already three in the afternoon and my stomach was so upset, I knew I would be able to get no further work done. I might as well go home.

As I drove, I realized how much of a struggle life had become in the short time we had been married. We were supposed to still be in the newlywed stage of the relationship, each of us so enamored with the other that we would do anything to please one another. Instead, I felt as though I had stepped into a horror movie in which I was going to be the victim who never heeded warnings, never escaped the violence that lurked in the shadows.

I arrived at our apartment, parked the car, and sat for a moment, forcing myself to breathe more slowly. My heart was racing, my breathing rapid when I faced the door, a common condition of late. However, it was not an emotional state I wanted The Queen to witness. And if Lauren was there, I knew she would be hurt by my anxiety, convinced that she had done something to offend me yet genuinely having no idea what might be wrong.

I entered the living room and heard noise coming from the bedroom. Once again I was at a disadvantage. I had no idea who would emerge—the malicious one who had been calling me, the woman I once might have joined in the shower if I arrived home early, or someone else. All I could do was sit and wait.

The clothing was the clue. She emerged in her miniskirt, tight blouse, and high heels. Hannah was back. "I'm going out!" she announced by way of greeting, then slammed the door behind her. When she returned fifteen minutes later, she had a glass of wine in her hand and the bottle nearby. She sat on the rocker and began moving back and forth, back and forth. When she looked at me, I saw the face of the Dark Rider from my nightmare. Her eyes seemed glowing red, yet I looked away, fearful that the dream had become a waking nightmare and that at any moment I might be looking up the shaft of a sword.

As quickly as it started, it came to an end. The rocking slowed and became gentle. Lauren returned. I heaved a sigh of relief knowing that, at least this time, I had escaped verbal or physical abuse at the hands of Hannah. I was safe for one more night.

But the peace did not last long. Matters went from bad to worse. Lauren and I had discussed several times what we wanted in a marriage during those wonderful days before the ceremony. I talked about my children, whom I adored, and my ex-wife who had once been so important to me. I explained to her that the one thing that had worked in that marriage, the thing I truly wanted to have with Lauren, was friendship. My ex-wife and I had been friends, true friends, in those years before so many interruptions had caused us to irrevocably drift apart. I needed that relationship with Lauren, and to my delight, she said she needed it with me. What neither of us understood was that such a declaration was ammunition for the Queen of Hearts to use against us and a reason for Hannah to want to turn me against Lauren.

The Queen of Hearts must have been present when I spoke of my relationship with my ex-wife before. Now, over a year later, she brought her up again, asking if Patsy was my best friend.

At first, I couldn't understand what she was getting at. Lauren knew full well what had happened between us. That life was over. This life had begun and Lauren served in the friendship role, at least in the beginning. I had become so fearful of late that I was tense even around Lauren, fearful that the change to someone else would occur the moment I let myself be emotionally vulnerable to the love I felt for her.

"Look at me! Look at me! Listen to me, now!" the Queen of Hearts began chanting. "Tell me, is she your friend?"

It was going to be a long night. "Tell me, is your ex-wife your best friend?" There was nothing to say, nothing that would matter. The Queen had decided how to try to hurt me and I would have to endure the endless questioning.

"Answer me! Answer me! Answer me, now!" Her eyes were wide. They seemed like at any moment they could send beams of hate piercing my heart. "Is she your best friend? Answer me! Answer me!"

I left the room, going into the bedroom, the demon following at my heels, repeating her question over and over again, then following with the demand, "Answer me! Answer me!" She was screaming by then, yet a smile was fixed on her face. She was enjoying the game of verbal violence, delighting in taunting me, seemingly trying to see if I would react.

"Is she your best friend?"

Quietly I answered, "No."

"Answer me! Answer me!"

Frustrated, I pushed past her and went back into the living room. To my surprise, she followed me, then kept going out the front door. She started her Mustang and drove from the lot. I had no idea where she went. I dared not ask and she had no intention of offering an answer.

A few minutes later she returned, stalking right into the bedroom. Soon a different woman emerged. Dressed in black, her white face and mulberry lips contorted, the demon walked over to the rocking chair, sat down, and said, "Look at me, you son-of-a-bitch! Listen to me! Listen to me now!" Her voice was harsher than before and the smile was gone. She was now making her diabolical plans clear.

"The children," said Peg, Lucifer's Daughter venomously.

"What children?" I asked. "My children?"

I had full visitation rights with my children, and we talked frequently on the telephone. Lauren and I had visited my son and daughter during the holidays when we first were dating, and she seemed to enjoy them almost as much as I did. But that was before the change. Lauren continued to care about the two of them, wondering why we didn't have them to our home. She had no sense of the danger I felt existed because of Hannah, the Queen of Hearts, and the others. After all, if she would attack me with a butcher knife, knowing I was a trained law enforcement officer, how much less hesitation would she have about hurting children fourteen and twelve? It was best to keep their lives separate from the life I was sharing with Lauren.

"What children?" she repeated mockingly. "Your children. The little heathen bastards down in Blacksburg." She rose from the rocking chair and walked rapidly to the kitchen, returning moments later with the butcher knife in her hand. My stomach muscles contracted and I forced myself to concentrate on her eyes.

When you're trained in hand-to-hand combat, you're taught to watch the body, not the eyes. A skilled fighter will have a blank expression, the body moving swiftly when he senses an opening. If you watch the weapon, if you watch the person's hands and feet, you will be better able to react swiftly than if you are studying the person's face.

Lauren was different. Her eyes again seemed to be the key to what was going to happen. As I had already perceived, each personality I was seeing had a different appearance, and the eyes were the first thing to change. I could sense the danger by watching her eyes, and so I went against all my training, ignoring the knife and looked deeply into them.

Her eyes were black as a moonless night. "I'm going to slit your children's throats. They can lay them out in caskets side by side!" she screamed. She made no move to lunge at me, no threatening gestures. She was simply telling me a truth. There was no question in either of our minds that if she were around my children, she would do everything in her power to kill them.

Peg, Lucifer's Daughter's voice lowered. She spit her words out. Then her voice changed. The tone became almost playful. Having established the fear she desired in me, she added to the threat diabolically. "I'm planning to take care of your ex, too," she said. "They can lay them out, one on each side of her!" She watched me, her eyes narrowed.

I said nothing, watching Lucifer's Daughter in all her evil. There was much I could have said. There was much I wanted to say yet dared not. I feared this woman. I knew what was happening but not why. Lauren was not some crazy, believing she was receiving messages from Mars and communicating in an unintelligible language. Lauren was not a paranoid amassing weapons in hidden caches so one would be in easy reach wherever she walked because of her certainty that she would become the victim of physical assault. Lauren, my Lauren, was neither mad nor violent. She was a gentle soul, capable of great loving kindness. Yet within her lived demons I could neither exorcise nor tame nor keep away.

The Daughter raised the knife over head, ready to strike. Suddenly, she became enraged. With all her might, she heaved the knife which narrowly missed me, instead striking the floor, bouncing and coming to rest in the hallway. Without a word, she walked out the front door, slamming it behind her. I heard her car as she drove off.

I picked up the knife, returned it to the kitchen, and went into the bedroom. All I could do was pray, and I feared that no answer would keep me safe.

Perhaps if I could get a good night's sleep. Perhaps if I could go twenty-four hours feeling so safe that I was able to do my work, relax over meals, and consider how to handle the situation. Instead, my adrenaline was constantly keeping me alert to the subtlest potential danger. I was living with a time bomb that was constantly resetting itself in a random pattern so there was never a way to know when it was defused and when it was time to run.

I may have been concentrating on my concerns or I

may have been so exhausted that I dozed off for a moment. All I remember is that suddenly there was the Queen of Hearts standing over me, again asking, "Well, is she your best friend?"

"Lauren, stop it! Why do you insist on doing this?" I asked. "What's the point?"

"Is she your best friend?" she asked. She was smiling, delighting in my discomfort as she stood in the doorway, deliberately blocking any escape from the room.

I rose from the bed and pushed past the Queen. Outraged, she followed me, screaming, "Listen to me! Listen to me now! Is she your best friend?"

The Queen was not interested in an answer. Instead, she went into the bedroom closet where there was a large cardboard box in which Lauren had placed old financial records, old letters she wanted to save, and other memorabilia. It was a box that was rarely, if ever, opened, that most couples have in their possession. You put things in it you feel are important but not immediately necessary for your life, then move it to your new home. You never get around to unpacking it because it really is not critical, and so it rests in a closet or other storage area until the next move and the next. The box seems to stay with you throughout much of your adult life, though you're never certain why and you regularly vow to go through it to see if anything within really matters.

I doubt that Lauren had opened the box since we moved to our apartment, but apparently Hannah and the Queen were using it as a safe storage space, a location neither Lauren nor I would check.

As I watched, the Queen disappeared and Lauren's body changed once again. Her jowls sagged, the scar returning to her right cheek. Her shoulders slumped, her breasts seemed to droop, and her face had the look of angry sadness.

Hannah had returned and walked straight to the box, throwing things out it until she found something obviously hidden near the bottom.

To my amazement, Hannah had several photographs of John Anthony Taylor that she removed from the box and began placing around the room. His image was set on tables and windowsills, and when there was only one picture left, she took it, sat on the rocking chair, and said, "Admit it! Admit it! Admit that John Anthony Taylor is a better person than your children." Her lips were quivering and I half expected to see her eyes start to glow with fire. She was a mad woman beyond my comprehension.

"Admit it!" she screamed. "ADMIT IT!"

The demon was raging out of control. There was nothing I could say, nothing I could do. I knew from past experience that she did not want conversation.

Suddenly Hannah exploded. She raced to the dining room and pulled the framed picture of my children from the wall shelf. She smashed the frame and tore the photograph, a cherished new present from my kids, into pieces so small, it might have been through a shredder.

As I approached, she turned towards me, the look so intense I immediately backed off. The violence was escalating in ways which I could not anticipate.

There was a blur of movement and Hannah threw herself over the coffee table, landing on top of me, smashing something hard against my head, obviously trying to break my skull. I grabbed her wrist, twisting it away, and realized she was using the cordless telephone as a weapon. I grabbed at her hair, jerking it back to try and cause her enough pain to stop her assault.

Suddenly she was still, neither attacking nor resisting. I released her hair, let go of her wrist, and rolled out from under her. I moved to the far end of the couch as she sat calmly on the other end. Her face was expressionless. The scar was gone, her flesh no longer sagging, yet none of the women I had come to know was identifiable. Barely able to breathe, I waited to see what would happen next.

Lauren's hands went up to her head, each fist grasping a quantity of hair. Then, soundlessly, she began pulling small clumps of hair from her head. She was torturing herself, yet not responding to the painful action she was taking. Horrified, I moved to reach for her, at which time she stopped, again becoming motionless. The demon had left as swiftly as it appeared, yet I was not certain who or what had taken its place.

The calm restored, I took Lauren's hand and led her into the bedroom. It was time for her to sleep. Perhaps with rest...

"Richard," said Lauren, her voice, soft, sweet, loving. "My head is pounding. Won't you come with me to bed?" She lay down and it was obvious that she wanted me beside her. It was the same way she looked in the early days of our marriage when we delighted in each other's closeness, in the quiet touch of lovers who do not need the intensity of sex to rejoice in the person with whom they plan to share one another's lives.

"Yes, Lauren," I said, my voice choked with emotion. "Very soon." How I loved this woman I saw all too seldom. How I longed to be with her. How I longed for the days when she was the only person I knew in this so familiar yet so strange body of hers. And how I grieved with the knowledge that they would never be again.

Eventually I did what I had done for too many nights. I went into the bedroom, lay down on the bed, and tried to slow my breathing enough to sleep. Instead, I listened to Lauren, trying to discern in the gentle rise and fall of her chest who was controlling the body, who was controlling the mind.

I fell asleep just before dawn, awakening at six. My head was throbbing. My body ached. My mind was fogged as though a blanket had been stuffed inside my brain. Thank God Lauren woke beside me, recognizing something was wrong, mistakenly thinking I had a virus that was wracking my body and making me miserable. "Are you going to work today?" she asked, concerned about me. Her hand gently stroked my forehead. Her words were as soothing as a medicated balm. I wanted to give in completely to her, laying my head against her, becoming totally vulnerable as once I would have done without hesitation.

"No, I don't think so," I said. "I don't think I can."

I hated the tension I felt as we spoke. I had to force myself to be a little distant, fearing that Hannah, the Daughter, or the Queen would return when I least could handle them. It was a horrible feeling to have to build a wall between yourself and the woman you love, yet it was critical.

Lauren picked up the telephone and called the security desk at my office. She told the staff that I was sick and would not be in for the day.

Ironically, the one time in recent weeks that they heard the voice of the woman I considered my wife, they did not trust her. They assumed it was the violent harridan whose endless telephone calls had caused so much disruption. I was told later that they worried about me and discussed among themselves how they should react.

As I lay on the bed, I realized action had to be taken immediately. Perhaps if I went directly to the court and gained a restraining order against Lauren...except the demon would ignore a restraining order. I had learned over the years that when there is domestic violence, a restraining order is only good for building a case against the spouse who violated it. Instead of keeping the couple separated, it is yet another point for argument by the violent individual from whom the complainant is seeking protection. Lauren would be hurt by a restraining order, yet respectful of my privacy if I moved out. Hannah, Lucifer's Daughter and the Queen of Hearts would use the existence of the order as grounds to attack me physically or mentally. My life would likely be worse than it was at the moment.

Exhaustion took hold and I fell asleep for an hour or two. When I awakened, Hannah was lying in bed next to me, eyes wide open, staring angrily, saying nothing. Unnerved, I went into the kitchen to make coffee. When I finished, Hannah was in the rocking chair, moving fiercely back and forth. "You're going to get the police, aren't you?" she said, her voice barely controlled.

"No, Lauren, I'm not," I said. She began to get more agitated as I reached into my pocket, found my car keys, and started to ease my way to the front door. As I passed the window, I glanced over at my parking space and saw that it was empty. I suspected that while I was asleep, Lauren had moved my car as she had done once before, hiding it somewhere in the complex.

Lauren's red Mustang was parked outside, but she had the keys. Any thought of a rapid escape was gone. Pretending I never had any intention of doing anything else, I went over to the couch, sat down, and tried to figure out if there was any way to get the keys to her car. That was when I remembered the old spare key in the candy dish.

Although it had never been used, I had to take the chance that it would work. It was my only chance.

Pretending I needed to go to the bathroom, I walked past the hallway table, looked down, and spotted the spare key. I continued on to the bathroom, staying long enough so there would be no suspicions. Then I flushed the toilet, turned on the water in the sink, and casually walked out into the corridor between the dining area and the kitchen. As I passed the table, I reached down and picked up the key.

Not waiting another instant, I went through the front door and began running towards the Mustang. I couldn't remember if Lauren routinely locked the door. *God, please let the door be unlocked. Please let the key work.*

I glanced over my shoulder and saw the enraged demon coming out the front door. My heart was racing and I had to force myself to stay calm, in control. I pushed the release on the door handle, slid onto the driver's seat, and locked the door.

I pushed the key into the ignition, but it did not fit. I turned it, jiggling it in the ignition, trying to work it inside. I turned it again and again. Finally I found a way to slide it in far enough so I could work the tumblers. The engine sputtered for a moment, then came to life.

I was still not in the clear. It had taken only seconds for Hannah to discover what I was doing. I was faster, but the time spent working the ignition was time she used to catch up with me. Before I could put the car in gear, she threw herself against the driver's side door.

The window was partially open, and when Hannah leapt, she grabbed the top of the window, then planted her feet against the side of the door. Her arms were like wire hooks, so powerful was her grip. I could hear ripping and tearing noises as the window strained against the door frame.

Suddenly there was a loud popping sound and the window gave way, dropping Hannah to the ground, still holding the broken window. I did not look to see if she was all right. I did not care. I threw the gear into reverse, the engine whining as I accelerated backwards out of the parking space.

I shifted into first and began racing around the main street of the complex. I had no intention of stealing Lauren's car. I just needed to find my own, and there was no way I could do that on foot without being vulnerable to another physical assault.

At last I found my car parked in front of another apartment unit. I pulled the Mustang into a space, opened the door, and got into my own car. I left the Mustang with the engine idling.

Aside from our court date last summer, the Henrico County Justice Center was a familiar building in that it housed the Henrico County Police Headquarters. I had been in and out of such buildings many times, first as a law enforcement officer and, later, as a detective. Even though I was there as a private citizen, there was something comfortable about the sense of familiar.

Now I walked inside and gave the police desk officer a brief summary of why I was there. She asked me to take a seat and wait for the Magistrate who agreed to see me ten minutes later.

The Magistrate proved to be the same man who had arraigned me the previous June. I wondered if he remembered me. He certainly was less than attentive as I detailed my situation. "Do you want to sign an assault and battery complaint against your wife?" he asked.

Once again the magnitude of what was taking place overwhelmed my emotions. No, I did not want to sign an assault and battery complaint against my wife. Lauren was on probation. If I signed a complaint and she was convicted, she would return to Goochland for the eight years remaining on her sentence. My wife would be in the state penitentiary. I couldn't stand the thought.

"You have another option," said the Magistrate, seeming to sense my reluctance. "You can call County Mental Health and request a green warrant. With that, you can sign an order placing her under observation in a mental facility for forty-eight hours."

Forty-eight hours in which to sleep without fear and work without needless interruptions? Forty-eight hours during which doctors could try to determine what was wrong with my wife? That would be the best option for everyone, and I immediately went to a pay telephone to place the call.

"I need help for my wife," I said when the person on duty answered the telephone. "I just spoke with the Magistrate at the Henrico County Public Safety Building and he suggested I call you."

"What type of help do you need?" he asked.

"I need an order of protection. Are you the people I need to talk to?" I asked.

"Is your wife currently being treated by anyone for mental health reasons?"

"Yes," I said, giving the person on the telephone the names of her therapist and psychiatrist. To my surprise, he explained that nothing could be done until there was a discussion with her therapist. I supplied the number and was told to wait by the pay phone while contact was made.

I waited for what seemed like hours but was probably only a few minutes. When the pay phone rang, I leaped from the bench and grabbed the receiver.

The therapist's words were mindboggling. Dr. Carter did not think such hospitalization was necessary.

I was shocked, though I probably should not have been. Lucifer's Daughter and the Queen of Hearts were both expert manipulators. They would have allowed the therapist to see only what they wanted him to see. He probably was unaware of her admission about holding the knife on me during the previous court case. So far as he was concerned, Lauren in all her guises was charming, bright, articulate, and ever so gentle. He was never physically assaulted. He never had his children threatened. He never...

And suddenly I wanted to drop to the floor and weep. I was out on the street with little money in my pocket, no extra clothing, and not even a toothbrush. I had no idea who was waiting for me back at home, but I knew that I could be greeted either with a warm kiss or an angry demon still furious over my moving Lauren's car. Nevertheless, I would have to return to the apartment. It seemed the only option I had.

CHAPTER 14

Danger, Danger

Patty Cat, our cat who adored both Lauren and myself, began to alert me when I was in jeopardy. She would come to whichever one of us was sitting watching television. With one eye on the parakeet she would curl up on our laps. There she would contentedly purr herself to sleep.

Hannah, Lucifer's Daughter, and the Queen of Hearts were quite different matters for Patty Cat. When she sensed that they were around, she would hide in the closet. Then, when they were gone, she would again come out to be held and stroked.

One evening I was sitting in the living room watching the network evening news on television. Suddenly Patty Cat rose up on her front legs, her ears alert, sensing danger. She was staring down the hallway towards the bedroom.

Before I could react, the cat dug her claws into my leg in order to spring off the couch and head for the bedroom closet as Hannah came rapidly down the hall.

Hannah was more agitated than I had ever seen her. She moved to the rocker, a place of comfort for some reason, but this time it brought her no pleasure. Her body was tense, as though she was fighting a battle within for control of her emotions. "Listen to me..." she screamed, never finishing the sentence, never breaking into the singsong repetitions with which I had become all too familiar.

Hannah rocked back, then forward, using the momentum of the chair to seemingly spring into the kitchen. She returned almost instantly, a butcher knife in one hand and a long, serrated edge bread knife in the other. I had barely moved to the edge of the couch when she was in front of me, completely out of control. "Get the fuck up and sit over there!" she ordered, motioning towards the dining room table. I moved around her cautiously, trying to keep as much distance from her as I could. It was not enough, though. The bread knife caught my chest, penetrating my shirt and slicing in my skin.

The sight of blood seemed to excite Hannah. She began lunging at me, slashing with both knives. I ran around the dining room table and I maneuvered to keep it between us.

Hannah started screaming incoherently, as though overwhelmed by a need to stab something. When she realized her arms were not long enough to overcome the barrier of the table, she began stabbing wildly into the wood.

I could not fight Hannah. There was no way I could avoid getting hurt, and if I got hurt, if I stopped being able to resist, I was certain she would stab me as viciously as she was attacking the table.

I watched Hannah as she moved first this way and then that. For a moment she seemed to become confused, stepping back a short distance as though to catch her breath and think how better to hurt me. I took that instant to run to the bedroom, closing the door and throwing myself against the wood.

Hannah pounded the door an instant after I was in position, and her strength was incredible. It was as though each time she was angry, her strength became greater. It was all I could do to hold the door in place.

There was a pause, then a violent stabbing sound. Hannah had switched to using the knives, attacking at the door, sending the blades deeper and deeper into the wood with each thrust. If she were able to penetrate, if I was standing in the wrong place, I would be severely cut this time.

Suddenly, there was a moment of silence, the blades no longer slashing at the door. There was also no pressure. I glanced around the room, spotting the cordless telephone on the nightstand by our bed. Praying she would not hear me, praying I could get back to the door in time, I left the door, grabbed the telephone, and returned to brace the door once again. I was just in time. Hannah attacked within seconds.

Somehow I was able to dial 911.

"911. What is your emergency?"

"I need help now. My wife has gone crazy! She has a knife!" I yelled into the telephone.

I tried to calm down and answer the operator's questions. She confirmed my address, then told me a police cruiser would be on the way.

As I depressed the disconnect button on the telephone, I realized there was silence. The pressure against the door had stopped, and as I strained to listen, I thought I heard Hannah's footsteps in the hallway. The front door opened and slammed shut. I cautiously left the bedroom, checking the apartment. She was gone.

I ran to the front door and slid the dead bolt into place. Moments later she was back, demanding to be let inside.

Safe for the moment, I stanched the bleeding from the cut ascertaining that it wasn't deep, and then I used the telephone to call Hannah's therapist, Dr. Carter. I reached his answering service, but this time I left a message that I had an emergency. Within five minutes he called me back.

I explained to Dr. Carter what was happening. I told him about the knives. And when I was done, there was silence.

I figured that the therapist was as shocked as I was. I figured he would arrange for her to be committed. Instead, he quietly said, "Well, I'm going to see her on Friday."

I could not believe what I had just heard him say. "For Christ's sake! Have you heard anything I have said? She's got a knife and she's trying to kill me." The therapist did not reply.

I heard a noise from somewhere behind me. Hitting the disconnect button, I turned around and looked towards the bedroom. Hannah had torn the screen and was climbing through the bedroom window. I felt like I was in the midst of one of those horror movies where the villain never dies.

As Hannah started moving towards me, I went out the front door and looked for the police. There was no sign of a patrol car so I called 911 again. The operator had assured me that a unit was on the way.

I reached into my pocket to get my car keys, only to realize that I had left them on the hall table. Before I could think what to do next, I saw Hannah climbing back out the bedroom window. She must have thought I was bracing the front door when I was not. However, once I saw her, I immediately went back in the apartment, again locking the front door.

There was no more cursing and slashing. As I watched from a corner of the room, my back to the wall, I saw Hannah start her Mustang. As she drove out of the complex, I called 911 and provided a description of the car she was using. Perhaps the officers could stop her on the road.

Exhausted, terrified, I stood in the apartment trying to decide what to do next. Several minutes passed, then the car returned. I heard her at the front door, though there was no slashing sound this time. Instead, she must have gotten on her knees for she was raising the mail slot, trying to see inside our apartment. Barely breathing, my senses alive to every sound, I heard the strangest noise. It was a whimpering sound like that of an animal hit by a car, dying slowly by the side of the road.

The pain in Lauren's voice was so intense, it tore at my heart. Whoever had tried to stab me was gone. This was not Lauren, yet I suddenly felt the same overwhelming desire to help, to comfort that I had experienced in Goochland. I felt responsible for helping my wife, even with the knowledge of what she could become in the space of a heartbeat.

The whimpering grew louder, the sound not meant to get my attention but reflecting the apparent internal turmoil she was experiencing. The demon was gone for the moment. The police car still had not arrived. Not certain if it was wise, I called 911 and canceled my earlier call.

"Are you sure you want to cancel the call?" the operator asked. Her voice was filled with concern and compassion.

"Yes," I said, as certain that it was the right thing to do as I was equally certain I would pay the price for it in another few minutes, few hours, or few days.

That night I lay in the darkness beside her, thinking about my life, thinking about Lauren. We had been together for a little over a year, most of which time had been spent with her seeing a therapist and a psychiatrist, as well as consuming various medications. There should have been some change. There should have been some answers. Instead, her mental illness was getting worse. I was living with at least six different women, a concept as hard to believe as it was to deny. Within me I knew I had made a mistake in canceling the last 911 telephone call. But Lauren had been so out of control, I was certain that she would have violently acted out

had she been arrested. That would have prevented her counselors from being such fools. That would have stopped the
games that enabled Lauren to convince so many medical
people that I was the one with the problem.

My life was in pieces. My work had suffered terribly.
I was getting calls all day from Hannah, Lucifer's daughter,
and the Queen of Hearts. I could only call my children from
work now. I couldn't take the chance that harm would come
to them. I could not enjoy the woman I loved for fear that in
a moment of intimacy, she would suddenly leave me, and
then I would get a visit from someone violent turning ten-
derness into a fight for survival.

There was no sense pondering my mistakes. I had to
leave, and I had to do it immediately. I lay still, keeping my
breathing calm and even, as though I was sleeping. Then I
mentally located where I had left my shirt, my shoes, and my
pants, planning the simplest way to slip from bed without disturbing whomever lay sleeping beside me, dress, and flee the
apartment.

I rolled from the bed.

"Where are you going?" said a voice, sleepily. I
could not tell if it was Lauren or Hannah or someone else. I
felt chilled, frightened.

"To the bathroom," I said, trying to make my words
sound as though I was too sleepy to do anything but relieve
myself and crawl back into bed.

Lauren was silent, but I knew that she was awake. I
could not sneak away until morning. I needed to rise early,
then leave for work as though nothing was wrong. With luck,
the timing would keep me from disturbing her.

I went back to bed, staring at the ceiling, listening to
the change in Lauren's breathing, periodically glancing at the
digital clock on the nightstand, praying for 6:00 A.M. to come.
As I waited, I kept thinking, *Dear God, the person I love and*

who lies next to me may actually be capable of murdering me.

I knew I had to seek legal assistance. At 5:57 A.M. I lifted myself from bed and went into the kitchen to prepare coffee. I was convinced that my best chance to escape was to pretend this was a normal day; I would get ready and go to work as always. Within twenty minutes, I was in my car, heading towards the bank's operation center, Lauren or one of her demons still sleeping beside my pillow.

To my surprise, when I got off the elevator on the first floor, Arnie was waiting to see me. "You look like hell!" he said, his voice reflecting compassion and concern.

Arnie walked with me to my office, closed the door, and said, "Okay, what will it be?" he asked. "You are either going to take care of this situation right now or we are parting company."

I had known this talk was coming. Arnie was not only my boss, he was also a long-time friend. Other men would have fired me long ago. Arnie wanted to give me every opportunity to find answers on my own. He had come here only because the situation had become so intolerable for the bank that it was necessary for him to drive the 184 miles from Roanoke to see me.

I explained that I was thinking of filing a complaint against my wife. Arnie informed me we would go to the Henrico County Justice Center together.

When we arrived, there was a different Magistrate, Barbara Henley, on duty. For the next several minutes I explained to the Magistrate what had happened. Then I signed an assault and battery complaint against Lauren.

The Magistrate explained that it was normal to notify the defendant that she would have seventy-two hours to report to the law enforcement agency for booking. However, when Henley checked the computer for Lauren's criminal history, she announced, "There will be no courtesy contact." Two sheriff's deputies were dispatched to arrest her, and within the hour, the clerk of the Juvenile and Domestic Relationship Court issued a protective order on my behalf. Lauren would be subject to arrest if she attempted to make contact with my children, my former wife, my mother, or myself.

I knew a protective order would mean nothing to Hannah, Lucifer's Daughter, or the Queen of Hearts, and Lauren would not understand why it was issued. Instead, I was buying a tool, a way to get help without being blocked by her therapist who I had come to believe was either naïve, in denial, or acting like a fool.

By the time I returned to the Magistrate's office, the deputies had radioed in that they were on their way with a female subject in custody. *Female subject? Female subjects, more likely.*

How could it all have come to this? How could I have loved a mad woman? How could I love her still?

Lauren was facing seven and a half years in prison without chance for parole because of her actions. The jailing would be a relief if it occurred, much as we all felt when Susan Gabriel had been returned to prison after threatening the Bradfords. Yet I had promised to love, honor, and cherish this woman in times of sickness, not just in health. Was I protecting myself from harm or trying to end a nightmare too quickly, given my duty as a husband?

These were questions I wanted to share with Arnie, and I was glad when he invited me to be a guest in his home in Roanoke, almost two hundred miles away from my apartment and the jail where Lauren would be held. Together, that evening, we walked a mountain trail in southern Virginia, sharing the fresh air, the smell of the grass in the crisp evening on the Blue Ridge Mountains, and the sounds of our boots crunching the earth below.

Arnie is a man of great faith, a devout Christian who tries to bring his morals and ethics to bear in the way he treats others. He has a deep personal relationship with God, one of the reasons he had given me so much time to try to work through my own problems before intervening to save my job, my emotions, and my life.

We were silent for a while, walking perhaps a mile, before he looked at me and said, "Dick, are you wondering why you've stayed so long with Lauren? Are you asking yourself why you have taken what you do and don't leave?"

"Of course I am, Arnie. I've thought of many reasons, but I'm not certain of any of them. Maybe it's fear, though I know that in the beginning I was trying to help her."

Arnie, smiling, shook his head. "No, Dick," he said. "Maybe that is part of it, or part of the circumstances that put you into the jar. The fact is, you are living inside a brown glass jar and until now you couldn't see out." He put his hand on my shoulder and I felt as if I was talking to the big brother I never had. It seemed a simplistic answer to a complex question, but I felt it was accurate. I endured the demons because I could not see through the glass.

The talk that day brought me great respite. I did not realize that I was still in the glass jar, having only struggled to the top to look out. The devil was still at the door.

— CHAPTER 15 —

Through the
Looking Glass

B efore I left Roanoke, I called the Henrico County Jail
and was told that Lauren had made bail on Saturday
morning. I had no idea where she might be, but I knew
where I had to go. When I left Arnie's, I stopped by Saint
Mary's Hospital Emergency Room for a check-up. Most of
the abrasions and bruises I had received days before were
minor, but I didn't want to take any chances with infection.
The physician examining me knew immediately I had been
the victim of violence. As he looked at the cut on my chest
and the bruises on my legs, arms, and head, he said, "Who
did this to you?"

I hesitated for a moment. The truth was difficult for
me. It was embarrassing and a point of great sadness. Finally
I quietly admitted, "My wife."

"Would you like to talk with someone about this?"
he asked.

"Talk to whom, doctor?"

"The Richmond YWCA has a crisis hotline for battered spouses and abused people. Would you like me to put
you in contact with them?"

Battered spouse? Me, a battered spouse? I had never

thought of myself in such a way. Battered spouses were quiet, meek women married to large, brutal husbands. I had seen such women used as punching bags when I used to patrol the streets. I never thought about a man like myself falling into such a category. Yet there I was, sitting in the emergency room, being treated for cuts and bruises inflicted by an out of control wife. Was I a battered spouse? Was this what my marriage had become? And if it was, how had it happened to me?

"Do you want to talk to them?" the doctor asked again.

"Yes," I said, realizing I could not go on the way I had been. "I think so."

By the time I finished dressing and stepped from the treatment cubicle, the doctor was holding the telephone in his hand. "I have the crisis hotline on the line. Good luck." He smiled as he handed me the telephone and walked away.

A woman on the other end of the line introduced herself, then encouraged me to begin talking. At first I had no idea what to say. Then I began speaking, and suddenly I could not stop.

I have no idea if I spoke for five minutes or an hour. I told about the joyful early days and the first days of violence. I told about the growing fear, the helplessness, the desperate need to leave and the inability to do so. I told about the feelings of humiliation, and that on some level, I still loved my wife. And when I was finished, there was silence.

Startled by the lack of reaction, I said, "Hello? Are you still there?"

"Yes," said the crisis hotline volunteer. But she said nothing else.

I stood there holding the telephone receiver, listening to the silence. She was too well trained or too compassionate to hang up on me, yet she was at a complete loss concerning what to say.

In the world of spousal abuse, the violent wife is seldom

discussed. This is not to say that such women are uncommon. Some experts suspect that almost half of all abusers are women but their husbands are too ashamed to admit the problem.

A man is supposed to be dominant in modern society. He is seen as the hunter, the warrior, and the provider. A woman is to be the passive nurturer, the person who raises the children and supports her man.

Even with the changing societal reality, the image of women remains the same. Women are entering the military in record numbers, training for combat alongside the men in elite units such as the Marines. Women are aggressive enough to work their way to top positions in major corporations or take the CEOs to court when denied the opportunity. Women are demanding a switch in roles, having their husbands stay home with the pre-school children because it is better for their careers to not have a break in service. Yet despite all this evidence of equal aggression, equal stress, and an equal likelihood of being prone to the troubles that can lead to violent outbursts, women are perceived as the only possible victims in domestic strife.

The truth is quite different, of course. This is not to say that women are not brutalized within many cultures. From the genital mutilation in some African cultures to the raping of women as a weapon of invading armies, women are routinely subject to the horrors of the damned. But this does not change the reality today when spousal abuse may be committed by a woman as well as a man. It is just not likely to be reported.

I was in a minority, but it was a large minority hidden from the public because our culture does not allow for discussing such realities. Not even the hotline volunteer, a woman whose hours on the telephone were filled with stories of the hell one person can inflict upon another within marriage, could deal with my reality.

There were no comforting words for male victims of

spousal abuse. There were no shelters in which to hide, to heal, and to use as a base for returning to a life free from fear. And so I heard only silence.

I placed the receiver back on the cradle and walked out of the hospital. I knew what I had to do next. I had to get away from Lauren to think. I drove to the office of an attorney I had come to know through my work and talked to him about a divorce.

Afterward, I drove towards the apartment complex, hoping to get more clothes and some personal possessions. I had unused vacation time coming on my job and I decided to use it to drive to Florida to visit my family. The time away from home and work would help me sort out my emotions, help me to make plans for the future. However, there was one call I made before I left. I alerted the Henrico County Police Department that I would be out of town for a few days. I told them where I would be going and when I would return. I suspected that the Queen of Hearts would defend herself by accusing me of assault and battery. Such a counter-complaint would be the logical way for her to fight my accusations. Even if the evidence was overwhelming against her, the court would have to hear both sides. This would mean that I would be ordered to the police department within seventy-two hours, something impossible for me to do if I left. My call explaining my time away would head off trouble if the Queen acted as I suspected she would.

The closer I came to the apartment, the more nervous I was. Would Lauren be there? And if she was, would she be herself? The Queen of Hearts? Hannah? Lucifer's Daughter? Jenny, the twelve-year-old girl? I had come to think of each as a unique individual, yet I knew that they were not. I supposed that having been sucked into a world of insanity, I was no longer uncomfortable with the manifestations of madness.

I drove slowly around the parking area, assuring myself that Lauren's Mustang was not there. Frightened of what I might find, I walked to the door, turned the key in the lock, and went inside. To my great relief, she was not there. She had taken with her the cat and our pet canary, along with many of her possessions.

There was something strange about all this, so on a hunch I called the local veterinarian who also offered boarding services. Whenever Lauren and I took one of our weekend vacations, we would leave the animals with the vet. To my great relief, both the cat and the bird were there. At the same time I wondered how that could be. Surely Lauren would have taken them with her, and as for the others, I was certain they would have abandoned the animals...or worse. Then I found the letter.

It is hard to explain the shock I felt when I saw the writing. I knew Lauren's handwriting well, and this was not it. Likewise I had seen a very different writing from Hannah and some of the others. Once again there was a quality that was unique. Whoever had left the note was quite possibly someone I had never before encountered. Despite the intimacy of the words, this was not Lauren.

"Richard," the letter began. "Guess that I will see you sometime in the future at court. Kind of strange if you think about it. We met in court. Looks like we'll end there. You need not worry about my bothering anything of yours. After what you have done to me, I want no part of you or anything that belongs to you. Richard, if you had truly wanted a divorce, you could have told me so. My friends Cindy and Gordon are separated but at least they're civilized about it. It wasn't necessary to do all that you did. You knew I had a three o'clock appointment with my therapist. It was bad enough as it was. But it would have been a lot nicer of you to have picked me up after my appointment.

"I still have a hard time believing that you did all of this to me. We both made mistakes, Richard. Don't want to ramble on. I will get the rest of my things as soon as I can. Take care, Richard. As soon as I quit loving you I'll be okay. You have nothing to fear from me."

The note was signed "Love, Lauren" but the handwriting was not that of the Lauren I had married. Whoever had written it, I wondered if she had any knowledge of what had taken place in our apartment over the past several days. Somehow I doubted it, and that fact was as chilling as the violence had been.

I had never understood how battered women could find the hope that their husbands would somehow change just because they apologized or asked for another chance. I had seen the physical scars and bruising. As a police officer I had witnessed the psychological results of their trauma. I had seen women withdraw into an almost fetal position as they talked, closing in on themselves for protection against monsters I could not imagine. And I had seen many of these same women try to save their marriages once more, get beaten once more, and weepingly talk about the good men they married, the hope that in the future things would be different.

Now I understood what they were going through. Lauren was still my wife, and I knew that if I could ever get the right Lauren back for good, I would be happy. I felt responsible for her. I had intimately known the beautiful, gentle, oh-so-desirable side of her. I longed for her love. I longed for her touch. I longed for those conversations that sometimes lasted through the night and into the early morning hours.

I didn't want the police involved in our lives. I didn't want to have to answer the counter-charges Lauren did, indeed, file against me. I wanted her well, even though I knew that there was a good chance I would be hurt or killed long before anyone could exorcise the demons that had overtaken her body.

Even worse was the pain of knowing that Lauren, my Lauren, knew nothing of what was taking place. She was as much a victim as I was, only she could never escape the demons without help. I could not live with her. I could not abandon her. And there was no one to whom I could turn to discuss my dilemma.

On the third night following my return from Florida, I sat in the living room drinking a glass of merlot and watching television. I had not arranged to have the apartment locks changed, a foolish denial on my part yet one that had not yet led to trouble. Then, as I relaxed, I heard the unmistakable sound of Lauren's Mustang's engine in the parking lot. I hurried to the front door and opened it slightly, looking out through the drizzle. There was Lauren walking across the parking lot. When she was about twenty feet from the door, she stopped and looked at me.

"Richard, are you going to call the police on me?" she asked.

"Lauren, what are you doing here?" I asked. I studied her body, trying to determine who she was, the danger within.

"Are you going to call the police on me, Richard?" Her voice was quiet, scared, like that of a little child who had been severely reprimanded for misbehavior only to get caught acting in the same manner a few minutes later.

Was I going to call the police? I didn't know. If she became threatening. If she brought out a knife. If she...no, I wasn't going to call the police. I wasn't going to have her sent to jail. She belonged in a mental hospital, and that wouldn't happen if I called the police.

It began to rain harder. Lauren's blouse was soaked

and I could see she was shaking. She hugged herself, trying to keep warm. "No, Lauren," I said. "I'm not going to call the police." I paused, then added, "Not just now, anyway. What do you want?"

"I need to talk to you, Richard."

"All right, Lauren. Step up onto the porch."

As she walked, I could see that Lauren had a partially consumed six pack of beer. There were four cans still bound by the plastic wrap. If this were all she had consumed, she would not be drunk.

"Stop there, Lauren, and open your purse," I said as she approached the landing. "Lay it down on the step."

I walked outside and picked up Lauren's purse. Then I held the door open and let her into the apartment. It was the only thing I could think to do.

Lauren walked over to the sofa to sit down. Obviously this was neither Hannah nor the Queen of Hearts. Both of them would only sit on the rocking chair.

As Lauren hugged herself, trying to get warm, I dumped the contents of her purse onto a chair. There was no knife, no gun, nothing that could be used as a weapon. "Where are you living now, Lauren?" I asked as I began to put her possessions back in the bag.

"In Roanoke," she said.

"That's one hundred eighty four miles from here. Why did you drive so far? What are you doing here? You know you're not supposed to be here, don't you?"

"I needed to see you, Richard. I need help. Please help me, Richard," Lauren cried.

It was then that I recognized this woman. She was one I had experienced just before the Queen of Hearts exploded onto the scene.

It was as though the Queen of Hearts fed off the weakness, the sorrow, and the desperation of a woman who seemed an adult version of Jenny, the twelve-year-old who cried for her grandmother. This woman, one I never named but called an Intermediary, might be with me for an hour, a day, or a week. Her time in control was unpredictable. All that was certain was that the Queen would ultimately replace her.

Once again my heart was torn by her plea. "Please help me, Richard." How long had it been since I had heard such words? Ever since Hannah had attacked me, I had been the enemy, the person who was the source of all trouble, not a helper, a man who was genuinely needed in her life. I sat down next to Lauren who said, "Richard, I've got a problem." Then she pointed to the beer.

I nodded. I was right about one of her problems stemming from alcohol abuse. I rationalized that it was the overuse of alcohol that allowed the violent side to emerge. However, with all I had learned, to think that alcoholism was the main concern was nonsense. "Lauren," I said. "You've got more problems than that, but you can't stay here. You've got to leave."

"Please, Richard, let me stay. I need some help!"

How I had longed for a marriage of equals, to be part of a couple where our strengths and weaknesses intermeshed, each of us able to help the other in times of crisis. There had been a time when Lauren's words would have filled me with pleasure. Not that I wanted her to be in trouble. Rather, I wanted her to trust and love me enough to turn to me in crisis, just as I wanted to both be vulnerable to her and have her help me handle my problems.

My heart told me to embrace Lauren, to comfort her, to tell her that, together, we could conquer anything, even mental illness. My head told me to kick her out, barricade the door, lock the windows, and have the cylinder rekeyed in the morning. My mouth took me along a third path. "You can stay the night, Lauren," I told her. "But in the morning I'm going to call the psychiatrist and get you the help you need. If there is any trouble, you are out the door. Do you hear what I am saying, Lauren?"

She sat on the sofa, nodding her head.

I gave Lauren the bedroom, and I lay on the couch. There would be no sleep for me that night, as I lay there uncertain what was going to happen. To my great relief the Intermediary awakened just as she had been, still sad, still depressed. She reminded me of the way she had looked during her lowest moments when she had been hospitalized, so I called her psychiatrist to explain that she needed help.

I had been livid when I had called Lauren's therapist and he had treated Lauren taking two knives and attacking me as something seemingly routine that could be discussed in her regular therapy session later in the week. The response I received from the psychiatrist who managed her treatment was no more helpful. "I'm not sure that is safe," he said.

I was stunned. What kind of an answer was that? And safe for whom? For Lauren? For me?

I knew better. This time I can honestly say that I knew better. There were no surprises other than that I had been foolish. The Intermediary was almost always followed by Ali, the Queen of Hearts, and sometimes by Hannah or Peg, Lucifer's Daughter. I had recognized this reality well before I filed for divorce. I understood what I was facing when she had come to the door, so wet, so cold, so pitifully seeking help. The woman seeking solace was the gateway to Hell.

This time it took sixty-eight hours for me to experience the transformation. As usual, the Queen of Hearts came. She, unlike Hannah or Peg, Lucifer's Daughter, would not cross the line that would lead me to call the police. Instead, she acted like a school bully delighting in taunting children on their way to school. She blocked my path as I moved about the apartment. She laughed at me, mocked me, and cursed me. She never touched a weapon. She never resorted to violence. She just made clear that she was going to be in my face.

The only time the Queen reacted was when I started to remove some clothes for packing. She ripped them from my hands, making clear that even with the threat of an arrest hanging over her head, she was not going to let me do anything but go to work. Fortunately the following day she had an appointment with her therapist and I used the time to pack a suitcase.

I needed to find a hotel and looked for one near my work. The hotel room I found was tiny but clean, with two small windows overlooking the street. I realized that the people I had helped send to prison had more living space than I did, but I didn't care. In my cell-like room I was freer than I had been in months. I accepted the reality that this would be my new home for a while.

I sensed the car before I saw it. That happens sometimes with tailgaters. They get so close that they change the wind resistance of your car and through that, you sense their presence behind you without even seeing them.

I glanced in my rearview mirror, and that was when I saw her. I could not be sure if it was Peg, Lucifer's Daughter or Hannah driving the red Mustang so close to my car that I could see her as she pressed forward over the steering wheel. I accelerated, only to have the demon keep pace with me. I slowed down. I made a series of unexpected right and left turns, never signaling, never braking until the very last second. Still she remained with me. Finally I turned into the parking lot of a convenience store and ran to the telephone.

"911, what is the emergency?"

"Yes...ah...I have a restraining order against my wife,

and right now she is attempting to make contact with me. I need a police unit," I told her. I tried to keep my voice calm.

"Is she there now?" the operator asked.

"Yes. Please send someone," I said loudly. My voice was rising and I fought to remain calm.

"Is she there now?" she asked again.

"Jesus, yes! I'm not sure I can handle her. Hell, I know I can't." I shouted. Fear was making me angry. This was a woman who had shot her former husband, trying to kill him. This was a woman who had repeatedly slashed at me with large knives. I had no idea if she was armed, nor with what. In fact, I had no idea who she was this time.

"Okay. There's a unit on the way," she assured me.

I hung up the telephone receiver and turned towards my car. At that moment, the demon left the parking lot. She knew what would happen when the police arrived. What she did not know was how slowly a "rapid response" can be. It took fifteen minutes before a Henrico County Police unit entered the parking lot.

The officer confirmed who I was and checked my restraining order. I told him what had happened, but he was obviously frustrated by the wasted call. "There's not much I can do if she isn't here, sir," he said, explaining the obvious.

"Can't you have her picked up or something?" I asked, knowing better. There was no evidence of a crime. There was no proof Lauren had ever been there. There were no witnesses. There was only the word of an estranged spouse, and that wasn't good enough to make an arrest away from the scene. "Well, don't hesitate to call if she tries it again," said the officer.

A short while later I sat in a Burger King parking lot a little ways down the road. I parked my car at the corner of the lot where two thick shrubs intersected, providing natural cover. I purchased a cup of coffee and sat in my car, watching, waiting.

The minutes went by. Then, as I sipped the hot liquid, I saw the Mustang coming slowly up one street and down another. The Queen of Hearts was on the prowl.

I watched as she turned up another street, traveling north. She had been less than 150 feet away from me, but she couldn't see where I was sitting, nor could she see my parked car. Minutes later she was back, traveling in the other direction. She moved in a grid pattern, as determined as a starving lioness stalking her prey. For at least twenty minutes she drove the streets before heading west for the drive back to the apartment.

I waited a while, watching the streets. When I was certain she was not coming back, I returned to the hotel, parked two blocks away and walked the rest of the distance.

The evening was surprisingly peaceful. I had a portable CD player and a book I had been looking forward to reading. Unfortunately my sense of security was a false one. I had only read a few pages when I heard the unmistakable sound of her Mustang. I walked to the window and looked out. There was Lauren sitting in her car on the street outside the hotel.

Lauren never tried to come inside. She sat for a while, then drove away.

It was the next morning that I discovered how she had located me. Apparently she had made some assumptions about what kind of place I might seek. She assumed that I would be seeking a hotel room close to work so she narrowed her search to those near my office. She called each number, asking, "Is Richard Goetzke there?" She finally got lucky. My hotel's switchboard operator, who I'd befriended, rang my room but didn't get an answer. "I'm sorry, Ma'am. There's no answer, but I'm sure he'll be here later." She then made a second call a few hours later pretending to be interested in booking a room. It was from that call that she learned the address.

Ali, the Queen of Hearts, arrived that evening. I was sitting on the porch talking to two other guests when I suddenly saw her running across the front lawn. "Don't you play games with me!" she shouted. "Do you hear me? Don't you fuck with me! Do you hear me?"

I went over to meet Lauren, hoping to keep her away from the hotel where I had found at least a little peace.

"Lauren, what are you doing here?" I asked. "Do I have to call the police?" The word "police" seemed to subdue her. She let me take her arm and walk her to the curb where we stood talking. The traffic was extremely heavy at that hour, and several people slowed whenever she would begin yelling.

Finally I calmed her to the point where her voice was quiet. Then, without warning, she suddenly pulled up her sweater, revealing her bare breasts. "Don't you want these anymore?" she screamed.

I heard tires squealing as brakes were rapidly applied. One driver fishtailed as he tried to stop without hitting the vehicle in front of him. Another ran over the curb, narrowly missing a street sign before regaining control.

I ignored both the Queen's breasts and the reactions of the drivers. Instead I talked quietly, maneuvering her back to her car. I don't remember what we said, but eventually she was satisfied, and drove off.

Embarrassed, I walked back to the front porch with my head down. There was no doubt that the small crowd which had gathered there had seen and heard everything.

CHAPTER 16

Our Day in Court

L auren and I were scheduled to have our day in court at the same time. The judge would hear my assault claim against her and her counter-claim against me.

The day I had been treated in the hospital, hearing a sympathetic voice from the attending physician, made me optimistic about the outcome of the case. The passage of time changed my thinking, though. The Queen of Hearts had been constantly harassing me. I had to change my pager number to keep it clear for the important calls related to my work at the bank. I had to leave a copy of the restraining order with the guarded station at the bank's operations center so that the police would be called if she set foot on the property. Yet I still had to endure her telephone calls on the job and in the hotel.

"Richard, I am tired of all your lies. Your lies, Richard. I am tired of all your lies."

Without meaning to, I would get sucked in. "Lauren, I've asked you many times, what lies? What have I lied to you about? Can you be specific?"

"The truth shall be shown! The truth shall be known, you motherfucker!"

"Calm down, Lauren," I would say.

"I am calm," she would reply, her voice soft, almost a whisper. Then, louder, breaking with emotion, she would say, "Don't you put those heathen bastards before me."

And again I would ask her what she was talking about. The fixation on my children worried me. Even though I hid my calls to them and told them not to telephone me at home, she continued to threaten their lives. That was why I kept her talking through the same repetitious conversation. I hoped that if I let her rant about them by yelling at me, the violence might be defused.

"Those little heathen bastards down in Blacksburg. Don't you put them in front of me." I could almost hear Alice in Wonderland's Queen of Hearts screaming at the soldiers, "Are their heads off yet?"

The tirade, which might go on for minutes or, on rare occasions, hours, would end with a quiet click as she hung up the telephone.

It was all very agonizing, and I could see how the Queen or her lawyer could build a case for my erupting in violence. It was obvious from the reaction of the crisis hot-line volunteer that a battered male was not something easily understood. The concept could be accepted in theory, but in practice...? I increasingly feared the possibility that I would be found guilty in a knee jerk reaction. I was male, therefore a brute. Lauren was female, therefore a victim. Sadly, until I married Lauren, that would have been my thinking as well.

Everything seemed to be a warning that the trial would be a disaster. There were the looks of pity and wariness at work that often made me feel that many of my co-workers would have thought less of me for not striking someone who treated me as Lauren had. Not only that, I had lost my home. I was becoming tired of living out of a suitcase in a hotel. I wanted it all to end. Ironically, one thing I dreaded most—stepping into a courtroom—was the only thing that would bring about an end to it all.

Finally the court date arrived, and with it came even greater anxiety. No matter what happened, one of us would be in serious trouble. Lauren was now on unsupervised probation, but a conviction on the assault charges would send her back to Goochland to complete her seven and one-half year sentence.

When I arrived at the courthouse, Lauren was seated in the waiting room just outside the security checkpoint. I walked over, sat down next to her, and said, "Lauren, we have to talk before we go inside."

"What do we have to talk about, Richard?" she asked quietly. There was no scar on her cheek, no fire in her eyes. Lauren's voice was controlled, yet it wasn't Lauren.

"I was the primary complainant in this case. Your complaint was a counter-complaint. The chances are very good that the court will find in my favor. Do you know what that means for you?" Lauren looked at me without changing her expression.

"Richard, your abuse has got to stop," she replied with conviction. It was obvious that she believed what she was saying. The woman sitting next to me seemed to have no knowledge of the repeated knife attacks or the endless, harassing telephone calls. The woman sitting next to me was honestly repeating allegations she believed to be accurate.

"Lauren," I said, calmly, "There is no abuse on my part. There never has been. I realize that you have a problem understanding this, but the abuse is coming from your side, not mine. Lauren, this is Richmond, not Roanoke. In case you haven't realized it yet, no one here is buying your story."

My words were greeted with silence. I reached into my wallet and removed a copy of the order of protection. Showing it to her, I said, "Have you read this, Lauren? This order was issued by this very court and it is against you. Now, are you willing to go in there and risk being sent to Goochland today?"

"What are you saying, Richard?" she asked.

"What I am saying is that you and I should move for dismissal of the charges and then walk out of here and go on with our lives."

Lauren thought for a moment, then said, "All right, Richard. But your abuse has got to stop. Do you hear me?"

She really did believe that, I realized. "Yes, I hear you, Lauren. Look, we have to make a decision right now. Are you willing to move for a dismissal if I do?"

Lauren sat quietly, staring ahead. Then she turned to me and said, "Yes, Richard."

Relieved, I walked through the security checkpoint and went to the office of the Commonwealth Attorney located at the far end of the hall. I had to wait at least fifteen minutes, but at last I was escorted into the office of an Assistant Commonwealth Attorney. I explained the situation, beginning with my signing of the complaint and the issuance of the protective order by the court. I asked that a motion be made to dismiss both complaints.

"No, I'm not going to allow that. This is the second complaint that has been brought against you. I am going to insist that the court hear the case."

I was stunned. My worst nightmare was confirmed. I am male therefore I am automatically guilty. Being found not guilty was not an expression of innocence. It was luck, perhaps, or foolish judgment. Whatever the case, this time the results would be different. "Look," I said, trying to keep my voice calm. I was frustrated, angry, and scared, all emotions I dared not reveal. "I was found *not guilty* on the first complaint. It was heard in this court last June and I was found not guilty! How can you not take that into consideration?"

There was no reasoning with the Assistant Commonwealth Attorney.

Eventually the case was called and I entered the courtroom. After the preliminaries of signing a waiver for an attorney to be present, I addressed the court. "Your honor, it is the desire of both parties that the charges and counter-charges be dismissed."

The judge looked towards the Commonwealth Attorney and asked, "What is the feeling of the Commonwealth on the motion to dismiss?"

The Commonwealth Attorney said, "Judge, this situation involves a second time complaint against the defendant in the second charge. The Commonwealth intends to proceed with the hearing of the charges."

The judge removed a file and began shuffling through a sheaf of papers on his bench. He paused, reading several documents, then said, "But counselor, this man was found not guilty on the first charge."

"Your honor, we still want to proceed with the case," said the Commonwealth Attorney.

"Well, counselor, you're not going to because I am dismissing both charges. Case dismissed."

"Thank you, your honor!" I said, my voice jubilant. All the tension in my body was eased. The judge had been fair. The system had worked. I vowed that I was never again going to get myself in such a position.

I lied to myself. Again.

There was a brief digression from the demons' madness, a time when I would be taught a lesson that would later have great significance. Lauren showed up at my door one day with a small package wrapped in brown paper. This was Lauren, no one else, and she looked heartbroken.

Lauren had no idea why our relationship had soured. She believed she had done everything she could to make our marriage work. She loved me with a passion that brought both of us greater joy than we had possibly ever known. Yet, in her mind, I had suddenly grown distant. She sensed I was fearful of intimacy, loving her yet holding back for reasons she could not fathom. She had no idea of the violence that could greet me almost without warning. To kiss her took courage. To make love to her would have been the act of a fool. Yet how could I describe something so horrible about which she had no memory?

When Lauren showed up, she was reeling from what she felt was another blow by me for no reason. "Is this your idea of a joke?" she demanded to know.

"I don't understand," I said, taking the package from her. There was a perfume box wrapped in pink ribbon with the label "White Shoulders" on it.

I moved the wrapping aside, lifted the lid, and looked inside. Instead of perfume, the box contained what appeared to be a high grade of marijuana. I closed it and looked at the postmark on the wrapping. It was from some backwater town in Texas.

"Did Gary do this?" Lauren asked angrily.

Gary was a friend of mine who lived in Texas. I had mentioned him a few times, though Lauren never met him. He was someone I had come to know through law enforcement and bank security conferences, and while we were casual friends, he would never have committed a crime. And sending marijuana through the mail was very definitely a crime, especially in the quantity Lauren had received.

"No, Lauren. Gary would never do anything like this and neither would I."

I was as puzzled as she was by what she had received.

"Then who did?" she asked again.

"I don't know, but I want that junk out of my apartment right now," I insisted.

Lauren left, and that was the last time I saw the package. It was only later, during a call from the Queen of Hearts, that I learned the truth. Angrily she asked, "Where the hell is my package from John Taylor? Did you take it? What did you do with it?"

"You mean the marijuana?" I asked, surprised.

"That's none of your goddamn business," she said, slamming down the telephone. I did not know what Lauren had done with it, but I suspected it had been destroyed. The fact that the Queen could not find it was a great relief.

How do I describe what I did next? Sleep deprivation, constant stress, poor diet, and a serious commitment to the vows I took with Lauren all came together to cloud what should have been my better judgment. Or perhaps I was just being a damned fool as Arnie undoubtedly thought. All I know is that I began having more and more contact with Lauren—not the Intermediary. Not Hannah. Not the Queen of Hearts. Not anyone but the woman I loved.

Lauren was hurting, confused, desperate to make our life together succeed even as it was being torn apart. She had no knowledge of the violence. She had no understanding of actions that had made me extremely cautious about being around her. She did not know when the physical loving had stopped or why I was hesitant to take her in my arms.

The woman was mentally ill. I knew that. I also knew that marriage was a commitment I took seriously.

Yes, I reminded myself that I had failed once. Maybe this knowledge was a driving force. I went back over the fact that my ex-wife and I had been young, naïve, and seemingly only capable of focusing on the wrong priorities. I told myself that I had learned when we had parted, that if I had been more sensitive, more sensible during the time when we stopped working on our relationship, my kids would not have had to endure their parents' separation. My children would not have had to question our love for them and their involvement, if any, in our break-up.

I knew I had grown in the time between marriages. I

had considered my failings again and again. I had taken my vow with Lauren very seriously, vows that included a willingness to work through troubled times. Certainly there could be times no more troubled than when one of us was mentally ill. And equally important, if I was the one who had become irrational, I would want Lauren's love to be so strong that she would stay with me until I became well. My hope would be in her strength, her unfailing love, and perhaps that was what was necessary for Lauren.

The psychiatrist and therapist seemed to have failed. And medications, too numerous to recount, had either done nothing or made Lauren even more agitated. Perhaps I was the bridge between madness and the domination of the woman I thought I was marrying. At least, that's what I hoped.

I suppose that from the vantage point of my brown glass jar I thought I was buying time until a miracle occurred. My health insurance had limited benefits for both psychiatric care and medication, and we had exceeded most of them. This meant I was dipping into savings. But it didn't really seem to matter. If she was any closer to self-understanding from all the therapy, it was not obvious to me. And at least one of her therapists seemed to stay in denial, perhaps overwhelmed by the complexity of her case, perhaps never seeing, and thus not believing, all that I was reporting. An outsider looking at my situation could probably justifiably say that my waiting for a miracle was as realistic as expecting to win the Irish Sweepstakes, my state lottery's jackpot, and the Publisher's Clearinghouse Sweepstakes all on the same day.

However, despite all that I had endured, I still loved the woman and so now I quietly agreed to live with Lauren on a trial basis. The divorce was on hold, but I could still invoke the order of protection. But Lauren and I moved into another apartment I had rented with a short term lease at the beginning of the summer.

As when we were first together, once again we had a few idyllic weeks, but then the madness intervened.

Now there became a somewhat regular pattern to her outbreaks. First there would be the Intermediary. Then would come the Queen of Hearts. Next, I might be greeted by Hannah or Lucifer's Daughter. After that, depending on what I said or what took place, any one of those three might appear. I had learned to find an excuse to leave the apartment whenever the Intermediary showed up rather than staying for the inevitable trouble.

If I could not leave before the Queen of Hearts came out, I found I could briefly defuse her by agreeing to whatever she said. Yes, I was a liar. Maybe she couldn't articulate where and when I failed to tell her the truth, but I was a liar without question. Perhaps the worst liar the world has ever seen and certainly not deserving of her trust. Did she think I was abusive? Then yes, I was abusive. Without touching her, without yelling at her, without calling her names, I agreed with her that I was the poster boy for all abusers.

Nothing changed, of course, but it was a reaction she had not expected. There were no arguments. I just agreed with her until I could leave.

My coping mechanism was my own insanity, a fact that became clear by the first of July. It was July 6 and my cockiness about knowing Lauren's pattern, then avoiding the worst confrontations came back to haunt me.

I saw the body language change first. Lauren became tense, her jaws sagging, the scar forming, her eyes as focused as laser beams. I knew I had to leave the apartment immediately, but Hannah blocked my path. I went into the bedroom to pack an overnight bag, thinking she would stay by the door. Instead she followed, kicking and punching me.

Determined to not get into a fight, I pushed Hannah back and walked through the living room. She was right behind, a smile fixed on her face like that of a painted doll manufactured in Hell to assure all children that their dreams would be nightmares. She kicked me in the legs. She kicked me in the butt. She hit me with her fists.

"I know what you want," I said, turning on Hannah. "You want me to hit you, don't you? Well I'm not going to!" I pushed past her and continued on into the kitchen, a bright, sunny room with the refrigerator standing at the far end.

The demon moved ahead of me, turning so her back was to the refrigerator. Her nostrils were flaring in rage, and for the first time in weeks, I didn't care about the words I used with her. "Hannah, understand this," I said coldly. "I will go to any length to get you out of my life. I will do anything! Do you understand me?"

As I watched, everything changed. Hannah's smile slowly faded from her face. The sagging flesh became firm. The deep scar-like crease on the right side of her face disappeared, her skin becoming as smooth as a baby's. Years of age dropped away as she moved back against the refrigerator. Lauren was obviously the same height, though she seemed to get smaller.

Unable to move any further, she slowly sank to the floor, her legs folding, her body curving into almost a fetal position. Then, in the voice I had heard only once before, a young girl on the threshold of puberty called out, "Grandma?" Then, louder, "Grandma, where have you gone? Grandma, why did you leave me?" Suddenly she was sobbing uncontrollably, a lost, helpless child, confused by a life that had radically changed in ways I could not comprehend.

I stepped over to this child/woman and took her hand. She looked angrily at me and then held it, squeezing it as if in desperate relief. Jenny seemed to remember me from a year ago, and her eyes held trust as if she had been searching for me for a long while. I suspected that for Jenny, time was continuous based on when she was out. A year had passed since I had seen her, yet only minutes had passed in her mind. That was why I was a trusted friend. That was why I could comfort her, helping her off the floor, guiding her into the bedroom, laying her on the bed, gently stroking her hair as her sobbing slowed, her breathing relaxed, and she fell quietly asleep.

I sat, watching Lauren, listening to her breathing, wondering what kind of hell she had endured to turn into this tormented woman. Then, without knowing when, I fell asleep myself. At 6:30 A.M. I woke and went into the kitchen to make coffee.

As I prepared for the morning, Lauren shuffled by the kitchen on her way to the bathroom. When she came out, her face was strained and she had the transparent look of the Intermediary. I knew the Queen of Hearts could not be far behind.

I hurriedly showered and dressed, acting as if everything was as normal as possible. By the time I was opening the front door, the Queen was sitting on the rocking chair, moving back and forth, back and forth. I knew she would soon explode, but it was better to deal with her on the telephone than in person.

It was not the violence that at last brought me to my senses; it was the twelve-year-old girl crying on the floor in front of the refrigerator. I did not know what horrors Lauren had endured to make her act like this, but I reached an epiphany of sorts through the sight of that little girl. I realized that my staying with Lauren was not going to bring about a miraculous change. Her current therapist and psychiatrist were both out of their elements. The medication they were prescribing might be having some effect, but it was not doing enough, it was not really helping her. I felt sure that others were out there who could find a way to unlock the source of Lauren's trauma.

All I could do to help her and myself was to love Lauren from afar, because to insist that she was all right was to deny that all the "people" I was seeing were inside Lauren. The different names, the different behaviors, were all a part of the same woman whether I accepted that fact or not.

I arrived at my office before eight o'clock and within minutes the telephone was ringing. I knew who it was even before I picked up the receiver. It was the usual, irrational, near out of control rantings of a woman whose words were unintelligible. I hung up the telephone and turned down the ringer volume, buying myself a few minutes of peace before the rest of the staff arrived and I would have to again take the calls, to spare my secretary from Lauren's verbal abuse.

I also removed a micro-cassette recorder from my desk drawer and attached it to the telephone. I had taped earlier calls from Lauren, but I hadn't recorded any calls since we'd reconciled. I decided I should begin taping her calls again, ideally for use helping the therapists, though also to serve as protection for me. I was the victim of abuse, yet I was also constantly on the defensive. The tapes were proof that on any given day I was subject to twenty, thirty, fifty, or even one hundred separate calls from Lauren, backing my claims of harassment. What I did not realize was that the hell I had already endured was about to return with renewed fury.

CHAPTER 17

The Terror at Hand

Ali, the Queen of Hearts called, but before I could free myself, a business call came in on my second line. I excused myself, putting the Queen on hold, and took the business call. Within seconds, the blinking hold light went out, indicating the Queen had hung up on me. Not thinking anything of it, I finished my call, put down the receiver, and the telephone rang again. "Ahhh, we got disconnected..." The voice was a rasping whisper, calmer now, more intelligible. Yet something was wrong. I had a feeling like a faint charge of electricity coming through the line.

"You'd better not hang up on me like that again," she said.

"Yeah, I know," I said. I was becoming agitated. I had work to do. I didn't want another day of this. I knew I had to end the relationship once and for all. There had to be no more lying to myself. I had told Lauren we would move into a penthouse apartment when the short-term lease expired. That would not happen. I would have to go back to court for another restraining order. I would have to figure out when Lauren would be away from our place so I could remove those personal possessions the Queen would destroy when she realized our relationship was over. I would have to talk with my divorce lawyer to put everything back on track for the divorce.

"Who were you speaking with?"

"It was a business call," I said. Then, excusing myself, I stood up and closed the office door to assure some privacy and switched on the tape recorder.

"What are you doing?" she asked when I returned to the telephone.

"I was closing the door," I told her.

"Why are you closing your door? Why was I put on hold? Don't you want your secretary to hear?" Her whispered voice was taunting me.

Another business call came in and I again put the Queen on hold. This time she did not hang up. Instead, when I returned to the line she demanded to know, "What was I put on hold for?"

"I had another call coming in that I had to handle," I said.

"From who?" she asked, her voice rising. "The police?"

This was becoming explosive I realized. "It doesn't matter," I said, my stomach tightening.

"The police!" she repeated, her voice filled with rage.

I tried to change the direction of the conversation. "Lauren, you have got to stop calling me and harassing me. You know that I have work to do. You are going to have to stop calling."

I knew there wouldn't be any cooperation from her. She wouldn't stop calling. It was always the same.

The Queen was yelling obscenities now. *God, please make her go*, I prayed silently, though I knew she wouldn't hang up. Quietly I said, "You're just going to have to do what you have to do, Lauren. I can't tolerate this any more."

"Okay," she said, her voice deepening. Something

was happening again; something as different as the first night I met Hannah. "I can't live like this..." There was a long silence, and then Lauren said, "Okay, so you're ready to get your things and go?" Her voice had become agitated. There was an excitement to it that was unfamiliar.

I didn't answer. I felt as though anything I said would be wrong or needless. So many words... So much anger... So much confusion... So much pain...

"Well," said Lauren, her voice a whisper. "Sit down and calm down like you told me."

Even in a whisper, I knew this was a cold voice I had never heard before. This wasn't Lauren or Hannah or Ali, the Queen of Hearts, or Peg, Lucifer's Daughter, or Jenny, the twelve-year-old girl or... The hairs on the nape of my neck stood on end as the profanity flowed. From what level of Hell was the latest demon rising to meet me?

"I am calmed down, Lauren." My words were soft, deliberately neutral, meant to neither alarm nor excite her.

"Then you meant what you said...when you said...you would do anything to get me out of your life?" Her voice, which started in a whisper, rose to a scream. "Well, I want to know what you want?" Her anger seemed to explode through the telephone. "Do you hear me? Do you hear me? Tell me what you want!" Her voice was shaking with emotion.

Scared and fed up, I, too, yelled, though mindful of how far sound would carry with the office door closed. "I've had enough of all this!" I shouted. "I'm leaving here right now and I'm going to Juvenile and Domestic Court."

I heard my own words as though listening to a third party. I knew better than to verbally attack her. I knew that yet another demon had made its presence known. I knew she was a bomb with a fuse so short that, once ignited, there would be no defusing the explosive. I knew I had just lit that fuse.

"Nooooo! Nooooo!" It was not a cry of pain but of rage. I could hear crashes and thuds. Things were being thrown about the apartment. God knew what possessions were being smashed. "So, you're on your way to the police department," she said, a poisonous snake calmly stalking a rodent in which it is about to inject its venom.

I tried to calm down. I knew I had to lower my voice and act rationally if I expected to defuse the situation. What I really wanted was to take back my words, find new words, do something to end what was happening, but it was too late. The connection went dead. A few minutes later the telephone was ringing again. When I answered it, Hannah was on the line.

"Tell me! Tell me! You're going to court, aren't you?" Hannah, the impulsive, potentially deadly Hannah was screaming.

"Lauren, that's enough."

"Answer me! Answer me! You are going..." Again I could hear the sound of things being smashed against the wall. I had the sense that, if she could, Hannah would tear down the entire building, brick by brick, her frenzy feeding on itself.

Later I would learn that the ferocity was as loud in the building as it was listening over the telephone. The two women who shared the apartment directly overhead had been discussing calling the police. They thought I was in the apartment with Lauren, and if I was, they were certain I was in grave physical danger.

"Lauren, get hold of yourself," I said, quietly, trying to get the woman I married to come on the line. As odd as it sounds, even to myself, I could no longer think of the woman I loved as having violent sides. I was married to something out of Greek mythology. I would not have been surprised to see a half dozen heads, each with a unique personality, all emerging from the same body. "Please, you need help, Lauren. Let me call your therapist."

"No. No. You said they all were a bunch of quacks!" she screamed. "Do you remember that?" Her voice was out of control. "Huh? Huh? Isn't that what you said?"

At that moment they were worse than quacks. In my mind, the so-called professionals were criminal in their incompetence. This nightmare was the pay-off for a year of therapy? If love alone could have healed, my Lauren would have been the world's healthiest woman. When love was not enough, I relied on the skills of experts who, at that moment, I blamed for failure. Yet could they have done more? Could anyone have done more?

I chose my words carefully, waiting to answer until I had thought through what I could say. "Yes, that is what I said, Lauren, because I haven't seen anyone helping you. I said those words out of frustration. Did you know I even apologized to your therapist for saying that?"

There was yet another voice, deeper than the rest, calm, controlled, a schoolteacher confronting a pupil who thought he had gotten away with cheating in class. "You're the one that lied about the eagle."

It was a statement, not a question. It related to something so minor I thought nothing of it. Back in April I had removed an expensive porcelain sculpture of an eagle from the apartment. It was something both Lauren and I loved, but I did not remove it to keep her from having it. I knew she would not want it ruined during one of Hannah's rages or the episodes of calculated violence inflicted by Peg, Lucifer's Daughter. I did it on the spur of the moment and had no intention of keeping it from her. She had never said anything. I had thought nothing further about it. Neither of us had seen it in weeks because it was simply packed away while Lauren got progressively more violent. Suddenly it was a major issue, and her comment caught me off-guard. "What the hell are you talking about, Lauren?" I asked her.

For a second I heard nothing. Then, suddenly, the telephone was hurled against the wall and went dead.

Within minutes the telephone rang again. I picked up the receiver. Apparently Lauren had destroyed the wired phone and was now using the cordless.

"I have a knife and it's at my jugular vein! And, I've already cut myself!" said the new voice. It was deep and strong. It was the type of voice I had heard in hostage situations where the person speaking is holding someone else against her will. "I'm standing in the window, and if I see any cops, I'm going to cut my throat! And, if anyone comes near me, I'm going to take them with me!"

The voice seemed to leap from the telephone. But what made the incident most disturbing was the way she was talking. She sounded as though she was planning to commit a murder, not a suicide. It was as though the person talking did not realize that if she cut one woman's throat, all would die. Instead, she seemed to think she would only be killing Lauren or perhaps one of the others. The madness of it made me even more frightened for her.

"Lauren, for God's sake, you have got to calm down!" I cried.

Lauren or Hannah or whoever was on the telephone became increasingly incoherent. Her words were intermingled with the low battery warning beeps from the cordless phone. Unable to communicate, I grabbed a piece of paper and wrote the words, "Call 911....tell them Lauren is threatening to kill herself. If she sees any police, she is going to cut her throat, and she's threatening to kill anyone who comes near her." Then I added the address, ran to the office door, and motioned to my secretary to come into my office.

As soon as Gail, my secretary read the message, she took off on a run for her desk. I tried to keep Lauren on the telephone, hoping the battery would survive while a police response took place, but she hung up. I grabbed my jacket and started to leave the office.

The telephone rang one more time. I was almost out the door and I ignored it, anxious as I was to get home. But I thought it might be Lauren again, so I raced back and picked up the receiver.

The voice on the line was soft and weak. "I just wanted you to hear your wife's voice one more time before she died." Then the battery failed and the line went dead. I pulled the tape recorder from my phone, shoved it in my pocket, and ran to the parking lot.

The drive from my office to the apartment took twenty minutes under ideal circumstances. I used every pursuit driving tactic I had ever learned, weaving in and out of cars, slowing for red lights and stop signs, then flooring the engine when I knew no traffic was coming from the other side. Part of me hoped there would be no cops patrolling where I was driving. Part of me was hoping for a police escort.

By the time I arrived, it seemed like only five or ten minutes had passed. I drove into the apartment complex looking for any sign of the police. If they were there, I could not see them.

I parked directly in front of the apartment, then glanced over my shoulder as I walked up the sidewalk. That was when I saw a plain, dark blue Chevy Caprice with an alert looking driver in plainclothes idling on the far side of the parking lot. Even if I hadn't been a police officer, it was obvious to me that it was a policeman sitting in the unmarked car.

I took the six stairs leading up to the apartment two at a time. My key was in my hand, but when I turned it in the lock, I discovered the privacy chain was on. I could see in but I could not open the door.

I started to step back, planning to kick in the door, when I saw Lauren crossing the living room, moving rapidly towards me. She was bleeding, naked, screaming incoherently, and holding a twelve-inch butcher knife in her hand. She started to unlock the privacy chain so I backed down the stairs and stood at the bottom. I feared her using the knife on herself if she felt trapped by my being at the door. And if someone else had come along who did not want the body to die, I feared her attacking me. Staying at the bottom of the steps would give her space and provide me with escape routes.

The woman I faced was the same murderous/suicidal one I had heard on the telephone. She stood screaming incoherently while holding the knife close to her jugular vein. There was a wild-eyed look on her face as she stared at me.

Suddenly something distracted her. She looked up, noticing the unmarked police car. I don't know if she recognized it for what it was or if she just did not want a witness. She said nothing, just backing into the apartment and slamming the door.

Not certain what to do next, I looked back towards the officer. He motioned to me, pointing down the street. I walked down about three apartments and stood behind a tree. That was when he shouted, "Go to the corner and meet an officer!"

I walked across the front of the apartments and turned the corner. It was there, well out of sight, that several Henrico County Police cars were idling. I went to the closest one, opened the passenger side door, and sat next to the uniformed officer who was behind the wheel.

"Sir," he asked. "Are there any firearms in the apartment?"

"No. Not to my knowledge, but she has a butcher knife, she's bleeding, and she's threatening to kill not only herself but anyone who gets in the way," I assured him.

"We need to know as much as possible, especially if she has other weapons."

The officer wanted a definite answer that I could not give him. For weeks Lauren had asked me to purchase a firearm. She wanted it to give her a sense of protection.

I knew better. Even before I discovered that she was on probation and could not legally own a firearm, there were other concerns. I had carried a gun for several years. I had regularly gone to the police firing range to hone and maintain my skills. Yet I knew from my training and the experience of others that even the most highly skilled marksmen are likely to miss their target when under stress. In the movies there can be intense firefights where the hero is able to shoot accurately with all hell breaking loose around him. In reality, police are taught to shoot to kill because the instructors know we are going to be scared, our adrenaline racing, as we try to hold our weapons steady. If I shoot for so large a target as the chest, I will be lucky to wound the person in the arm when the pressure is on. And if police officers have trouble with all their training and constant practice, how much worse will the average citizen be on the rare chance the gun will be needed?

When I left the police department, I walked away from gun ownership. However, I knew that Lauren's business had regularly taken her inside private homes where a gun might have been available. She would never touch a weapon, but impulsive Hannah? There was a chance she would steal one, and though Hannah might get caught, I suspected Lucifer's Daughter could take a weapon without the owner ever connecting her to the theft. That was why I could only assure the officer that I knew of no weapons in the house.

Sitting in the front of the police patrol car should have made what was taking place a little easier. This was familiar territory for me. This was the type of vehicle in which I had logged hundreds of hours on the road. These were men whose careers and concerns had once been my own.

After I had fully described the bloody scene in the

apartment, I began talking about Lauren, trying to explain her condition as best as I understood it. At first the words came easily. "I began to tape record these bizarre conversations..." Then, as I listened to myself, I realized what the officer must have been thinking. He wasn't relating to an ex-cop who had gone into bank security work. He was seeing a damned fool husband with a crazy, violent wife he continued to live with. If I was in his position, I would have either held myself in disdain or questioned my sanity.

"One of the Sheriff's officers back there says he knows your wife," the officer told me. "He said he arrested her a few months back on an assault charge."

I sat inside the police cruiser, waiting for what seemed like an eternity. I listened to the radio transmissions, most of which were routine. Then I heard a supervisor notifying all the cars surrounding the apartment that "the suspect might exit from the building nude." That was the word he used. "Suspect."

When did Lauren become a "suspect"? She was my wife. She was...

And I remembered the knife held aloft by the latest demon. I remembered her nakedness. I remembered...

I don't recall how much time was passing or what was taking place. It was as though I was going in and out of my own world, in and out of shock.

Unexpectedly, the officer sitting next to me said, "Sir, my supervisor needs to know if you are willing to sign a green warrant on your wife."

"I'll sign it, anything to make this stop," I said desperately.

Finally it had come to this. The involuntary commitment Dr. Carter refused to allow had been taken from his hands by Lauren's now public madness. Perhaps I could at last get her the help she needed. The only trouble was she might be dead before the green warrant could be executed.

"The officer pulled the microphone from its holder. "A one-zero-six. That's affirmative on the GW."

"Ten-four. Meet a unit at the entrance for transport to the center," a voice replied.

The officer then said to me, "Sir, we are going to transfer you to another unit for transport to the Public Safety Center where you can sign the warrant for the Magistrate."

The officer drove his patrol car to the front entrance of the apartment complex, still out of the line of sight of my apartment. Lauren would be aware of nothing other than the plainclothes officer she had spotted, and I still did not know if she even realized he was with the police.

The day had grown hot, mid-morning. The temperature had risen into the nineties and the humidity was becoming so thick, it seemed as though you could chew the air. I had been in the air conditioning of first my car and then the cruiser. But when I stepped from the patrol car in order to get into the supervisor's unit, I was overwhelmed by the weather. I could see the heat rising from the car's hood, then felt what seemed like a blast furnace. I began sweating profusely, a wave of nausea sweeping over me. It took me a moment to recover when I entered the supervisor's car.

"Sir," said the supervisor, scanning my face. "I want to be sure you know what a green warrant is. It's a legal document authorizing us to take your wife into custody for a period of psychiatric evaluation not to exceed forty-eight hours. Are you willing to sign the warrant?"

I nodded my head, "I know what it is and I'll sign it." His only response was to place the car in gear and drive from the complex onto the highway. Within a few minutes we were on our way to the Henrico County Public Safety Building. I stared out the window, thinking of Lauren. I wondered who she was at that moment. I wondered what she had done to herself. Was she alive? Was she trying to flee the building?

It had been so odd to see her that way. There had been a time when the idea of Lauren greeting me naked at the door of our apartment would have left me with the erection of an adolescent. The love and desire radiating from her face would have filled me with feelings both lustful and joyous. I would have kissed her with a passion, tearing at my suit, kicking shut the door, fighting to get off my clothes as we lowered ourselves to the floor to share our passion.

But the woman who had met me at the apartment door was a parody of all that was good in creation. Instead of a Siren of mythology whose voice could lure sailors to their death in pursuit of one moment of bliss, she was something from a nightmare. There was nothing erotic about her body. She might as well have been covered with poisonous snakes.

I could not stop thinking that the woman who met me at the door was homicidal, never comprehending that the person she wanted to kill was herself. I had no basis for making such a judgment, yet everything about her body language, everything about her actions indicated to me that she thought she could kill Lauren and still live.

I had to stop thinking about the meaning of the madness and concentrate on the terror at hand. The Magistrate with whom I had spoken at the trial was waiting for us. He prepared the warrant, never saying what I was thinking, that all of us could have been saved from this experience if I had acted differently a few months earlier.

But I hadn't done that. God help me, I had let matters ride, fantasizing that I was helping Lauren in some way.

CHAPTER 18

Dire Explosion

Countless police cruisers, a fire engine, and ambulances were positioned around the parking area when we returned to the apartment complex. I didn't realize it at the time, but the Henrico County Police Department's Incident Management Team is routinely called when a suicide is mentioned.

My initial call had resulted in a uniformed patrol officer checking to see if there was a problem. The moment he knew Lauren was acting as I had stated, he moved swiftly back, calling for back-up. Other officers arrived to seal the perimeter of the large complex, a supervisor rolling through to oversee what was taking place.

Between her threat and rap sheet which a member of the Intelligence Division pulled as a routine precaution, there was no question that there could be serious trouble. An intensely emotionally disturbed woman with a history of attempted murder and aggravated assault was threatening to take her own life and those of anyone who got in her way. That, in itself, was cause for concern.

The County Police Incident Management Team prides itself on saving lives. Their goal is to help whoever is in crisis without jeopardizing anyone else around them. They know that some want to commit suicide by cop—threatening a police officer with such violence that the person had to be shot. And they know that their goal is to coordinate all units and services necessary to avoid the loss of life, of bystanders as well as the person making the threat and then to help the person after he or she is in custody. They would use all the skills at their disposal. Fire power would be their last resort.

The men and women moved into position. The complex was large and sealing it off took quite a few officers. Some of the people were evacuated from their apartments. Others were placed in "enclosed custody" for their safety, police jargon for being asked to stay inside until Lauren could be removed from the apartment.

Twenty SWAT officers in full body protection gear armed with high powered weaponry took positions. They were placed so that some could observe what was going on inside my apartment, some were positioned as snipers if shooting Lauren would prove necessary, and the rest were positioned to take Lauren safely out of the apartment if they were able to do so.

Three hostage negotiators were present, along with two members of the mental health community. A young officer named Paul Siers was the crisis negotiator. He had a back-up and a supervisor in case there were prolonged negotiations or serious problems. The three of them and the two representatives from the mental health community were linked by wireless headsets so everyone heard what Paul and Lauren were saying to each other. However, Lauren could only hear Paul.

The apartment leasing center had become the command center for all emergency services. Luckily, the building was large enough to handle the men and women involved, and the office had records of everyone living in the complex.

They could coordinate any movement of residents that remained in their apartments that might be necessary to protect them in case Lauren had a gun.

When Siers saw me he said, "I know you taped her. Can I have the tape recorder you used?" I handed it to him and the five member team went into another room in order to play back Lauren's calls for the day. "We're hoping," Siers explained, "that with the playback there will be some clue that will help us bring your wife out without anyone being hurt."

The apartment leasing office staff was both shocked and angry. This was not the way they expected their day to progress in a luxury complex. Several of the women who worked there sat at their desks, trying to keep some semblance of routine.

There was a surreal quality to what was taking place. Officer Paul Siers came out of the office after listening to the tape. "Sir, are you positive there are no firearms in the apartment?" he asked. The Intelligence Unit officer had filled him in concerning the shooting of Lauren's previous husband. If she had a gun, the stakes were enormously higher than with a suicidal woman with a knife. She might decide to kill as many people as possible with the gun as a way of forcing the police to shoot her.

"To the best of my knowledge there are none," I replied. In the other room, the tape had been rewound and was being played a second time. My words to the hostage negotiator were punctuated by the screams of my wife's disembodied voice filtering through the doorway. "What's going to happen now?" I asked.

"We're going to attempt to make contact with her by telephone, and then we'll try to talk her out. Is there anything you might be able to tell us that would help us in getting her to come out?" he asked.

"You should know that our cordless phone went dead. I think the battery needs recharging. She destroyed the only other phone we have."

The negotiators carry telephones they can place within reach of a barricaded subject so they can talk but Paul didn't want to send a man close to the apartment to get a telephone to Lauren unless it was absolutely necessary. Paul began dialing our home number and said, "Let's see if I need to use one of ours." As it turned out, I was mistaken; the wired telephone Lauren had hurled at a wall was better than I thought. A moment after he finished dialing, Siers heard Lauren's shaky voice on the other end. She quickly hung up on him, but he looked relieved nonetheless.

"Well, your phone works well enough to receive calls. Is there anything else?" he asked.

"Look, I've been having a lot of serious problems with my wife in the past year. She has been treated by several doctors. No one seems to believe me when I try to explain that she is a deeply troubled person."

Paul smiled sympathetically. "Sir, for some reason I think that people will start believing you now. I think your wife just got their attention."

For a moment I smiled back. Paul was right. Lauren had repeatedly gone too far in her actions, but this time her madness had become a public spectacle.

Some of the neighbors might view the action as street theater, but I knew what was taking place. The law enforcement men and women who had gathered had but one job— to protect the greatest number of lives possible. If they could get Lauren to leave without any resistance, that would be the best thing. But if Lauren attacked them, or if Lauren went after a neighbor, there was a good chance they would kill her. They would sacrifice one madwoman for the sake of the rational neighbors. Their job was to do that which would save the greatest number of lives, yet if someone had to die to save the others...

I began praying. I prayed for Lauren. I prayed for the men and women whose job it was to try and protect her from her own violence. I prayed for myself.

In minutes the negotiations began.

"Mrs. Goetzke, this must be a very hard time for you," said Paul. "I'd like to help. Can you tell me what's wrong?"

His voice was gentle but firm. He went on.

"I understand you're having problems. They must be awful for you to feel like this. I'd like to see if maybe I can help you. I don't know if you're aware that the county has a lot of services available to you, whether you're having financial problems, difficulties with your husband, on the job...."

A detective hurried to where I was sitting. "Your wife was just seen at one of the windows. It looks like she put on some clothes." he told me. The SWAT team was in position, snipers and spotters on rooftops overlooking the window. Others were doing an analysis to see how they could rush the apartment if they had to break inside. Speed was critical so that they could subdue Lauren before she had a chance to hurt herself or resist them, or worse, kill someone.

I knew the longer you could keep someone from committing suicide or murder, the less likely such a person will act on his impulses. I prayed for time. I did not realize that in this case, time was a luxury the officers could not afford.

Hostage negotiations will continue as long as practical, whatever that means. If someone has a group of hostages in an abandoned warehouse, it might be practical, depending upon the circumstances, to talk and talk and talk. The negotiator might work through the night. He might go through the next day. With three negotiators always on the scene, there is a chance for relief while slowly exhausting the perpetrator. And when there are no hostages, only a person threatening violence against his or her self, there is no reason to risk lives by rushing a building when the individual can be worn down over time.

But Lauren had created a situation that had its own deadline. She was holed up in a massive apartment complex, and she had threatened to kill anyone who came near her. It was now afternoon, and by five o'clock the police would be faced with the prospect that hundreds of people would be returning to their homes. They could not keep the building sealed off all that time. They also could not risk anyone getting hurt. "If she's not out by seventeen hundred hours, we'll have to take her out," one of the SWAT team members said grimly.

Two other members of the SWAT team approached the bedroom window in the rear of the apartment, then radioed what they found. "Your wife is at the window, screaming," a young detective reported. "We're going to try to calm her down."

But who was it? Maybe the woman who had come to the door always went around naked. Maybe someone else was in charge of the body. Maybe someone else had no intention of hurting anyone. Maybe it was Hannah. Maybe it was Peg, Lucifer's Daughter. Maybe it was Ali, the Queen of Hearts. Maybe it was...

"It must be terrible for you to have him lie all the time," Paul sympathized with her. "We can help you get marriage counseling if that's what you want. Or we can hep you get a divorce. The county has many services to help you through this terrible time. All you have to do is come out. I can't talk with you very well just on the telephone. If you come out, we can work together to get you what you need."

And then I thought of Lauren, my Lauren, the

woman I thought I was marrying. What if she had no awareness of what was taking place? What if she was suddenly
given full use of the body and discovered that the apartment
was filled with armed police officers? She would be terrified.
She would have no idea what was happening. She would
need comforting. She would need me to hold her, to explain
things to her. She would need me to...

I still could not let go. After all that had happened, I
continued to separate the woman from her illness and to love
that woman with a passion that kept me from walking away
from her and the demons that haunted her.

I had to be a realist, though. If Lauren was there and
I went to her, Lucifer's Daughter or Hannah would probably
take control, attacking me with a knife or shooting me, assuring that a SWAT team sniper would shoot her. It was a vari-
ation of that military horror story. Instead of someone
destroying a village to save it, I would in essence be taking my
wife's life in order to save her from the demons.

I had to sit quietly.

Paul tried again. "Do you want me to call you
Lauren? I understand that you hate Richard Goetzke. I'm
not here for him. I'm here for you. I want to help you. I want
to make things right for you."

The place where I waited was air-conditioned but I
was too restless to stay inside as the hours passed. Morning
became afternoon. The temperature hovered between 97
and 100 degrees. The humidity rose so high that your body
sweat could not evaporate in order to cool you. Uniform
shirts clung to the officers' bodies, the SWAT team members being especially miserable because of the extra protective gear they had to wear. I felt as though I had just stepped
out of a shower taken with my clothes on.

As I stood on the sidewalk watching, two television crews arrived with their video cameras and their trucks with satellite link ups. They also brought their perky announcers who needed to check their hair and their looks of solemnity as they reported the unfolding drama.

Through my mind passed images of the first day I met Lauren and my efforts to protect her from the prying eyes of the media. Now they were on our doorstep, the result of her actions. There was no more protecting her.

Two detectives walked up the sidewalk towards me. One of them, genuinely sympathetic, said, "Sir, our negotiator is still talking with your wife. She says her name is Hannah. We have to ask you some question about your wife's background. Do you mind answering them?"

"No, I don't mind," I answered. I was relieved that Hannah was talking. She would not be violent so long as they kept her on the telephone. "What do you want to know?"

One of the detectives held a sheet of paper in his hand. It was her NCIC sheet, her criminal record. "Do you have any information about these various criminal charges that were brought against your wife?"

I told him what I knew about the shooting of Lauren's ex-husband and the property damages that were caused by some of her rages. I did not explain that it was Hannah or Ali or Peg, not Lauren, who had done the damage. No matter what happened, Lauren's name was on the criminal record.

"Are you positive that there are no firearms in the apartment?" the second detective asked.

"I don't think there are."

The two men carried two-way radios which allowed them to hear what was going on with the SWAT negotiator. The detectives and I listened. I heard Paul's voice again. Hannah was gone, or at least he was using Lauren's name.

"We're here to help you, Lauren. We care about

you. We know things have been rough for you and you haven't known where to go for help. But we know, Lauren. It's our job to know. Whatever it is you need we can help you. You don't need to use the knife. But I do need you to come outside. I can't help you so long as you stay in your apartment.

We walked over to the leasing office and stepped into the cool air inside. My apartment was out of sight of the command center, the reason the leasing office had been chosen for use. I recognized some of the men and women moving into position. I knew an ambulance was just out of Lauren's view but ready to roll the moment anyone got hurt. I was also aware that there were snipers trying to keep Lauren in the sights of their weapons, ready to pull the trigger yet undoubtedly praying, as I was, that it would not be necessary.

"Any firearms?" one detective said, asking again.

"I don't think Lauren has any." But I knew and they knew she was on record for attempted murder with a firearm. Of course they were nervous.

"If you're mistaken," he said quietly, "someone could get seriously hurt or killed. She has a history of violence with guns. If she got hold of a weapon, we have no doubt she will use it." Given the impulsiveness of Hannah and the violent planning of Peg, Lucifer's Daughter, I had no reason to doubt their thinking.

"Perhaps she might," I relented. "I can't be sure."

Again Paul's voice came over the detective's radio.

"If you will just step outside, I'll have a man meet you. Lauren, you'll be safe. Nothing will happen to you. We just want to protect you from everyone and help you."

The afternoon inched by. Lauren had placed the officers in one of the most stressful situations police encounter. Their job is to save as many lives as possible, including someone like Lauren who, if she had a gun, might try to kill them just for approaching her to help. The constant tension was palpable. Minute after minute the officers had to be ready in case Lauren came out shooting or attacking someone. At the same time, when nothing happened, their adrenaline was wasted and their bodies became tense. The reaction was much like hypoglycemia and many men and women had trouble with the strain.

Through it all Officer Paul Siers stayed on the telephone with Lauren. His voice was calm, soothing, accepting. He listened to everything she had to say. At the same time, I could tell that there were moments of extreme frustration for him. I was certain he had never encountered anyone like Lauren and her minion of demons before. Nevertheless, Paul tried to reason with her:

"But Lauren, I did explain to you who I am. I told you I want to help you. We have been talking quite a while. Lauren? Don't you remember me? You can trust me."

More bits and pieces of Paul's side of the conversation, which was filled with frustration, filtered towards 'me. Periodically he obviously covered the mouthpiece of the telephone and I could hear such comments as, "Who the hell is in there?" He was meeting woman after woman, all different, and he could not tell what was happening. He knew there was only one. He knew she was alone. Yet he, too, experienced the shock of meeting everyone. And unless today was radically different, I suspected that whenever Lauren was on the telephone, she had no knowledge of what had happened with the Queen of Hearts, Lucifer's Daughter, Hannah, or anyone else. In many ways, frightened as I was for Lauren, I felt relieved and vindicated. But I also felt despondent and hopeless. Finally, there were witnesses to the explosive situation with which I had been living. Finally there were people who would not question me. Yet their very belief was leading the woman I still loved to the brink of death. I had no idea now who was in charge of Lauren's body.

Seventeen hundred hours was getting closer. Paul tried to intercede again:

"Lauren, I want you to come out. There will be a man wearing a helmet near your door. If you open it a crack and look out, you will see him. I want you to go to him and he will help you. He's your friend, just like I am. I'll join you when you're with him. I'm not going to leave you. I'll join you when you're with him."

The residents of the complex began returning from work, only to be stopped from going near our section of the complex. It was six and a half hours since Paul had begun talking to Lauren on the telephone. The clouds were rolling in, indicating an early dusk for a July day. The stakes were going up. I sat down with the officer in charge of SWAT and quickly began drawing a sketch of apartment's interior. I gave him the layout, the furniture, and what would be encountered as they moved from room to room. When I was finished, I prayed that Lauren would be all right and that no one would be hurt in the assault.

Then we heard what sounded like a gunshot. The men around me tensed. I watched as they and the others moved into position. The next thing we heard was the shattering of glass. They could wait no longer. It was a signal of Lauren's deepening crisis which could not be ignored. An entry team moved to the side of the apartment, close enough to quickly grab Lauren and far enough so she could not see them. The SWAT team members moved a 40mm grenade launcher in. One took careful aim and fired, the gas grenade pierced the upper pane of the bedroom window. The canister was propelled across the ceiling, skimming the surface and leaving a pink trail in its wake. Then it burst, the contents I knew would engulf Lauren as it fell directly on her.

At the same instant, the SWAT team, gas masks in place, burst into the bedroom. Despite the choking fumes, Lauren was screaming and kicking as they disarmed and restrained her. They took her from apartment. Thankfully, both she and the officers who risked their lives to bring her out safely were unhurt.

Despite everything, as I watched my poor, lost love, I could not help but move toward her, hoping to offer her some comfort. But I stopped myself. It was not appropriate. It was useless.

As I left the command center, one of the Henrico County detectives I had met earlier approached me. I held out my hand and thanked him for his work. "Your wife is going to be all right," he told me. "She is being transported to Saint Mary's Hospital for treatment of chemical burns. When they are finished with her there, they will transport her over to Charter Westbrook Psychiatric Hospital for observation." He shook my hand, then added, "Good luck, sir."

I had heard that remark before. Now I had little hope that it would come to pass.

PART III

Living With the Truth

— CHAPTER 19 —

Destruction's Wake

The night was calm, quiet, as I walked back to my apartment. Outside my unit, several firefighters moved around a fire truck, and several more were inside, the front door open as they worked. They were using fans to drive the gas and fumes out of the rooms, yet the air was still heavy with the odor of the chemical agent. My eyes began to water and burn, though I first checked on the parakeet, which was singing as though nothing had happened, and the cat that, as usual, was hiding in the closet.

I felt a strange euphoria in the midst of the devastation. There was a jagged hole in the upper corner of the bedroom window. A pinkish-red streak spread across the ceiling like a jet's vapor trail. The bed and carpeting were covered with the residue of the chemical agent so that every time I took a step, fumes rose up and stung my face.

The telephone receiver on which Lauren had been talking earlier in the day lay on the bed. I picked up the receiver and replaced it in the cradle.

All around was the wake of the destruction left by the women who comprised my wife. Yet there was relief in having survived the violence. There was peace in being alive, in knowing that the lives that mattered were also physically untouched. The arrest of Lauren Goetzke was a tribute to the skill and compassion of large numbers of law enforcement officers.

Later, I learned how fortunate we were. The Henrico County Incident Management Unit was trained to do battle with violent people but they were committed to helping people like Lauren—the depressed, the mentally ill. Unlike other states where such incidents result in death, they genuinely cared and did everything in their power to save human lives.

Tonight I could relax. I would not think about tomorrow.

The security manager for the apartment complex stopped by to see me, suggesting that I find alternative housing. He was shocked by the destruction caused by both Lauren and the SWAT team. I was relieved. Never again would I face the disbelief and unspoken accusations when I tried to explain that my wife was dangerously violent.

When the security manager left, I sat on the bed, oblivious to the residue and the odor that still stung my eyes. My home had been shattered. I had no idea whether I would still have a job. Yet I felt relief for no one would again question what I had been telling him or her about Lauren. She had acted out in a way so extreme, there were no more questions. Perhaps my nightmare was coming to an end.

I phone Arnie who told me, "I'm with you. You have to be strong now."

I felt that I needed to be the first person to telephone Lauren's parents. I had no idea what involvement, if any, they had in her mental illness. My relationship with them had been minimal and not particularly friendly. However, they were her parents. Presumably they loved her. And I knew that if something like the forced incarceration for psychiatric care happened to my daughter, I would want to know about it right away.

I spoke with Lauren's mother in Roanoke later that evening. I did my best to explain to her what had happened to Lauren, then waited for a response. At first there was only silence. Then her mother said, "Richard, somebody is going to have to kill her!"

"What did you say?" I asked, shocked.

"Somebody is going to have to kill her, Richard. You're going to have to kill her!" Her voice was calm, quiet. Chilled by her words, disbelieving yet knowing what I had heard, I hung up the telephone.

Although my heart was heavy, there were mundane tasks to consider. There was the clean up. There was the packing of each of our possessions in preparation for the move I knew had to be made to avoid a forced eviction. There was dinner. But my first concern was preparing to take Lauren's Mustang to the hospital where it would be waiting when she was released. I did not want to have to see her any more than necessary. I certainly did not want to have to meet her at the hospital.

I looked all over for the spare key and could not find it. The police had allowed her to take her purse in which one of the keys was kept. But the other should have been at home.

Frustrated, I tried to remember where she might have left it. My suspicion was that it might be with a dealer in Richmond where she had taken it for servicing the week before. The dealer had not been asked to rush the work, but Lauren had become upset when she found that the car had sat in the garage overnight, no one even looking at it. Instead of getting a fixed time to do the work, she just took the car back and told them to forget it. I thought that in her anger, she might have left the key behind, and a call to the garage proved me right. I drove to the dealer and retrieved the key from the service department.

Returning home, I decided to go through the car to see what I could find. I'm not even certain why I did it.

Over a period of months, much of my personal property had mysteriously disappeared. I was missing a very expensive watch, two cameras, a light meter, and my CD player. I never suspected Lauren of taking them. There was no reason to be suspicious. And when I looked in the rear storage compartment of her car, I did not expect to find any answers.

The missing equipment was not in the compartment, but a secret unraveled with the discovery of a brown paper grocery bag stuffed with more than one hundred letters. Some of them were in envelopes postmarked Leavenworth, Kansas, the city where a Federal Penitentiary is located. Most of them were from John Anthony Taylor. After finding the letter from the Queen to John long ago, I suspected they wrote to each other on occasion, but I was shocked at the volume of correspondence now before me.

I brought the letters into the apartment and began reading them. I quickly learned about the affair I had no knowledge of, of clandestine meetings in prison trailers. I was surprised that Lauren, a convicted felon, could even get in to see John. However, as I read on, it appeared that Lucifer's Daughter, the Queen and whomever else was corresponding with Taylor pretended to be a relative of John's to have an overnight visit with him. There were a couple of other letters from Lauren, though whether they were copies or never sent I do not know. What is certain is that the woman I had married did not write them. They had her name, and the return address was the same post office box to which John's letters had been sent. But the handwriting was different, obviously the work of one of the demons.

Certainly all the demons must have been writing to the convicted felon because even he experienced her odd behavior. In a letter dated July 5, for example, he wrote of how glad he was to get the letters. There was anger, though, because she was writing one thing to him and doing another. While there was no indication as to what she did that so upset him, it was obvious that he was dealing with more than one person. I suspected that most of the time, the letters were written by the Queen and Lucifer's Daughter, Hannah being too impulsive to spend her time manipulating a relationship or writing letters.

In the aftermath of the hell that had been my day, I was finally able to find a little humor in what was taking place. The Queen of Hearts, one of Lauren's selves, had been manipulating John Taylor, and Taylor had been manipulating the Queen, neither with much success.

John was often seductive with his outrageous plans. Some of the plans required his release from jail to accomplish, something that was not going to occur for more years than the Queen ever considered. However, one letter discussed the plans he had been making for a wedding while he was imprisoned. The fact that he was going to remain behind bars was irrelevant. He was weaving a fantasy in which he was Prince Charming and she was Cinderella, the high security Federal prison serving as their castle. What was not said was that there would be no need for rodents to bring her coach. The prison was already filled with rats.

Of course, during the early part of their relationship, I assumed that Hannah or the Queen convinced John that she was not married at all. Increasingly, though, I began to think that whomever was writing John wasn't married—to me, to Norm Graybill, or to anyone else. My relationship with Lauren did not involve any of them, especially Hannah. She hated what Lauren did and refused to participate. Hannah would stay around as a witness, but I'm certain she also did not take the wedding vows Lauren and I so cherished.

John continued talking about money he must have spent on gifts or some other purpose that was special. He explained that he had gotten money from others. The debt was upsetting to him, apparently keeping him from concentrating on his beloved, my wife. He wanted her to send money to him to ease his burden, erase his debts, and presumably to better move forward with their relationship.

John was also receiving declarations of love from one person that went counter to what was taking place with the others. I could only guess that among the different personalities writing to him, one was buying into his fantasy and seeing herself as single, and others knew the truth and told him about the wedding she witnessed. The letters were confusing to John and frustrated him. He would repeatedly talk about how she would have to show him her love, not just tell him things she didn't follow through on. Had his relationship been with someone other than Lauren, I might have been amused by his frustration.

I knew just how John felt. He could not stand the confusion, something I decided he deserved. He would never experience the hell of having a wife create what became a war zone. Let him be confused by letters from the demons from Hell.

Then came the attempts by John to manipulate Lauren. John wanted money and pornography. The money had not been a problem. The Queen had been sending him money orders for small sums. I could not tell if this was her money or money she got from me.

Again there was humor to the request. Apparently the Queen had been sending money orders figuring they were safe. Cash might be taken and a check would leave a paper trail I would eventually see. A money order was the same as cash. All John had to do was go into any bank, any check-cashing outlet, or even most supermarkets and he could get the money. That was the trouble. John Taylor would not be seeing the inside of such places for many years to come. He apparently had a stack of unusable money orders, the Queen having "proven" her love in a way that assured he would be unable to take advantage of it.

The other request was different. John specifically wanted three pornography magazines mailed in a single envelope, apparently in order to meet a restriction of the penitentiary. He did not specify what he wanted them to show. He just stressed that they should be the most obscene she could find.

Sex, or the perversions of sex, seemed to be one of John Taylor's obsessions. It was understandable, of course. This was a man who had always been successful in getting what he wanted from women. He had seduced a woman young enough to be his daughter, lived with her, and led her into circumstances where she ultimately died for him. He had managed to catch the attention of Hannah when he was in a jail holding area. To suddenly be deprived of sex with a woman, to know he might never again have intercourse, must have been shattering. For sex to be an obsessive focus seemed logical for a man in jail.

In each letter there was always a section that encouraged her to see him as a kindred spirit, a man who understood the troubles she was telling him. The two of them began referring to me in terms that ironically matched the way I thought about the violent sides of Lauren. It was with John that the Queen shared a fantasy world of physical and emotional abuse, of denial of necessities, of a life so hard she needed a protector to take her from me. She knew she would never be caught in her lies, and he knew that his commiseration cost him nothing. He could rant and rave about me. He could talk about wanting to hold her, to love her, to care for her. They could both talk about marriage and plans for the future because nothing was going to happen. John Taylor didn't have to consider the possibility of marrying the Queen of Hearts or Lucifer's Daughter, much less living with them. And the Queen did not have to worry about John seeing her in her car, buying clothes, going anywhere she wanted whenever she wanted rather than being trapped in a filthy house with nothing but a broom and dust mop for company as she had led him to believe.

There was also one other common demand, one that the demons fulfilled for John. He wanted her to take sexy pictures of herself.

The requests were frequent. Usually they came in the same letters as the ones that had requests for money. A letter from July 8 was typical in that he expressed his concern about her hospitalization, stressed their relationship, mentioned the pictures, and asked for money. Always he needed more money. Always there was no other person to whom he could turn. Yet, despite the two photos I had already seen, it was the photography session that both sickened and intrigued me.

The person in the images I now found was most often Peg, Lucifer's Daughter, but at other times the Intermediary. The face was not Lauren's. There was no life in the eyes, no joy, none of the spark that made Lauren such a delight. There was also no scar, something very evident with Hannah. Unlike the two pictures I'd seen earlier of the Queen, this woman was the type one saw in erotic movies, her hair high and glued with hairspray, her face heavily made up. She seemed to portray sexual experience of every kind.

The woman in the picture wore seductive leathers, a garter belt, and fishnet stockings. The provocative way she wore them was not only quite different from Lauren's tastes in clothes, but her attitude. There was no sense of caring what John Taylor thought. And when she showed herself touching erogenous zones, it appeared that she was fascinated with herself. She set up the camera and let the timer take the picture as if she was displaying herself for her own pleasure and cared little what anyone else thought.

Then came the pitch. He had told her he liked looking at her. He told her that others had hurt them both. Now he wanted her to send him money before she entered the hospital. He seemed to be taking no chances. She would be vulnerable with the stress of entering the hospital for her surgery, and there was always the chance she would refuse to send money when she came out. It was best to request the payment while he could.

There was also an implication that somehow there should have been or could have been a committed, involved relationship despite the fact that he was going to be doing extensive time in prison. Lauren's marriage to me was supposedly insulting to John, a rather odd situation since she knew him from little more than a moment's glance. However, Hannah loved the fantasy of the man she had woven in her mind from the newspaper accounts of his exploits, capture, and trial. The fact that neither she nor any of the others had ever spent meaningful time with the man was irrelevant. Still, she seemed to believe him when he spoke of love and commitment, and his betrayal by her when she married someone else.

The letters were hard to read. There was something at once intimate and obscene about the writing. Had these been letters addressed to the Queen of Hearts, Lucifer's Daughter, or one of the others, I would not have minded. Instead, these were addressed to Lauren, the woman I loved and who loved me.

It is difficult to explain the emotions that swept over me as I read those letters. My relationship with Lauren had been intense and deeply loving. Even though the demons that held her captive were trying to destroy our life together, I loved the real Lauren and felt that it was a blessing that we were brought together. But the letters were a slap in the face. I felt like I had found explicit sexual comments about my wife scrawled on a telephone booth or a bathroom stall. I tried not to think that Lauren had been with John Taylor physically, but I was sickened that he put into writing the things he planned to do with her, to her. There was something so venomous about his words that I become nauseous, wanting desperately to vomit.

I hated Taylor for being so verbally intimate with my wife. I hated Hannah for bringing the bastard into my life. And I hated dealing with the letters, trying to keep in mind that he did not know the Lauren I wed. At times, he seemed to be writing to impulsive, violent Hannah who had struck out at one husband, at others to violent, manipulative Lucifer's Daughter, who was trying to kill me, and still others to the Queen, who enjoyed wreaking havoc throughout her adult life. One of the most difficult to read was one he wrote on July 11. The bastard had the nerve to tell the Queen that she needed to take better care of me for his sake. He was worried about what our estrangement might be costing him. The money she sent, the material she bought, all were dependent upon the money the Queen could get from me. At least in his perverted fantasy. It was an arrangement that, if true, would have made the woman who undertook it little more than a whore.

Perhaps that was the way this man saw all women. Certainly the relationship with his girlfriend killed during the escape attempt seemed cold-blooded. I could not know without talking with him. All I had were the letters, and I was certain that if sweet, vulnerable Lauren had seen the letters, not the Queen of Hearts, she would have been disgusted by the man's lack of respect for her, not to mention the pain he was causing me.

Taylor explained how much he needed the Queen to be his partner in life. He briefly proposed a sex and business arrangement be made between them. She would take care of his matters from the outside. She would be his partner in every way. And she would sexually service him whenever he was able to have a conjugal visit.

He admitted that his one and only lover actually had competition. With all the talk of a long term relationship and total commitment, the man was egotistical enough to mention that he was writing to another woman, apparently in an equally intimate way. She was expendable, though. She was kept warm in the bullpen in case the pitcher couldn't go the distance. But in this game, the pitcher was the Queen of Hearts, and he foolishly let the pitcher decide whether or not to take herself out of the game.

At the same time, the Queen built a fantasy life that included claims that she she was totally dependent on me, kept in isolation and forced to endure my abuse. In response, John blustered and threatened, making clear that he would be her brave protector. He knew how to handle someone like myself. He was a tough guy, a bank robber, and an important man. The fact that he was locked away never seemed to interfere with the lying manipulations of them both.

The relationship between Taylor and the Queen had continued through his change of prisons. Through September, John Taylor had been in Lewisburg. However, Taylor made more enemies than just myself. Another inmate made a knife and took a length of pipe to use as a club, then hid in the garbage shack when Taylor was working a detail transporting garbage. Taylor was caught unaware, badly hurt, and transported to Leavenworth, Kansas after hospital treatment and recovery in isolation from the other prisoners.

Taylor's brush with death did not change him. The letters continued to be manipulative. The Queen of Hearts had apparently been talking about my "cruelty" to her and suggesting that she wanted to divorce me. In a letter written after she was arrested for assault and battery, she complained to him about the indignities of her jail stay in a way that he must have found humorous. No matter how horrible a night or two in jail must be for someone, it is nothing compared with the emotions of facing years of your life behind bars. Still, in his reply he comforted her and suggested it was time they became life partners. Together they could triumph. John Taylor advised her to go to a lawyer and sue me. He also expressed anger so great that he had to take a walk around the prison yard to cool off, as though we were sitting at separate tables in a bar and he might come at me. Always the aggression was cartoon-like. Were these idle threats from an impotent man or did Taylor have connections on the outside?

Taylor had sided with vengeful Lucifer's Daughter, a woman who had viciously attacked me and seemed to take delight in the attack.

The transfer had taken John to a prison he felt was less desirable. He wrote to the demon that each prison was different, some were better than others. It was a little like a weary traveler finding himself at a hotel chain whose quality was lacking compared with that of a rival down the road. He told the Queen that he needed money in the new prison. There was little supplied that he needed. Everything had to be purchased, including bags for laundry, and he was without funds.

The letters began answering questions about some aspects of the madness I had been enduring. I sometimes thought that more than the violence I endured at home, the hardest part of the previous year was her threats against my children and the harassment at work. I had chosen to stay with Lauren because of my wedding vows, my love for the woman I thought I was marrying, and my concern that she got help. It was my business what I endured in private. It was my business whether I lived at home or took a hotel room to escape when that seemed appropriate. It was my business that I tried a reconciliation, or at least returned to living with her after initially filing for divorce because I still loved the Lauren I had married and thought I could help her recover. I knew it was all a gamble but I was willing to take that chance with my life.

The workplace was different. I felt my work was important. I was helping to protect the lives of the men and women who handled the money in our banks, and I was helping protect the savings of the people who used the facilities. In the hierarchy of prison life, the bold directness of the bank robber made such an individual highly respected. This was why bank robbery was often the crime of choice of the career criminal. Help stop one such individual and I would be resolving what might have been dozen or more past crimes, as well as preventing dozens of future crimes. At the same time, it was eight or more hours where I did not have to think about Lauren's evil sides if I did not wish to do so. I could focus on the good, or I could think about ways to help her. What I would not have to do was talk to the Queen of Hearts, Lucifer's Daughter, Hannah, or anyone else.

But there was more. I loved the work and I liked my co-workers. I didn't want to lose the friendship and respect of the people with whom I shared so many hours a day. Until now I did not realize the extent to which Hannah, Lucifer's

Daughter and the Queen of Hearts harassed other employees in my office.

The manipulative side of John Taylor had touched
the viciously creative side of Ali, the Queen of Hearts. She
had been telling him about my hostility towards her and the
way I kept her in isolation from the people around her, and
he devised a plan for revenge.

John Taylor's idea was to have Lauren call Arnie and
other executives. She was to be sweet and polite with everyone with whom she spoke. There was to be none of the hostility the woman who called my secretary used. However, she
was always to choose a time and a day when I would not be
around the person she was calling.

Once the Queen got hold of Arnie, she was to discuss a personal problem with him. She was to sound as if she
was confiding in him because she cared about me and cared
about what happened to me. Then she was to explain that
during the marriage she had discovered that I had a violent
side. She didn't know what caused it. But she was an innocent victim who loved me and would never do anything to
harm me. Yet for some reason there were times when I
would hit her. When I read the passages that explained this
scheme, I didn't know whether to laugh or cry.

Ali was to be extremely naïve. She was to explain that
people shouldn't hit other people when they didn't do anything to them. She was to be the poor, innocent waif trying to
make the marriage work, not understanding how she could
become a victim of a man who seemed to have two faces.
That she would be putting a mirror to herself was not said.
Admittedly, it was also not known.

The idea was a good one and probably had an
impact at work. I never heard about any of this, and once
word got out about the SWAT team, I was certain people
like Arnie would look at her statements quite differently. But

I was equally certain that the idea had forever cost me the respect I desired. After all, why else would she call like that? No one in his or her right mind would create such havoc with the telephone. *No one in her right mind...*

The final letter I scanned was one that took the scheming to a new level. John Taylor wrote in depth of an idea he had briefly alluded to in an earlier letter. He wanted to go into a business partnership with Lauren. He had an idea for making money using her considerable skills as a creative writer (if he only knew).

According to Taylor, men in prison were lonely for female companionship. They liked the idea of writing to someone who would pledge devotion, talk about sex, and generally act as though they were truly taken by a man they had never met. The fact that the man might have been a rapist whom they would never have wanted to meet did not matter. Serial killer or petty thief, if the man was in jail, he fantasized about women and delighted in telling himself that some strange woman was anxious to engage in every possible sex act or perversion with him.

John knew his scam would get him in trouble with the warden so he did not put too many specific details on paper. He told her they would talk later, a fact that indicated he had found a way to contact Lauren by telephone without my knowledge. Whatever the case, the basic idea was for the Queen of Hearts to take a post office box, then write to men who advertised for a relationship in a number of popular men's magazines and pornographic publications they could receive in the prison. She would tell the men anything they wanted to hear, then ask them for money.

Avoiding the issue of his own resources, which I suspect were more plentiful than he ever told Lauren, he said that not everyone in prison was broke. Enough had large sums of money that establishing a correspondence with them could lead to a very good income that I suspected he wanted to share.

I could not tell if the Queen of Hearts decided to participate. The SWAT team had cancelled any hope of additional correspondence at least momentarily.

Taking the letters with me for safekeeping in my office, I went out for something to eat. I still had at least twenty-four hours before the doctors finally might be able to tell me what was wrong with Lauren and whether I would ever again have the woman I had married back.

— CHAPTER 20 —

The Minds of Lauren Goetzke

Lauren had been taken to ward E of the holding facility for the criminally insane and those individuals considered dangerous. Ironically, it was the same building where Susan Gabriel met Randy Gladstone and plotted the destruction of the Bradfords. A sanity hearing was scheduled for July 15.

By the time I returned to my office that Thursday, my secretary told me that Lauren had been telephoning every few minutes since the office had opened.

"Richard?" said Lauren when I reached her in the locked ward of the hospital. Her voice was slow and somewhat slurred. I could not tell if this was someone new or just the result of the medication she was on.

"Lauren. Are you all right?" I asked.

"I'll be out of here very soon, maybe tomorrow."

It was twenty-four hours since the time the SWAT team had surrounded the apartment, twenty-four hours since she had stood nude with a butcher knife to her throat. It was twenty-four hours since Lauren had been led away in handcuffs.

"How do you know that?" I asked. There was no way she could be released so soon. Yet there had been no way her therapist could have failed to believe me when I told him of the attack I had endured months before this, and he did.

"Believe me, Richard, I will be out of here probably tomorrow." There was no anger in her voice, no threat of violence. It was a simple fact, like hearing, *Hi, honey, I've finished my business in the "loony bin" and I'll be home in twenty-four hours. Make sure the knives are sharp and the guns loaded. I'm really looking forward to seeing you.*

Then, as happily excited as when we were newlyweds, she said, "Richard, what about our new apartment?"

She was asking about one-time plans to move into a penthouse apartment in the same complex. We had been scheduled to move there at the end of the month. But that had been before the violence, before the SWAT team shot tear gas into our bedroom, then stormed inside to arrest her. Could she seriously think that the management would welcome our continuing to stay there?

"Lauren," I said, incredulous. "You don't really think that they would rent us an apartment now, do you?" I said. I didn't give her a chance to answer. I suspected the Lauren speaking to me now had not been in our apartment the day SWAT team was called in. "They've given us notice. We have to be out of the apartment by the end of the month. Do you understand that?"

There was silence on the other end of the line. I could not tell if she did not comprehend what had happened or if someone else was now talking. Finally she said, "Richard, I am going to need a ride home after the hearing tomorrow."

"I will have your Mustang at the hospital for you," I said.

There was a long silence. When Lauren spoke once again her voice was shaky. "How...how can you? You don't have the key," she said. She sounded like a teenager who has just discovered that her mother could read her diary any time she desired. I wondered if she was thinking about the letters. For that matter, I wondered who the hell I was talking to and what my having the key would mean.

"I have the key, Lauren. Your car will be there in the morning if they let you out." There were no other words. The line went dead.

As soon as she hung up I told my secretary I needed to transact some family business out of the office. Once again I went to the Juvenile and Domestic Relations Court. I applied for and received another restraining order. It would immediately be served on Lauren in the hospital.

Early the next morning accompanied by Arnie, who had come to town at my request, I drove Lauren's car to the hospital, parked it in the visitors' parking lot, and then had him drive me home. I went in to work and for the first time in over a year, the morning went quietly with no calls from Lauren.

After lunch I drove back to the hospital where I met Dr. Carter standing in front of the entrance. I shook his hand, then asked, "What do you think is going to happen now? Are they going to release her?"

"I don't see how they can after what's happened," he said as we walked in the door and headed down the corridor. We were both going to ward E.

As we walked, I wanted to ask him if he remembered the telephone call I made to him in desperation that previous April. I wanted to ask him if he thought that had he done something then, none of this would have happened. To be truthful, I think I wanted to hurt him, to make him suffer for his sin of omission in a critical time in Lauren's unstable life. I wanted to believe that early intervention would have helped me retain the woman I loved.

I was silent, though. As angry as I was, I was gradually accepting the fact that there were no magic pills for Lauren. Perhaps it would not have mattered what anyone did in those early days. Perhaps today was inevitable. Perhaps...

Ward E was sealed by a heavy steel door with a small viewing window whose glass was impregnated with mesh screening to assure no one could break out. The lock was a solid one, and the nurse who answered my ringing of the entry bell was alert for both patients and visitors who might cause trouble. The nurse took the car keys from me, then directed me to the hearing room that was in another part of the hospital. The staff wanted to keep the patients as isolated as they could. Transporting them to another building was a high risk. A hearing room within the hospital was the safest approach.

The hearing room was down a long hallway. I expected someone from Lauren's family to be there but there was no one evident when I entered the room. There was only Lauren, heavily medicated, staring down at the table in front of her. She never looked up when I entered, never acknowledged anyone's presence.

I was asked to testify before a hearing officer from the county mental health department. I recounted the events of the previous day as well as my efforts to find help for Lauren over the preceding months. It was difficult for me to speak, and I was extremely emotional during the course of my testimony. I fought back tears when I said my final words. "I just want my wife to get the help she needs," I choked.

Next came the state appointed psychiatrist who examined Lauren when she was brought in. I looked at him and wondered what he would say. Ted Carter had told me he was certain Lauren would not be released. Lauren was certain she would be. I worried that this new doctor would tell the judge that she was a victim and I the abuser. I was afraid that this would be a repetition of so many unspoken accusations, all of which indicated I was lying and Lauren was the person who needed protection. I was not ready for the words I heard next.

"Lauren suffers from what I refer to as an exotic multiple personality disorder. Unfortunately, the state statute is seriously flawed. There is a loophole caused by the wording requiring the forty-eight hour time. I can not state that she will be a danger to herself or another person within the next forty-eight hours, as the law requires. I am certain there will be some point in the future when she will be. It could be a week, or a month. Due to the wording of the statute, we have no choice but to release her."

Although because of her behavior I should have suspected it, I sat in stunned silence. My entire focus was on the words "an exotic multiple personality disorder."

For more than a year I had been desperate for someone to put a label on Lauren's condition. Each person who interacted with Lauren saw only the personality who was in control of the body. Some people came to know her as the sweet, loving woman with whom I still wanted to spend my life. Some knew the hot-tempered, out of control Hannah. Some experienced the manipulative Queen of Hearts or the premeditated evil of Lucifer's Daughter. But few had experienced any two of the personalities on the same day, much less the gamut I had encountered. Until now. Obviously Lauren had revealed enough of herself for the doctor to make the diagnosis I had instinctively known without being able to label it. What I agonized over was even with such a diagnosis, was it possible to gain a course of treatment which might make Lauren well? And even if it was, how could that occur if they were going to release her without even trying to cure her?

The hearing officer turned to Lauren and asked, "Do you have anything to say?"

Lauren never moved her gaze from the tabletop, but her voice changed and I suspected that if I could better see her face the scar would be present. Angrily she said, "I just want to go and do my work! I just want to go and do my work!" The demon was about to be released back on the streets.

I left the hospital as quickly as possible and began to drive back to my office. Less than ten minutes into my trip, my pager activated. I glanced at the number and realized it was a call from someplace in or near the hospital. Perhaps Lauren had been allowed to check on her car after I dropped it off and had discovered that the bag of John's letters was missing. Whoever was in control was not someone I wanted to deal with. I ignored the page and went to my office. I needed to get work done, forgetting about Lauren for a while. There would be another hearing on the court order of protection on July 29. With all the time off I had to take because of the court appearances, I needed to spend as much time as I could on the job, not sparring with the demons from Hell over the telephone.

As I sat at my desk, however, I began thinking of the diagnosis I had heard that morning. Multiple Personality Disorder. I had heard of the condition, of course. I once saw *The Three Faces Of Eve* on late night television. I remembered Sally Field starring in *Sybil* and David Birney starring in *The Five Of Me*. They were all about people who had radically different personalities—some child like, some violent, some gentle, some...

As I thought about the women with whom I lived, I realized that Lauren was like those others, a mind so divided that I might as well have been a polygamist. I loved the one woman who truly loved me, and my backing off from her must have been extremely painful because she had no idea how many different people shared her body.

During the next few hours I began making phone calls, talking with experts in the field to learn more about the condition. They all said the same thing, that though television and the movies have popularized the disorder, it is actually quite rare. It is triggered by excessive trauma before the age of seven, and the trauma often has a sexual component to it.

One doctor mentioned Christina Peters, a woman who was kidnapped and raped by her father when she was five years of age. Her mind was so overwhelmed that her original personality vanished. The personality was replaced with a child who was all rage, all violence. She tried desperately to hurt or kill her psychopathic father, a man who years later committed suicide in a penitentiary. However, the man was far more powerful than his daughter's new, violent personality, so she hid and created someone to endure all pain and suffering in life. Finally, when the rape was over, she created a personality to run the body. "It took years before Christina was properly diagnosed and treated by Dr. Ralph Allison who then practiced in Santa Cruz, California," one psychiatrist explained to me. "The original personality never showed herself. Depending upon her stress, there might be the nice Christina who ran the body, the Christina who endured suffering, or the one whose rage led her to attack her husbands and commit crimes that sent her to prison. When Dr. Allison eventually integrated her, she was emotionally five years old until she could assimilate all the knowledge and information of the alter-personalities."

I remember Lauren telling me stories about when she was two years old and had been found under her bed with a knife, apparently trying to protect herself from something. I knew she had little contact with her parents, and I had learned that the parents or some close relative often cause the trauma creating multiple personality. It also could have been a stranger or a trusted caretaker such as a sitter or preschool teacher. Whatever the case, it was the violent, psychologically overwhelming action of a very sick adult who had created the condition that led Lauren to develop the demons who tormented our life together.

The saddest part of what I learned was what I had instinctively come to understand. Lauren, my Lauren, the woman I loved, had no knowledge of the others. She lived her life unable to remember large segments of time. The doctors said that if she was typical, she had become adept at covering her confusion. She would pretend to remember people she had never met. She would pretend to be proud or embarrassed or whatever other emotion was appropriate for experiences she could not remember because one of the other personalities had actually lived that time. It would only be with intense therapy leading to the integration of all the personalities that she would finally discover the lost pieces of her life.

I realized then that Lauren never wrote the letters I had found. Lauren never read them. And when the letters were hidden, it was one of the other personalities who had stuffed them in the bag, then placed them in her car. Unfortunately, the letters also created my next problem. I became convinced from reading them and, after receiving a phone call, that one of the personalities would shortly commit a crime, probably as soon as Lauren would be released from ward E.

True crime books had always fascinated Lauren. Criminals fascinated Hannah. It was Hannah, so in control that I originally thought it was Lauren who called me when she was released to ask about establishing a new identity.

"You want to do what?" I asked her.

"I want to establish a new identity. You know, a new name, Social Security number, all the records I'd need to pretend to be someone else."

You already have that, I thought to myself. There was something almost humorous about a multiple personality talking about creating a new identity. She already changed with a moment's stress. Instead of setting myself up for verbal violence, I took her seriously. "Why in the world would you need another identity?" I asked Hannah.

"Somewhere out there is a lot of money hidden away. If I could get in to see John, he would tell me where it is. We could keep most of it. All we would have to do would be to keep plenty of money in John's prison account."

I noticed the subtle shift to inclusiveness in her suggestion. I had no idea if the various personalities realized I knew who they were. I suspected they did not. That was why I referred to everyone who came out by Lauren's name. I wanted them to think they were fooling me. It seemed somehow easier that way.

There was no way I was going to go along with receiving stolen money, though I don't think Hannah understood that. For Hannah, morality was something that was a convenience. She would do whatever resulted in personal pleasure. Because of her narrowed ability to think, she assumed that everyone else was impulsive and immoral as well.

"What makes you think there's any money at all out there?" I asked. "The government confiscated all of John's property. Don't you think they would have found it?"

There was silence. Then she said good-bye. I obviously was not going to offer her the help she desired.

I thought about the money. From what I knew of the case, there could be as little as a few thousand dollars to as much as $250,000 hidden somewhere. Perhaps the girlfriend who had been killed in the shoot-out with the Federal Marshals had hidden the cash. She was in a position to obtain it. She was in a position to hide it. And she must have believed that after she "rescued" John Taylor from his captors, together they would dig it up. Perhaps she carried the secret of the missing money, if that was what there was, to her grave.

The call from Hannah convinced me I had to call the appropriate authorities. This meant alerting a friend of mine, Special Agent Charlie Brooks, a man with whom I had worked for years. He was the agent who coordinated the Bureau's local "Fast Track" program, a concentrated effort by the U.S. Attorney's office, the FBI, and local banks to vigorously prosecute crimes involving fraud against local financial institutions.

As I dialed the number, telling the receptionist whom I wanted, I again thought of Lauren. No matter how many personalities she had, she was the one who would suffer. She would be the one who would be thrown into jail for reasons she would neither remember nor understand. I was jeopardizing my own wife, forcing her to face the consequences of another personality's actions. For a moment I wanted to hang up the phone, to pretend I did not know what I knew. Instead, I told Charlie when he came on the line, "I've got an urgent matter I need to talk to you about. Something I think will be of interest to the Bureau."

"Does this involve your bank?" he asked. "Is it a Fast Track issue?"

"No, it's something that involves my personal knowledge about some past crimes," I told him. "There may be something to what I have, or it may end up being pure bull. I think you should bring in somebody from the bank robbery squad." I could feel the knot in my stomach. I was doing my duty as a former law enforcement officer and as a man responsible for bank security. I was doing what was right and proper. Yet there was a chance that my actions would send the woman I loved, a woman extremely disturbed from some overwhelming childhood trauma, into an even greater nightmare world than she had endured before.

"Okay," said Charlie. "When can we meet?" I could tell by his voice that he was excited. There was an adrenaline rush when we worked such cases.

"Later this afternoon. I still have some documents to get together."

"Okay. Our office at five o'clock. I'll see if I can get one of the men from robbery," he told me.

Trying to divorce my feelings from what was happening, I got right down to business. Turning to my computer I started typing a detailed report of everything I knew. I photocopied some of John Taylor's letters from Leavenworth, then attached the copies to the report. By the time I finished, the report was over an inch and a half thick.

The field office of the FBI was in suburban Richmond in a small shopping center style office park. As I walked up the sidewalk towards the one story office building, I thought, My God, here I am at the FBI's office to implicate my own wife in a possible crime. I became nauseated and my skin was cold. I began to sweat. For a moment I thought I might pass out. I stopped for a moment and loosened my tie. After a few deep breaths, I felt that I had regained control. I entered the building and told the receptionist I was there to see Charlie Brooks.

Charlie had Special Agent Wade Marlowe with him. Wade was a man I had known from past bank robbery cases. They were both capable agents and I knew I could trust them both.

"What's on your mind, Dick?" asked Charlie after I was led to a small, windowless interview room barely large enough for the three of us.

I explained the SWAT team encounter to the men. They looked at me incredulous. I didn't know if they were shocked by Lauren's actions or the fact that I had stayed with this woman through so much hell. I didn't ask. I didn't want to know. I just assured them that what I was telling them was the truth, then showed them the report I had prepared.

"I just found out that a convict out at Leavenworth, a guy named John Anthony Taylor, has been writing to my wife," I told them. "He is doing time for bank robbery. In the past his name came up in conversations with my wife so I knew she knew him or knew of all the banks he robbed. Anyway, she called me today. She seems to think there was a sizable amount of money squirreled away, maybe as much as $250,000. To tell you the truth, I thought she was confused or joking. But when I thought about letters I found from John Taylor, I decided to go over some of them again. I started to wonder if she was serious about it. That is why I came here. I thought you should know so that you could look into it."

Charlie and Wade were both interested. They were kind enough at first to not ask more questions about my wife but focus on John Taylor. He was notorious in Virginia, and Wade Marlowe had worked the Roanoke office. Certainly his escape attempt had left a lasting impression on everyone who worked that type of case. However, eventually Lauren/Hannah's role had to be discussed.

"Do you think she's going to make a run for the money?" Trencher asked.

"It's possible, if there is any money. First she has to find out where it is. I don't think she has that information yet. You guys should be able to find out how much money was not recovered, shouldn't you?" I asked.

There was no reply and I suddenly realized why. I had called Charlie as a colleague. The moment I brought the documents involving my wife with a career bank robber, I became something else. I was a possible accessory. Certainly I was not a safe person with whom to share information because I might take it to my wife. They were going to ask me everything they could, everything they needed, but they were going to share nothing with me. It was not a good feeling.

"Hey, Dick, make yourself comfortable while we sort some things out," said Wade, rising from the table and taking the report.

"We'll be back in a few minutes," said Charlie, smiling. And then I was left alone.

Interrogation rooms are frequently designed so that questioning can be observed. Sometimes this works to the advantage of a suspect. A supervisor can see into the room and witness any acts of coercion or violence that might be taking place. A criminal suspect can actually be protected.

Usually the observation is not for anything quite so dramatic. Instead it is to get an idea of the guilt or innocence of the person. How does he or she react when under pressure? When the interrogating officers leave the room, what does the person do? In many instances an innocent person will become quite agitated when alone, looking all about, pacing, and generally showing a high level of discomfort. A guilty person, by contrast, will often relax, sometimes falling asleep. None of this is evidence, of course, but the pattern is consistent enough that it helps the officers.

I wondered if I was in such an interrogation room. Was I being watched, my actions studied to determine if I might be an accomplice in the crime scenario I was reporting? I had always lived my life on the side of the law. To suddenly feel as though such actions might no longer be believed, my word no longer trusted, was unsettling.

I began to wonder if I had done the right thing in going to the FBI. I knew that many of my wife's personalities lived in a fantasy world. For all I knew, I was being paranoid. Lauren's sanity hearing was scheduled for the next day. Perhaps I should have waited. Perhaps...

Charlie and Wade returned to the room. Wade was

holding some papers that I guessed were Lauren's criminal record. The look on Charlie's face was similar to one I had seen with Arnie. It seemed to be saying, *What is someone like you, someone with your background, doing being married to a person with Lauren's background?* His words did not broach that subject. He just said, "Dick, what do you want us to do?"

"Well, Lauren said she was going to Roanoke as soon as she was released from the hospital," I told them. There was no point in trying to explain that Lauren would not be the guilty person. Lauren would be kept as unaware as if she was blindfolded and locked in a closet. "It's my guess that at some point soon she will try to visit John at Leavenworth. She will attempt to find out the location of the money, if there is any. That kind of information isn't going to be in their letters. That would be too risky.

"When Lauren called today, she asked if I could get her a phony identity. I asked her why but she wouldn't tell me. My guess is it would allow her to get on the visitors' list at the prison. Then she could find out from John where the money is."

"Well, we could set something up when she pays this guy a visit," Marlowe said.

"Yeah, you could, but there is a small problem there. As a convicted felon, Lauren can't get on the visitors' list at a correctional facility. She used a phony identity and posed as his relative to visit him in the past, but I don't know if she can get in to see him at Leavenworth with those tricks."

"I know about your wife's record," said Wade. "I have a copy of her rap sheet right here. It makes for interesting reading."

My wife's rap sheet! Just hearing those words uttered out loud set my mind spinning. My wife was a criminal with enough arrests to make up several pages. I had come to understand this fact, even though there were mitigating circumstances. Even though the women committing those crimes were not the woman I had married. Lauren was not Hannah or the Queen of Hearts or... Yet how could I explain all this? I didn't know what to say.

"What do you think?" I asked.

I didn't want to continue the conversation. I didn't want to have to deal with the fact that I had married a woman like Lauren. I wanted to focus on the prevention of further crime and the recovery of stolen money. But even that was not possible. They no longer saw me as a colleague. I had become just another informant. The FBI never tells informants anything.

"Hey, look you guys! I know from the letters that John is trying awful hard to get Lauren on the visitors' list. But she's a convicted..."

Charlie cut me off. "Believe me," he said, "she's on the list."

"And we'll make sure a close watch is put on his mail and his visitors," Wade added.

"Anything else?" Charlie asked.

"I would like you to read through everything here. I'd like to know if this dirt bag might try something. You know, try to have somebody hit me."

I paused, then looked at my friend and said, "I don't know, Charlie. Maybe I'm paranoid from all of this. Maybe I've seen too many movies."

Marlowe, shaking his head, broke in. "Look, you know and we know this guy is dangerous. You're a professional. Take all the precautions and call us if anything occurs."

Charlie looked at me searchingly. "Richard, get a divorce," he paused, "as soon as you can." With that he stood up, dismissing me.

I didn't mention the marijuana package. I didn't mention my first-hand knowledge that John Taylor remained well enough connected to the outside to be able to arrange for an illegal shipment. If he was that well connected, then there was good reason for my fear.

— CHAPTER 21 —

Searching for Truth

D ay after day, week after week, and month after month I had been reacting to Lauren's abnormal behavior. While I tried to save her and our relationship, now I knew the body of the woman I loved was a dormitory from Hell and I never knew which woman might come after me. Now with Lauren out of town and my having gone to the FBI, I could no longer continue responding to the events of the moment. I felt I had to learn the rest of the truth as soon as I could.

I drove down to Roanoke, hoping I wouldn't run into her. My first stop was at the Roanoke Public Library where I searched through the microfilmed back issues of the newspapers that might have covered Lauren's violence against her first husband. Finally, under a headline that read: "Man Shot In Domestic Quarrel In Serious Condition: Wife Jailed," I read the details of the story I already knew the outline of. I read about the shooting I suspected Lucifer's Daughter was responsible for and thought about what might have happened.

I had long had doubts even about Lauren's version of events surrounding her previous marriage. Was her husband really an abusive bully? Or had she goaded and physically assaulted him and had he fought back? I had heard her repeated stories claiming abuse at his hands, but I never knew what his side of the story was. I knew that in my case, it was very clear which one of us was the abuser and which one was the abused. After my experiences, I had to believe Lauren's previous husband had received his share of abuse. So, even if Lauren's claims of abuse were true, what had he endured before reaching the point when he could take no more, when he lashed out and attacked Lauren back?

I was a police officer trained to keep violence from escalating. When I joined the department, the Academy training was designed so that we would never hurt anyone more than absolutely necessary. I became accustomed to that style of defending myself physically. It was that very style that made it so easy for doctors to find cuts and bruises on my body after Lauren's assaults. Lauren, on the other hand, never showed signs of the "abuse" she alleged.

Most men don't receive the training I had. If they go in the army, the idea is to fight in a way that results in death or such severe injury that the enemy can not get up again. If a man's experience with self-defense is limited to street fights and barroom brawls, he learns to punch and kick as hard as he can so the person he is fighting can not get up.

What was Hannah's husband like? Had he taken all the abuse he could stand? Had he waited until he was certain that severe injury or death was likely if he did not fight back? The impulsive way Hannah wielded the knife was such that she could do intense harm. A man without training might easily have hurt her severely while fighting for his life, then been unable to defend himself against her accusations. After all, her body would bear the bruises. Her body would reveal the effects of great violence. She could easily talk the courts into believing her.

I also wondered what triggered the rage her ex-husband had endured. Did she shoot him realizing that an act of passion would not be construed as premeditated since she had filed several police reports against him for the abuse she had suffered? Did she shoot him because he was divorcing her and she refused to accept rejection? And more to the point, would I one day turn around on the street and find Lauren standing with a rifle, aiming at my heart?

Lauren's attorney had taken custody of all of her husband's firearms after the two of them separated. I assumed that he had done that because he feared her husband might become violent. Now it seemed that there might be something more to what had taken place. Had the attorney met Hannah? Did he know the Ali, Queen of Hearts? What about Peg, Lucifer's Daughter? Did he realize that within Lauren was the potential for overwhelming violence?

The newspaper article mentioned the name of the gun store where Lauren had bought the gun used on her ex-husband. I remembered Lucifer's Daughter calling the store clerk a "punk" because he had testified for the prosecution in her shooting trial. I decided to go to the store in the hope that, even after several years, at least one of the people who had worked there at the time would still be employed.

Gun shops were often the type of places where the staff loved their work, enjoyed the customers, and stayed for years. Fortunately the store where Lauren had bought the gun was no exception. I found the clerk who had testified, but when I started asking questions, he became suspicious. "What are you, a cop or something?"

"No," I told him. "I'm the husband of the woman who purchased the rifle."

"Jesus!" he exclaimed. "Are you the guy she shot?"

"No, I married her last year after she shot him," I explained.

"You're kidding!" he said, laughing.

"No, I'm afraid I'm not. I'd appreciate it if you could tell me a little about your knowledge of my wife."

The clerk stared incredulously. "I testified at her pre-sentencing hearing," he told me. "Did you know that?"

"Yes. I know you did. That's why I'm here. She told me about it. She called you a punk."

"She did? Hey, man, that lady has ice water in her veins!" he said, shaking his head.

"What makes you say that?"

"Well, she bought a handgun and the .22 rifle. Then she asked me if I would teach her how to use the rifle. She said she already knew how to use the handgun. We went downstairs to the range. She asked me to show her how to load the rifle and fire it. The lady spent about an hour load-ing and firing the weapon. She bought three boxes of ammo. That's about all there is to tell."

"Is that what you testified to at her hearing?"

"I sure did."

"Thanks for the information." I said, turning to leave.

"Come on, are you really her husband?" the clerk asked. "Or are you putting me on?"

"Yeah, I am," I assured him.

"Hey, there's one thing I didn't mention," the clerk called after me.

I turned around. "What's that?"

"Well," he began, "when she was on the range firing, she just stood there firing the weapon with a real weird smile on her face. She told me afterward she liked guns, that she was going to start a collection of them, and that she had been to a few gun shops in the area. She was still smiling that weird smile. She was real scary."

I knew exactly what he meant. I was certain I had seen that same expression when I was attacked with the butcher knife, though I wasn't about to share that information with him. "Thanks again," I said.

Before I could leave the store, he said, "Hey, mister, do you want to buy a gun? You should have one. She might have bought more guns from other dealers like she said."

I shook my head and walked out. I had carried a weapon for a number of years. It is as much a part of being a cop as putting on your shirt and pants each morning. Arnie had offered to loan me a weapon when I was visiting him in Roanoke. It was a .38 police special with a two-inch barrel. The weapon fits easily in your pocket, in a side holster, or even an ankle holster hidden under your pant leg. It's meant for close range shooting, the reason many detectives carry it. The gun is a defensive weapon for men and women who might suddenly find themselves in a life or death situation in close quarters. If my desire was to kill Lauren, then it would have been the ideal weapon for me, a man living with demons from Hell. But it was not something I could use.

As I walked to my car, I mulled everything over in my head. I thought about how I had once asked Lauren why she had a loaded rifle with her the day she shot her husband. She had said that it was for protection. She was afraid he would become physically violent. I believed her then. I still believed her to some extent. Maybe Lauren was afraid. Maybe Lauren had no idea why she had the gun and convinced herself of the most logical reason—self-protection. Lucifer's Daughter had done the stalking, Hannah had done the shooting, and I suspected that the Queen had created the "battered wife syndrome" because it was the one chance she had to go free. Even if Lauren had been abused—and increasingly I wondered about the veracity of that claim—the shooting was almost certainly attempted murder even if not premeditated. My head ached as I tried to figure out who had done what and why.

I opened my car door and sat in the driver's seat, my

mind swirling with thoughts of Lauren, her ex-husband, the stories she had told me, the claims of abuse. As I pulled out of the store's parking lot and headed back to Richmond, I continued going over it all in my mind. I needed to look at each piece of this puzzle that Lauren was, that my life had become, and try to find a way to make sense of it all.

I recalled another story Lauren had told about her ex-husband punching her in the side of her head as they drove home from therapy. It was a story that always disturbed me. But now, with all I had learned about her mental illness and all I had experienced with her, I wondered what really happened in that car. Perhaps she had told the truth, or more likely, that incident mirrored the experience I had with Lauren while driving down Broad Street in Richmond.

I thought back to that day. We were sitting in silence, as we always did after Lauren's sessions with Dr. Carter. Before I knew it, Lauren was caressing my leg, cooing words of love in my ear and giggling like a school girl. It was as if she had completely forgotten the growing tension between us. She had gotten little response from me so she moved her hand inside my thigh, laughing at my pleas to stop so I could safely drive. Then, as if honoring my request, she stopped. Looking back, I now realize that in that instant, her body became rigid and then relaxed.

Although I didn't know it at the time, Peg, Lucifer's Daughter, was suddenly in Lauren's place. It was Lucifer's Daughter who squeezed my testicles as hard as she could. Even with all my police training and the love I felt for Lauren, in that moment, I wanted to hit the creature beside me. I wanted to smash her head. I wanted to make her hurt as she had hurt me.

There had been times after that in which Lucifer's Daughter or Hannah had attacked me similarly, trying to create intense pain and illicit a violent response. The only thing that kept me from striking out at the demons was that it was not Lauren who was doing these awful things to me, but it would be Lauren who would endure the pain. I could not retaliate. But what about her previous husband? Did he realize who and what he was dealing with? Or did he let his anger take control and lash out at the demon beside him as fiercely as I fought to contain my rage?

I thought about all this as I drove home from Roanoke.

I had the diagnosis I was seeking. I had married a woman who had multiple personality disorder. She had endured childhood hell I could not even imagine, and now she was seemingly possessed by demons that wreaked havoc, damaging her life and the lives of many others.

Most upsetting was that Lauren was not being helped. She had been diagnosed. The enemy had a name. But the enemy was still free, taking control of her body at will, causing chaos, then disappearing to let her take the punishment.

What would be the next evil to be faced, I wondered? Would I be stalked as Lucifer's Daughter had stalked her previous husband? Would my children? Especially after speaking to the gun store clerk, I no longer believed the story once told me that the .22 rifle was bought as a gift for her ex-husband. He had been a hunter and a gun collector; his large collection already included several .22 caliber guns. He was a man who knew weapons, understood their firepower, and was well aware of their limitations. He might have purchased a .30-.30. He might have purchased a shotgun. He would not have been interested in a .22-caliber rifle, especially when all his other guns were in the hands of his wife's lawyer. It was neither a weapon he would use for hunting nor a gun meant for protection against one of Lauren's demons. It was an assassination weapon, and I became increasingly certain that it was bought for that purpose only.

Then there was the money John Taylor supposedly

had stashed, the money Hannah wanted for herself. I had spent enough time in the library to determine that the last robbery spree Taylor and his partner went on netted them just over $58,000, only a portion of which had been recovered. Presumably there would have been a stash of cash available for the getaway Taylor had planned following his hoped-for escape. Yet there was no money found in the car. There was no money found in the home where his girlfriend lived.

The more I thought about what Hannah had said, the more I was convinced she was right. While I did not think there was a $250,000 stash, I did think there was enough money to live comfortably for a year or two wherever Taylor had planned to go. Certainly it was enough for Hannah to try to obtain. It was also probably enough for her to kill for.

When I returned to Richmond I began putting my affairs in order. The routine of establishing a new life helped me avoid obsessing about the danger that still seemed to be lurking around the corner. I knew Hannah would continue her harassment. I knew the Queen of Hearts would stay in my life. But I could not live in fear. Instead, I had to take the actions necessary to adjust to the aftermath of the violence and the court proceedings.

My first concern was my children, whom I took a day off to visit and talk to about these agonizing events. I wanted to reassure them that I would always be there for them and that no one would harm them. Next, I turned to the divorce proceeding. My costs had reached $150 an hour for the attorney and my savings, by then, were almost non-existent. There was a property settlement draft my attorney had completed, a document I would try to get signed by Lauren at the first opportunity. Beyond that, I needed to get more cash before the full divorce could be completed. In the meantime, I needed to get completely away from my wife. I needed a fresh start.

I moved out of the apartment in which I had been living, taking a one-bedroom unit on the west side of town. The bed we shared was dragged to the dumpster, a note attached warning any scavengers that it was permeated with tear gas. SWAT teams and naked knife wielders, tear gas and a ruined bedroom. Just another routine day in my life, I thought as I leaned the mattress and box spring against the dumpster.

I gave Lauren's upholstered rocker to a neighbor who was a casual acquaintance. She was delighted and I chose to not mention my fears. To me, the rocker was the location of change. The moment Lauren or the Intermediary sat on the chair, Hannah, Lucifer's Daughter, or the Queen of Hearts appeared. In my fantasies, the rocker was itself possessed. Anyone who sat on it would become one with the demons.

It was an irrational belief I knew. The change in Lauren was the result of a horribly disturbed mind, not a chair that was a conduit for the creatures of Hell. That was why I said nothing to my neighbor. That was also why I said a silent prayer, seeking God's blessing, as I carried it to her apartment.

The surviving objects in the apartment led to other thoughts. I realized as I looked around that our life together had gradually changed from all love to almost constant explosive violence. I never thought I had anything to fear from Lauren, a belief I still held. The problem was with the different personalities and the failure of the medical community to help her.

Lauren had been given the medication of the moment rather than the intense counseling she needed. Prozac was tried, for example, yet it only seemed to make matters worse. I did not know if she was having an allergic reaction to the popular prescription anti-depressant or if the drug made it easier for the violent personalities to take control of her body.

I had to face the fact that my life might be in real danger. I had obviously recognized the explosive potential I was facing with Hannah, the Daughter, and the Queen, but that was only when I was around them. Now that there was no question that a divorce would take place, I realized that I might be stalked in the same manner as her ex-husband. This time she would not get away with claiming to be an abused spouse, but would she understand this? Would she recognize that what had happened with the SWAT team would forever end any credibility such an excuse might have? I doubted it. I felt certain I might be stalked and killed by one personality, leaving the rest amazed to be arrested and charged with first degree murder.

To add to my worries was an incident that once seemed so minor, I had dismissed it from my memory. It was during the period when I first met Hannah but was mostly involved with Lauren. There was tension, but it had not changed our still positive relationship. Lauren dominated our time together, and I had not yet learned to fear her.

I remember renting the movie *Basic Instinct* from the video store one night. It was the story of a female killer who dispatched her lovers with an ice pick as they were making love. It was one of Lauren's favorite movies.

The story involved a detective who finds himself lustfully drawn to a beautiful woman, who happens to also be the prime suspect in the case. The questions of whether or not she is the killer and if she is, whether or not she will turn on him, constantly pervade the movie. Then comes the chilling final scene in which the two are in bed, making love. The camera pans down to view the floor beneath the bed where an ice pick is laying on the carpet.

The movie had been chilling but fascinating. We both enjoyed it and nothing seemed out of the ordinary after I returned it to the video store that same evening.

Still nothing seemed abnormal the next morning as I was getting dressed in the bedroom. Then I accidentally dropped my watch on Lauren's side of the bed. When I leaned over to retrieve it, I saw that Lauren had placed a

butcher knife with a twelve-inch blade in the same position as
the ice pick in the last scene of the movie. It was a sick joke,
I thought, nothing more. I did not mention it to Lauren,
replacing the knife in the kitchen. I figured that when she
said nothing, it was because she had seen that the knife was
returned and would know I had gotten the joke.

The incident had seemed so minor that I forgot
about it. Now that I knew she had multiple personality disorder, now that I had been repeatedly assaulted, I was no
longer certain. I suspected that Peg, Lucifer's Daughter had
enjoyed at least a part of the movie and that I had been too
absorbed to recognize the change. The psychopathic character had been an inspiration, a role model, and a mentor of
evil. Lauren did not say anything about finding the knife,
because Lauren never knew it was removed from the
kitchen, placed under the bed, and put back in the kitchen
by me. So when would there be another attempt? When
would I face another confrontation?

The answer came in August when I went to
Lightfoot's, an upscale club located in the Hyatt Hotel in
Richmond. It was a place popular with locals as well as hotel
guests. Lauren and I had been there occasionally and I still
liked to stop in at times.

I went to the bar, sat down, and ordered a drink. The
place was crowded, the dance floor jumping, but I had my
back turned to the action, listening to the music, lost in my
own thoughts. Then, just as my drink was served, I heard a
voice say, "Richard."

I knew it was Lauren before I recognized the voice
or saw her face. It was the electricity in the air. The hairs on
my neck stood on end just as she slipped onto the empty seat
next to me.

"Lauren, you're not supposed to be talking to me.
The court order..."

"Bullshit!" she replied, though not in an angry way. It was the gentle tone of a lover. "I'm just here to order a drink," she said, quietly.

Then, softer, in a loving manner, she said, "Richard, I've missed you. How are you?"

"Fine," I answered her. I deliberately kept my voice a little cold, distant. This was the woman I loved, the woman whose voice could lull me into peace, happiness. I wanted to kiss her, to talk through the evening then take her home to my apartment and hold her in my arms. Yet I knew if I did, there would be a demon from Hell terrorizing the neighborhood before morning. "Look, let's cut through the niceties, Lauren," I said, laying a five dollar bill on the bar and starting to rise.

"Richard, I still love you," she said, gently touching my arm.

"Lauren," I said. "You sure have a strange way of showing it."

"What do you mean, Richard?" Her face showed genuine confusion and concern. She was hurt by my words; she did not understand. "How can you say something like that?"

"The letters, Lauren. All those letters to and from John." I sat back down.

I felt the electricity, sensed the change in her body. "Richard, don't take any of that too seriously," she said, smiling. Lauren was gone. There was no scar, but the voice and body language told me a change had taken place. Who was with me now? The Queen? Lucifer's Daughter?

"How else can I take it, Lauren?" I asked.

"Don't call me Lauren," she said, brusquely. The smile was still on her face, though her attitude was harsh. Her words were a surprise until I realized that she had frequently made the same comment in the midst of our arguments. "Don't call me Lauren." I had once thought she would say that because I used a patronizing tone of voice or because I acted in a manner that was offensive to her. Only now, with the diagnosis of Multiple Personality Disorder, did I realize the meaning of her request; this was not Lauren and she did not want to be called by that "other woman's" name.

"You didn't wait very long, did you? Let's see, if my calculations are correct, you started writing him less than three months after we were married. Isn't that right?"

I wasn't going to wait for an answer. This was no longer Lauren. Lauren knew nothing of the letters. In fact, John's writing indicated that there were long gaps between letters at times, and when he did hear from the Queen of Hearts, she acted like no time at all had passed. I realized this was because they were times, like during the early days of our marriage, when Lauren was in charge, and Lauren wanted nothing to do with any man other than me.

I pushed back from the bar and stood up.

"Leaving so soon, Richard?" The voice was cold now, deeper. Peg, Lucifer's Daughter, spoke. "Why don't you stay for a while and talk with me."

"No thanks, Lauren," I said as I started to leave. "We are not supposed to be talking to each other."

"Don't call me Lauren," she seethed as I left the bar, never looking back.

I walked rapidly to the parking lot, then turned suddenly just before reaching my car. I half expected the Furies from Hell to attack from the sky. Instead, all I saw was the doorman and the bright lights of the hotel. There was no Lauren, no Mustang with its engine revved, its tires screeching as it raced in circles around the parking lot.

I got in my car, then drove onto Broad Street. The traffic was fairly heavy as I slipped in and out of the different lanes. I was terrified the Queen, the Daughter, or Hannah might be following me, so I kept alert to all the cars around me. I used tactics I had learned during rolling pursuits of felons back in my days with the police force. I turned right and left, randomly choosing streets. Sometimes I signaled.

Sometimes I didn't. It was unnecessary, though. Lauren and her demons were not following me.

August rolled into September. I had changed to an unlisted telephone number and arranged for a new number for my pager, both of which helped assure my privacy. But I could not change my job or my telephone number there. Thus I was delighted when no one called day after day, at last allowing me to get on with my work. But my peace would not last.

It was the middle of the month when I received a telephone call from Hannah. I decided that even with the volatile woman on the other end of the line, I was not going to let fear prevent me from doing what must be done. "Lauren, we need to talk about a property settlement agreement," I told her.

"Are you divorcing me, Richard?" she asked. It was more a statement than a question. It was the type of challenge that had once led Hannah to attack her former husband. Any answer was dangerous.

"Before we can talk about that, we need to discuss a property settlement," I told her. I was dancing around her question, and probably we both knew it.

"Richard, I'm going to need financial support from you," Hannah demanded angrily.

Financial support was an issue I had hoped to avoid when I mentioned the property settlement. After all I had been through, there was no way I was going to pay for Lauren's support. She had built her own business, one that serviced some of the wealthiest families in the community. So long as Lauren was in control, the business thrived. Neither Hannah nor the Queen nor any of the demons from Hell wanted anything to do with the work, though. Whenever they took charge, customers would go elsewhere and eventually Lauren had to rebuild.

I had lost my home, many of my possessions, and almost destroyed my career. I would gladly share that which was appropriate, but the idea of paying regular sums of money was something I intended to fight. Maybe having nothing would encourage the therapists to truly treat her. Maybe the others would let Lauren run her business until they could sucker some other man. Maybe...

"Well, Lauren, you're not going to get any support payments from me," I told her. "Understand this. With everything I have, the letters from John and the court orders of protection, there isn't a court that would award you any support. Do you understand that?"

There was a long silence. Then a quieter voice said, "What about my medication and my visits to the therapist and psychiatrist?"

Lauren needed therapy. There was no question about that. The problem was that the two therapists who had been treating her were accomplishing nothing. She was worse, if anything, than she had been. Still, they were the only people she was willing to see at the moment.

"Lauren, I'm willing to cover all that until the divorce is final. After that it will be your responsibility. That is when your medical insurance stops."

There was silence on the other end of the line. I had not intended to say the word "divorce." I knew it might set her off. I was right.

"You damn pig! Do you think you're divorcing me and cutting me off?" asked Hannah. There was no mistaking her voice or the challenge it held. I was in trouble. It was only a matter of what kind and when it would happen.

Determined to defuse the issue, I said, "Lauren, you and I both know that we can't go on like this. We have to end this and go on with our lives."

There was silence, then a quiet click. Hannah had hung up the telephone.

I knew there was something wrong as I made my way home from the office that evening. There was nothing I could state exactly. A constant checking of my rear view mirror failed to indicate I was being followed. Yet nothing was quite right, and shortly after I arrived home, there was a knock on the apartment door. I looked out the front window and saw Lauren standing there.

I was not certain what to do. I could ignore her, of course. But she had undoubtedly checked for my car and knew I was home. If she became enraged and smashed a window, the management might ask me to leave. The same was true if I called the police. It was best to open the door.

"Aren't you going to invite me in, Richard?" asked Ali, the Queen of Hearts.

"I'm not even going to ask how you found me, Lauren."

"I've known where you were living for some time now." She smiled as I opened the door wider and stepped aside to allow her to enter the living room.

"What do you want, Lauren. Why are you here?" I kept looking at her purse, wondering if she had a gun inside.

"Richard, we need to talk," said someone else. Lauren perhaps. I was scared, uncertain what was right. Was I defusing the problem with Lauren inside or had I escalated it in ways I could not imagine. "Is there any possibility that we could get back together?" Definitely Lauren. There was a tone of helplessness in her voice. She was a woman in love who had been spurned by the object of her affections for reasons she could not comprehend. That was the trouble with a true multiple personality, I had learned. Until therapy begins the integration process, there is no shared memory. The actions of one personality are unknown by the others, even though other people around them are fully aware of what took place.

"Right now, Lauren...I think we should...just wait and see what's going to happen." I felt as though I was attempting to walk on cartons of eggs without breaking the shells. I didn't want to hurt Lauren. I also didn't want to trigger Hannah's violence. I had no idea how stable Lauren might be, when she might react.

"Are you writing to John?" I asked.

"No, Richard, I'm not!" Ali, again. The Queen of Hearts was back. My living room was getting crowded.

"I don't believe that, Lauren. As a matter of fact, if it weren't for your felony conviction, you would probably be on your way to Kansas right now." I was baiting her and knew it.

"If I wanted to, I could visit John now. I'm on his authorized visitor list. I just don't have the money for a trip like that right now."

I wondered when she would make the trip. My friends at the FBI had been right. "Why don't you ask John for some of the quarter of a million dollars he has squirreled away," I said, trying to keep my tone light.

"Someday..."

I interrupted Ali and said, "Come on, Lauren, you don't really believe in buried treasure, do you?"

"John has told me about the money!" The Queen was almost shouting. I couldn't tell if her reaction was one of fear that he had been lying or one of anger that I would dare question what he had said.

"Richard, are you going to divorce me?" The Intermediary had taken over.

"Lauren, when we discussed this on the telephone this afternoon, I told you that we would have to give it time to see what was going to happen. For the time being, we need to at least enter into a property settlement agreement."

The Intermediary was not there for a fight. She agreed to meet the following week to confirm the agreement the lawyer created, then left without incident.

On the day of the meeting, we gathered in one of the branch offices of the bank for which I worked. The branch manager had the papers involved with the settlement neatly arranged on her desk, waiting for the signatures. The manager was a notary and would witness what was taking place.

The manager and I waited several minutes until we saw the Mustang pull into the lot. The moment the driver's door opened, I knew there was a problem. The woman who emerged was wearing a tight orange top with a black micro-mini skirt. Hannah had returned.

Oh no, I thought, *This is a set-up.* I was sure Hannah had no intention of allowing Lauren to be involved with any settlement.

To my amazement, Hannah came in, read the agreement, picked up the pen, and signed it without comment. The branch manager notarized her signature and mine, made two notarized copies for Hannah, and then Hannah left.

Relieved, I thanked the manager who wished me good luck. Then I drove back to my office. I had no idea why matters had gone so smoothly.

The court order of protection expired in September. There had been no incidents serious enough to justify renewing it. In fact, after the order was lifted, Lauren visited me in my apartment many an evening, talking quietly, and leaving peacefully. I never went to see her. I never knew where she was living. In this period of limbo, we seemed to have become casual friends in a manner that would have been pleasant had we not had the history of violence together.

The one warning that all was not well was the way in which she sometimes left. Those times, Lauren quickly got into her car and drove away. Then, a half-hour later, Hannah or the Queen returned, cruising the parking lot to make certain my car was still there. She was checking on me, though for what reasons I had no idea.

Several days passed and Lauren never mentioned the property agreement she signed. She was still seeing both her therapist and psychiatrist. She was still taking medication. She never asked for money or assistance, yet something was certainly wrong. Finally, during one of her visits in early October, I asked her, "Lauren, do you still have your copy of our property settlement agreement?"

"What agreement, Richard?" she asked. Her face was a blank. There was no pretense. She genuinely did not know.

"Nothing, Lauren. Nothing," I said.

It was too late. I didn't know if Hannah had developed the ability to listen in or if Lauren was so startled that she instantly changed personas. All I know was that suddenly a raging Hannah was in front of me. She rushed towards the rear of my apartment, entering my bedroom, wielding a knife.

I followed after Hannah, grabbed the knife and dragged her to the front door. I opened the door and pushed her outside onto the front step. Then I slammed it shut and locked it.

Hannah exploded. She began pounding on the door, determined to break it down.

I no longer cared what happened. I went to the couch, grabbed her purse, opened the door, and threw it out. "Lauren," I said, "if you don't leave, I am going to call the police!" I shut and locked the door, then waited until I heard the sound of her Mustang leaving.

I went to bed, but had little sleep. Hour after hour, Hannah raced her Mustang around the parking lot, the distinctive sound of the car keeping me alert.

There was only one call when I arrived at work. It was the Queen of Hearts who coldly stated, "You're divorcing me, aren't you, Richard?" She hung up as soon as I tried to reply.

For the next four days there were no more telephone calls. Instead, each night I heard Lauren gunning the motor of her car as she repeatedly drove through the apartment complex. She wanted me to know she was there, watching me. What I did not know was why.

On the fifth day, as I was driving home, by chance I

spotted a red Mustang ahead of me. I recognized the license plate. I knew it was Lauren's. I followed at a discrete distance until I saw it pull into a house in Richmond's west end.

I recognized the place immediately. It was the home of Cindy and Gordon, Lauren's very first clients when she started her business here in Richmond. Cindy and Lauren became quick friends, and Lauren and I had dinner at their house once. They had two boys and a large dog.

I remembered they also had a locked gun cabinet in their home that Gordon had shown to me the night we were over for dinner. While the cabinet was certainly secure against the actions of children, I doubted that it would offer adequate protection from Hannah's prying hands. Worse, Lauren and the others in her head might have been shown where to get the key in case there was a need to protect the family.

I had also learned from Lauren a few months before that Gordon and Cindy had separated, Cindy remaining in the house, presumably with the gun cabinet. Such a separation would give Hannah, Lucifer's Daughter or the Queen even greater opportunity to get a weapon. I wondered if Lauren was staying there now.

I waited until just before dawn the next morning to confirm my suspicions. Then I dressed for work and left the apartment. I drove over to Cindy and Gordon's to check the drive. There was Lauren's car. The only question remaining was whether or not there were still guns in the cabinet.

Later that morning I found Cindy's telephone number. She answered when I called.

"Hello, Cindy? Is Lauren there?" I asked. I knew that Lauren would be running her business. Only Hannah, the Daughter, the Queen, or one of the others might have stayed back in the house.

"No, she's not here. Who is this?" Cindy asked.

"This is Richard. Lauren's husband," I said.

"Uh, oh!" said Cindy. I knew instantly that she had

heard and believed all the stories that Hannah, Lucifer's Daughter, and the Queen had ever manufactured. I was an abuser. I was a son of a bitch. I was evilness personified.

"Look, Cindy, I know what Lauren has told you, but..."

"She's told me how you abused her and that she's afraid of you," said Cindy, angrily. She sounded like a mother hen protecting her chicks from attack.

"She told you I had a real mean streak in me and that I beat her. That nobody should hit anyone," I said. I knew the drill. I had been there with the doctors, the social workers, the lawyers, and the judges. I had been there with the police. The story told was consistent.

"Yes..." said Cindy, calming. She seemed surprised by what I said. "Those were almost exactly her words."

"Not exactly her words," I said, thinking of John's letters in which he had suggested she bring those charges in order to discredit me. Maybe I should read her one of the letters I thought. But it was not worth saying the words.

"I don't understand."

"Nothing, Cindy. It's a long story. But I have something important to ask you and I would appreciate your trusting me."

"What do you want, Richard?" Her voice again took on a hardness. "Why should I trust you?"

"Cindy, when Gordon left, did he take his guns with him?"

"What?" she said, indignantly. "What business is that of yours?"

"Listen to me, Cindy. This is important. It could be a matter of life and death. My life or yours and the children's."

"Gordon's guns are still here in the cabinet. We always keep the cabinet locked because of the boys," she responded.

"Where is the key, Cindy?"

"We always keep it hidden on one of the book shelves." She was more anxious now.

"Is Lauren living with you?"

She hesitated and finally admitted that she was.

"Cindy, please do something for me. Right now, go check the cabinet and make sure all Gordon's guns are there. I'll hold on."

I was desperate and apparently she sensed my concern. "Just a minute..." she said, laying down the receiver. I could hear her footsteps walking across the floor.

Minutes later Cindy was back, no longer angry, no longer certain what to think. "I'm not positive, she said, but I think there is a rifle missing.

Suddenly I was terrified. "What kind of rifle, Cindy?"

"Ah... a twenty something. I don't know anything about guns."

"A .22 Caliber?"

"Yes, I think so." Cindy's attitude had changed. I had her attention now.

"Cindy, do you think Gordon has it?"

"I don't think so. He hasn't been here in more than a month."

"Cindy, this is important, more important than you could ever realize. You've got to find out if Gordon has it. If he doesn't, then you are going to have to confront Lauren and ask her if she has it. You also have to get the key and keep it safe someplace." My voice was shaking with emotion.

"What... what is this all about? What's going on?" Cindy was bewildered. I had to tell her the truth.

"Cindy, let's just leave it that Lauren could get into a lot of trouble if she is in possession of a firearm." I wanted to tell her as little as possible. The full story might be unbelievable.

"Richard, what are you talking about?" Cindy demanded.

I took a deep breath, then said, "Cindy, Lauren is a convicted felon. She can't even be near a firearm."

"What? A convicted felon? What was she convicted of?"

"Lauren shot her ex-husband."

There was a long silence and I wondered if she had hung up the telephone. Then she said, "Oh, Jesus! You're not making this up, are you?"

Before I could answer, she spoke again.

"Lauren, that sweet woman. She what? My God, she's my friend. I've left her alone with my children." Cindy's voice was breaking. She was frightened and near tears.

"Listen to me, Cindy. You have to find out where the rifle is. Call Gordon now, and if he doesn't have it, you are going to have to get it back from Lauren. If she denies it, then tell her you're going to have to call the police and make a report. That should do it. If she really did take it, then she won't want the police coming around to make an investigation."

"All right. All right. I'll call you back after I find out what's going on. Goodbye, Richard." Cindy hung up the telephone.

The rest of my workday was a tense one. I kept waiting for the telephone to ring or for an armed Hannah to arrive at the bank. Nothing happened. All was quiet until I returned to the apartment and the telephone rang.

"You son of a bitch!" screamed Hannah. "Because of your lies, I have nowhere to live. Cindy has told me to move out right away!"

"Did you give her the rifle back, Lauren?" I asked.

The response was silence. I knew I had been right. However, I wanted her to say something.

"Lauren, why do you think you need a rifle?" I asked her.

"I need protection from you, Richard!" screamed

Hannah. "You are an evil son of a bitch and I won't stand for your abuse!"

I shook my head in disbelief. All the therapy. All the drugs. Finally a diagnosis that mattered, and still no one was helping her. All was the same.

"Lauren, you are not using your head. Don't you realize that if you are caught with a firearm, your probation will be revoked? They will send you to Goochland for the next seven years."

There was silence. Then what I think was Lauren's voice came on, "Richard, where am I going to live?"

"Lauren, you're making a good living. Go somewhere and rent an apartment."

"Like most married women, I have no credit, Richard. They won't lease me an apartment." Her voice was shaking.

"Listen to me, Lauren. Go find an apartment and I'll sign the lease. Find something you can afford because I'm not paying a dime towards your rent. After you move in, we'll have the lease amended to your name."

The next day Cindy called to confer with me on the events of the day before. After a confrontation, Lauren had returned the rifle along with a box of .22 long ammunition. At least part of her potential arsenal had been taken and so we were all safer. But could she have more? The truth was I did not know.

CHAPTER 22

Pushing the Demons Away

It was nearly over. Lauren and I were separated, all papers filed for the divorce, just waiting for the court to finalize it. There were no illusions, no hope of reconciliation. I still loved the woman I had met long ago, but now I accepted that Lauren was one of several different personalities. She was the best, the gentlest, the most loving, but she was not the whole woman. Perhaps if I had met her when she was receiving meaningful help, things would have been different. Perhaps if we had found a therapist who could treat her disorder I might have stayed. Instead, I accepted the fact that if the woman I loved ever got well, it would happen too far in the future. Our relationship was over.

Lauren had moved into an apartment the way I suggested. The lease was in my name alone, though I arranged a meeting with Lauren to transfer the lease into her name. She might have credit problems getting the lease, but once signed, her credit would not be an issue for the transfer, provided she continued to pay the rent.

Lauren arranged to meet me in her new place. She told me to bring the papers for us to sign and I could be on my way.

It was strange walking to the door, not knowing who
would answer. It was the Intermediary who answered the
door. Whenever she was present, I knew the Queen was
close at hand. All I could think to do was get the damned
papers signed and get the hell out of the apartment.

"Hello, Lauren," I said. "Here are the papers you
need to sign." I handed her the lease transfer documents as
I stepped into the apartment.

The Intermediary walked to the coffee table, set the
papers on it, and began reading them. Then she left them,
stood up, and headed down the hallway towards the bedroom. I knew immediately that she was changing and followed her to prevent her getting a weapon in the bedroom.

"I wrote you a poem, Richard."

"A poem?" I said, unsure what was happening. The
Intermediary was leaving, the Queen of Hearts taking her
place. "Why a poem?"

She began reading. It talked of my abuse, my decep-
tion, and my lies. There were no specifics. The poem just
implied that they were so overwhelming, no one could ever
be so evil as I was. By the end, she was accusing me of being
Satan personified. It was all very strange, yet as I had discussed with her therapist, Lauren projected on to others.
Truth was relative.

I turned away and the Queen of Hearts said,
"Richard, don't you want your poem?"

When I looked at her, the Queen was gone. Her
eyes were aglow and hate filled her face. The crease was
forming on her cheek, and within seconds there was the scar.

Hannah smiled, grasping my right hand, then using
her free hand to jerk back my fingers. I heard them snap and
realized she planned to break them one at a time.

I twisted my wrist, grabbing her with my free hand,
pulling away. I shoved her away and Hannah fell face down
on the bed.

Suddenly she rolled on her back and began attacking her face with her fingers. She clawed at her flesh with her nails. She jabbed her fingers into her nostrils, tearing the flesh, drawing blood. When it started to spurt from the self-inflicted injuries, she started smearing the blood on my face and hands, chanting, "DNA, DNA! Let's have the cops look at this."

The demon was screaming, delighting in tearing her flesh, then smearing me with blood. Hannah was apparently trying to set me up by hurting herself, then smearing me with her blood.

I pushed the demon away and walked down the hallway to the living room. Suddenly she was off the bed and hurrying towards me. Instead of attacking, though, she sat down at the coffee table and began slapping herself across the face with both hands, striking herself as hard as she could.

"Stop it!" she screamed. "Stop it! I'm going to call the police!"

I was standing perhaps eight feet away, but anyone hearing the screams would be certain that the marks on her face were caused by my actions. They would believe the scene of brutality that would seemingly confront them if they came into the apartment.

I had been lucky so far that my employers and outsiders supported me despite what must be their own doubts, but how long would they continue if more charges were heaped upon me? If someone called the police, I would be disgraced. If someone called the police, I could lose my job. If someone called the police, I might go to jail for assault and battery. If someone called the police, my life as I had known it would be over, my good name smeared, my past triumphs as though they were nothing.

And suddenly I did not care.

I had been manipulated. I had been abused. I had been attacked. I had been thrown out of my apartment following the assault against Hannah by the local SWAT team.

I did not fear Hannah. I did not fear the Queen of Hearts. I did not even fear Lucifer's Daughter. I did not fear those who would not believe the truth. I just stood there. *If she is going to try to shoot me*, I thought, *let her do it now.*

I walked across the living room to a sliding door that led to a deck out back. It was a bright fall evening, and the sky was filled with tens of thousands of bright stars. I stepped outside and embraced the night with my heart.

"Dear God," I began to pray, ignoring the demon in the living room. "In the name of your son, Jesus, please let me have my life back. I know this is not the life you intended for me to live. Please free me now, or let my life end here."

And suddenly I found myself completely at peace. When I glanced back at the demon, the only emotion I experienced was complete disgust with what I was seeing. I knew I was finished with all of this and that soon I was going to take back my life, the life that I wanted so much. One demon or a hundred demons—the Legions of Hell would not prevent the future I desired.

I walked back through the apartment, heading for the front door. The demon was sitting on the coffee table, a smile fixed on her face. I turned my back to her and walked towards the door.

Hannah leapt from the table, ran into the kitchen, and within seconds was back in the living room, holding a twelve-inch butcher knife above her head, preparing to strike. I turned back towards her and could see the intense hatred burning in her eyes. The blade of the knife shook in her trembling hand, and I felt certain that if she suddenly decided to thrust downward, I would have a good chance of blocking the blow, grabbing hold of her wrists, and disarming her.

I also sensed that there was another way out. I could back away from her, moving towards the front door, turning the handle, and slipping out. I dared not turn my back to her, yet I was fairly certain I could escape if I kept my eyes on her while moving away.

Neither approach felt right. Why should there be more violence between us? Why should I use my training to disarm her, perhaps break her arm, only to have both of us in court again? And why should I back away when the reality was she would just track me down again. The demon from Hell would follow me for eternity if she could. I was certain of that.

Suddenly I knew what I had to do. Instead of moving away or staying where I was, I took a step closer. It was a move the demon had not expected. Hannah stood holding the knife, shaking harder than before. Her breathing was heavy, labored. There was a burning wildness in her eyes. Once again I thought that if I looked deeply enough, what I would be seeing was a gateway to Hell. And that's when I knew.

"Our Father, Who art in heaven, hallowed be Thy name." Lauren took two steps backward as I moved forward, reciting the Lord's Prayer.

"Thy kingdom come. Thy will be done..."

I had learned the prayer as a child. I had said it thousands of times in church. It was not an exorcism. It was not an acceptance of God's presence in the manner of the Twenty-third Psalm. It was the prayer Jesus had taught his disciples.

The demon kept moving backwards, stopping only when her back was against the wall, and there was no place else to go. "...On earth as it is in Heaven..."

Hannah began to slowly slide downward until she was sitting on the floor, her back rigidly against the wall, the knife still clutched in both hands, held over her head. As I finished my prayer, I realized that she looked a little like an ice cube melting away. "...For Thine is the kingdom, the power, and the glory."

I walked to the coffee table and picked up the papers that I had brought with me. They were the ones that would have assigned the lease to Lauren. As she sat, unmoving, I

tore the papers to pieces and threw them at her feet on the
floor. "Amen," I said. I turned and walked to the door.

I stepped out into the cool autumn air. The apartment was a third floor walk-up. As I made my way down the
steps, I did not look back. I knew I didn't have to. My days
of looking over my shoulder were finished.

I left a note on Lauren's car. It read, "You have
twenty-four hours to leave here."

That night I slept peacefully. Only once, shortly
before awakening, was I aware of dreaming. The dream was
the familiar one in which I am standing, watching storm
clouds gather. Lightning from the sky touches the ground,
and the sound of distant thunder grows louder and louder,
slowly changing to the pounding of a horse's hooves. The
Dark Rider appears astride the black horse. She lowers the
point of her sword toward me and shouts, "Look at me!
Look at me now! Listen to me! Listen to me now! The truth
shall be shown. The truth shall be known."

The Dark Rider began to turn her mount away,
preparing to ride back into the swirling abyss of darkness.
Instead of watching her leave, I spoke to her. "Rider," I said.
"Let me hear your final words. You have never allowed me
to hear them. I want to hear them."

She turned her mount back towards me. It was then
I saw Lauren's face as she spoke, "Look at me! Look at me
now! Listen to me! Listen to me now! I am the abused
become the abuser."

"Be gone in God's name!" I called out. And with
that, the Dark Rider turned her mount away and rode into
the gates of Hell.

Later that morning I drove by the apartment Lauren
had rented. She was gone, leaving not only the place I had
rented for her, but also the city itself.

— CHAPTER 23 —

To Live and
Love and Leave

The nightmare is over now. The prayer that came spontaneously to my lips on that last night we were together was not an exorcism for the demons inside Lauren. They are the result of mental illness, not a possession by Satan. The sins she has committed, the violence that overwhelms her alter personalities, are as much the fault of those who abused her as they are her personal choices. Experts in the field agree that a multiple personality experiences overwhelming physical and psychological trauma before the age of seven. They are the victims of the evil adults can do, and their responses are meant for survival, not because the possession has been passed to them like a vampire's curse.

The second period of abuse comes when they seek the help they need, the help they deserve, only to be further hurt by well-meaning or insecure therapists. Lauren's treatment was naïve at best, incompetent at worst. Even after the two mental health professionals working with her had a diagnosis that clearly identified the problem, they were unable to help her, unwilling to refer her. Their treatment, in my opinion, was almost as brutal as the original abuse, because they were entrusted to help her rise from the nightmare illness that has dominated her life for so long, and they let her stay captive to it.

While I do not believe that Lauren has been demon-possessed, I do believe that in some sense there was an exorcism that last day we were together. The demons that were exorcised were those of pride and false hope, and the person who was possessed was me.

To know Lauren, just Lauren, the woman I first met, as I did those first few months, was to know an aspect of human love in its purest form. That Lauren was a woman of passion and compassion, of great intelligence and an entre-preneurial work ethic. If she will ever let herself seek therapy from someone more competent to treat her illness than the people with whom she has spent so many hours in the past, she will be a woman loved and admired wherever she goes.

In talks with experts and in reading books on the sub-ject of multiple personality, it has become clear to me that healing—the integration of the different personalities into one normal being—does not guarantee that the person will match any particular character trait. There is the fantasy that if some-one was abused as a small child, then went through hell as an adult, therapy should make him or her happy, compassion-ate, and able to be a positive role model. In truth, people make good choices and bad. Some people look at their past and say, "After what others have done to me, I'm going to get mine now. I'm going to start looking after Number One, and to hell with anyone else." Other people say, "I never want anyone to endure what I experienced. I'm going to spend at least part of my life helping the abused and the troubled so they can end their suffering." And still others say, "Now that I'm well, I'm going to be like everyone else." People make good choices and bad, selfish decisions and altruistic ones, act in a mildly destructive way with alcohol or recreational drugs, or explore fitness, nutrition, and better health.

I now know that an integrated Lauren may be more like the Queen of Hearts than the woman I loved. Or an integrated Lauren may be a woman loved, admired, and respected by males and females alike. God gave us all free will, the ability to choose right and wrong. I do not know what choices she will make. I only know about my own.

I married Lauren for life. I know that sounds foolish coming from a man who had experienced a failed marriage. I had taken the same vows once before. I had made the same commitment with my first wife that I made with Lauren. But I had also made choices that caused the failure of that first marriage, choices I had no intention of repeating. And when I knew the love of Lauren in those early days, I was certain I had experienced the grace of God, the forgiveness of God, and the new chance that awaits us all when we are willing to change.

Perhaps this was also true for Lauren. Perhaps she believed the love we shared was meant to strengthen the good in her, to help her resolve to fight the others, to seek the psychological help she needed. Or perhaps I am flattering myself by thinking that she could feel towards me as I did towards her. What is certain is that I believe I would have done whatever was necessary to make the relationship work, including staying with a mentally ill woman while she went through therapy. I tried and failed. In the end, though I couldn't save her, I had to save myself.

Because of my overwhelming need to leave Lauren, I left my job, a job I loved with co-workers whose friendships on and off the job I cherished. I left Virginia and moved back to Florida. I am again employed in the security field. I again have co-workers I like and respect. And I am dating again, albeit far more cautiously than before.

Is my divorce from Lauren, at last finalized, a failure or a moving on? Lauren has access to all the knowledge she needs about her illness to seek help. The therapist and the psychiatrist who treated her have the same information. So far as I know, nothing has changed for her. There will undoubtedly be other men, other violence, other charges and counter-charges, and there is nothing I can do to help her or prevent the violence from happening to others who come into Lauren's life.

I believe that I tried to honor my marriage, to love Lauren in her most serious illness, not just in health. I believe that God did not want me to continue in a relationship dominated by demons which could not be stilled.

What I have learned from all this has driven me to write this book. Our assumptions about men and women, about mental illness, about marriage and domestic violence, are skewed by popular culture.

Child abuse, which experts tell me Lauren undoubtedly suffered to the extreme, is multigenerational. It takes as many as five generations before a child reaches adulthood with the decision to raise his or her children differently from the way that person was raised. I don't know who hurt Lauren, but I do know she was fragmented by the pain and became an abuser.

Her's was a mental illness with which society could not seem to cope. No matter how Lauren acted, the therapists who had been working with her over a prolonged period of time refused to admit the seriousness of her condition, a condition so readily apparent to psychiatrists who encountered her for just forty-eight hours in an institution. The time in jail did not help, because the personalities adjusted their actions to the circumstances, keeping Lauren out of trouble or meeting violence with greater violence when such was necessary.

Oddly, it was the institutionalization of Lauren that I fought, yet it was only when she was institutionalized that we got an accurate diagnosis. Again I was reacting to a stigma. I've always felt that human beings are meant to be free. I especially felt this way about my wife. As a police officer, I had denied freedom to numerous men and women whose actions warranted their being removed from society, yet I never felt good about it. I always thought that if there was a way to change someone's behavior, to help him or her make restitution for their past actions, without going to a jail or a locked mental ward, it was the better way. I did not want my wife to endure the regimentation and restrictions of a mental hospital. Yet such care might have led to change, might have prevented the violence I endured, might have prevented her criminal behavior.

And it might not have.

So many questions. So few answers.

I feel that we need to take a second look at how we treat the mentally ill. We need to look at what their families endure. We need to understand that domestic violence is not a cut and dried issue with men always the abusers and women always the victims. Some will endure what others feel is intolerable because of a deep and abiding love. Others will react in self-defense against someone whose relative size seems to belie the justification. And still others must face the fact that a woman or a man can be the abuse victim in one relationship, the abuser in another. She or he must be helped while they are victims. She or he must be stopped, their families helped, when they are the victimizer. Always a cry for help should be answered whether brought by a man, a woman, or a dependent child.

Since this happened there have been many new lives. The woman who haunted the Bradfords and led me to Lauren is now well, her obsession ended, and the couple she harassed are living in peace. Arnie and I have remained good friends. John Taylor remains locked away, and though Lauren or one of her demons did visit him as she promised, apparently there was either no money or he did not trust her with the secret.

There is an assumption with multiple personality that one or both parents were the original abusers. Certainly I feel Lauren's mother has been extremely harsh in her attitude towards her troubled daughter. But is she that way because she abused Lauren or because she was subject to so much abuse by her adult, mentally ill daughter that her angry statements came from frustration, not hatred? I do not know, nor do I want her falsely labeled as happened to me.

I still have great anger towards the therapist and psychiatrist who treated Lauren and should have been helping her. My personal belief is that they were incompetent or had inflated egos that prevented them from admitting they were out of their realm of knowledge and needed to seek expert assistance. Yet I also know that change must come from within. If Lauren was not ready, if she fought the therapy and manipulated the sessions, that is her fault, not theirs.

I do not want to hurt anyone with this story. I pray each day that Lauren will find the help she needs and have the inner strength to change. This is why I want to tell my experiences, to help others, yet in no way hurt the present or future of the men and women who have been part of the nightmare I went through.

Those who have listened, who have stood by me or at least made reasoned, objective decisions based on the facts, I want to personally thank. For them I will always be grateful. As for the others, I can only pray that God's light touches their lives as I pray it touches Lauren's, so that those victimized by demons of any kind will not endure the hell I have experienced.